2022

A N

Que disfrutes
la aventura !

(Enjoy the adventure!)

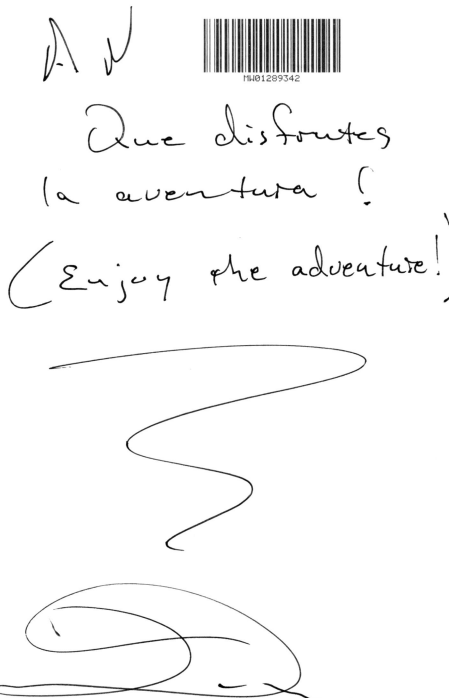

The Mexico Diaries
(A Sustainable Adventure)

By Daniel Theodore Gair

50% of all profit from the sale of this book will be donated to:

The Environmental Defense Fund

Cover Photo: View of Mayto Beach from the ranch
Cover Inset Front: Compañeros de la Calbalgata
(from left: Piri, Brian, Lupe, Chido, Jorge, Juanito, Cesar)
Cover Inset Back: Dan & Holly on Lover's Beach

All interior and jacket photo's by Dan or Holly except back inset
(photographer unknown)

Dedication

This book is foremost dedicated to my fellow goat-wrangling partner, Holly, who has put up with, loved, challenged, and inspired me these past twenty-five years. It's also dedicated to our adult 'children' Zachary, Aja, Hillary, Jessica, and Joshua, and our grandchildren Ava, Nathan, and Adam, who have given us reason to strive for a better world.

This book is further dedicated to all of the volunteers, apprentices, and other participants who have breathed life and love into the Rancho Sol y Mar project: Liz and Riley, Ty and Vanessa, Mateo, Joán, Juanito, Yamir, Victor, Edgar, Cedric, Miguel, Max, Grace and Michael, Tara, Patricio (Papa Dulce), Eric, Ana, Alex and Katy (The Brits), the other Alex, Marshal & Elja, Ali, all the amazing Cob'ers and PD-C'ers—the list goes on and on. Without all of your muscle and good will, Rancho Sol y Mar would be nothing but a sign swinging lonely and a patch of dirt.

Finally, this book is dedicated to the memory and inspiration of Brian Mitchel Wallace, the most go-for-the-gusto, Mexicanized gringo I've ever known. You showed me what true assimilation and courage in the face of dying looks like. There are chapters in here that you helped me write, amigo.

Contents

Section IV   117

Un Camino Mal (A Bad Road)
Autumn 2012 ~ Spring 2015

Section V   179

Finding the Flow (Summer 2015 on...)

Preface

"A book is a version of the world. If you do not like it, ignore it or offer your own version in return." ~ Salman Rushdie

In the autumn of 2005, things were going great. Having launched the last of our five kids, and with careers in full swing, Holly, a financial planner, and I, an advertising and travel photographer, were starting to imagine the next phase of our lives. Having attended a professional life-planning workshop, Holly was doing a lot of visioning and came up with the idea of us having a spot in Mexico to escape to winters, and possibly retire to permanently in the future. That winter we took a trip down to 'Olde' Mexico to find ourselves a little bungalow near the beach. What unfolded turned our 'normal' world on its head forever.

Now, more than a dozen years later, I'm writing this preface from the 100-acre working goat ranch and Sustainability Education Center, set in a rural village on the coast of Jalisco, that we call home.

The period between that first reconnaissance trip and now has been a rogue experiment that overran the lab, filling our life with joy and heartache, outrageous animal episodes, and an endless string of eccentric people that wash ashore like flotsam in our funky little beach town. It's also been a time of great growth and learning, particularly with regard to permaculture, the holistic management of land and re-sources designed to achieve a positive, even regenerative balance with nature.

With a few minor 'enhancements' or modifications to the timeline, the stories herein are all true. In a few cases, names have been changed to 'protect the guilty'.

With the scores of visitors we get to the ranch each year, we're often asked questions like, "How did you find this place?" and "Is it possible to own land here in Mexico?" For those interested in the nuts and bolts of living in Mexico, there is a posting at my Sustainable Mexico blog that describes the process we went through and outlines some of the bureaucratic gauntlet involved in owning property here. Those considering retiring to Mexico will likely find this book to be both a source of encouragement and a cautionary tale.

For answers to other questions like, "Are you happy here?", "Aren't you afraid?", "Don't you get bored?" or "If you had it to do all over again, would you?" I offer up The Mexico Diaries...

Section 1

Reconnaissance
(Autumn 2005 ~ Spring 2006)

"It's like driving a car at night. You never see further than your headlights, but you can make the whole trip that way." ~ *E.L. Doctorow*

1 - Soft Landing

It was clear that this wasn't going to be an ordinary trip. Within 48 hours of touching down in Puerto Vallarta, Mexico, I was nearly eaten by a lion (well, almost nearly eaten) and soon after that, Holly and I came close to drowning (this time I'm serious). Then, a few hours later, we crossed an invisible threshold that upended our lives forever.

Dropping toward the runway, we knew none of that, however. Instead, we were happily peering out our little plexiglass oval, watching the white sands, swaying palms, and royal blue Pacific rising up to greet us...

December 28, 2005 - January 1, 2006

Descending steep aluminum steps to the tarmac, we're struck by the first, humid wave. The dense tropical air is at once familiar, from many trips to Mexico and other similar places in the past, but also filled with a brand-new sense of anticipation. After exiting baggage claim, amid mariachis playing lively corridos (Mexican folk ballads) in the marbled airport corridor and rainbow-skirted señoritas offering margaritas and smiles, the magic of Mexico re-emerges to greet us as would an old forgotten friend.

Outside the airport, Holly and I feel like ants being tortured under a magnifying glass. This is a different sun than the feeble orb we've left behind in Maine. After gathering up our things and navigating the crush of cabbies and resort touts hanging around the main airport-arrivals door, we make our way across the parking lot toward the rental car agency, stopping for sweat breaks wherever we encounter a scrap of shade.

The puny little Hyundai we're given at the rental agency is going to be a challenging home for the next month, filled with camping, snorkeling, and fishing gear; backpacks; our Cocker Spaniel, Amy; and our infinite hopes for finding a hidden slice of paradise to run away to winters. Having grown up in sunny Florida, Holly has been particularly miserable throughout the long New England winters and, with both of us beginning to burn out from running our hectic, stateside businesses, our plan is to find a small patch of property—with a house near the beach perhaps—as the balm to soothe our seasonal ills.

After escaping the airport madness, we head into downtown Puerta Vallarta to provision and find a room for the night. With its box stores and miles-wide pearlescent bay festooned with a necklace of luxury high-rise hotels—all set against a backdrop of jagged, verdant mountains—our first impression is that mischievous aliens have snatched up Miami and grafted it to the rugged Mexican coastline.

That night, we toast the good life from the terrace of a seaside restaurant overlooking The Malecón, a gorgeous, miles-long oceanfront promenade. Offshore, a faux pirate schooner laden with tourists returns our toast with fireworks and sounds of drunken partying instigated by its boisterous crew.

The next day, after buying supplies, we turn our sights toward Sayulita, an hour north, the first stop highlighted in our *Lonely Planet* guidebook. Noted as a top surf spot with a funky charm and "still Mexican feel," we're anxious to finally be rolling unfettered after many months of planning and daydreaming back in dreary New England.

Arriving in Sayulita, we quickly abandon the image from the guidebook that's been foremost in our minds—horseback-riding vaqueros parading down cobbled main street amid banners and gaiety—and settle instead for too-narrow streets lined with hip, overpriced boutiques; lunch spots with names like "Choco-Banana;" monied couples in souped-up golf carts; and swarms of trustafarian hippie types drinking forty-ounce "caguamas" (tortoises) of beer and hawking cheap jewelry along the sidewalks. Toward the north end of town, we find basic digs in a small guest lodge and settle in for a few days of exploring.

After dinner, I pack up my cameras and check out a small circus that's set up in a dusty vacant lot on the outskirts of town. (As with all our trips, this one is doubling as a write-off for my photography business.)

Feeling like I'm on the set of a Fellini film, I find the circus to be a sad, poignant family affair: sparse crowd of spectators scattered across rickety wooden bleachers beneath hulking, patched, seen-better-days tenting. Members of the Jimenez family—whose names and photos are prominent on the signage out front—trade roles with each other, doubling or tripling as animal wrangler (the show boasts both a lion and an elephant!), candy vendor, clown, and trapeze performer. I introduce myself and, though rushing to make their preparations for the show, the family welcomes me enthusiastically and tells me to photograph wherever I want.

By the time the show gets underway, it's pitch dark outside, not ideal for photography, however, there's some colorful lighting I can use to experiment with the new remote flash setup I've brought. Making my way around back for an insider's POV looking out toward the spectators, I'm greeted by a stern, warning gr-o-w-l-l-l-l right beside me. "What the fuck?" I jump back thinking, nearly tripping over a lion chained to a post at the back entrance. Barely visible in the dim light leaking out of the tent, the toothy mound of flesh growls again, warning me off a second time.

As the show is winding down, some decent images captured, I head out across the parking lot, back toward town. Ahead of me, a group of partying teenagers—with a cherry red, '80s-vintage, Olds Cutlass as their centerpiece—has me on alert.

"Hey, amigo, you like circus party?" one of the more macho-looking boys with cutoff sleeves calls.

Another joins in: "Nice camera, friend. You wanna take our picture tonight?"

Boys showing off for girls can turn ugly fast. Running is not an option. With racing brain processing the only two choices—ignoring the group or playing along—I play along.

"Por supuesto, muchachos. Sunreisen a todo. Whiskey! (Sure thing, kids. Smile, everyone. Whiskey!)" I say, walking up to them, smiling, and pointing my camera.

My luck in not getting eaten by the lion earlier in the evening holds, and the group has a great time striking poses and getting blinded by the powerful flash. Tough guys, memorialized now as pixels, will be preening and posing for the giggling girls for all eternity. How lucky they are that they'll never grow old!

After a couple of shots of tequila with them, I'm on my way, with a collection of fresh images and a couple of new memories to file.

✳ ✳ ✳ ✳ ✳ ✳ ✳

Over the next several days, the transition to 2006 passed uneventfully. Everywhere in Sayulita, the buzz was about real estate. We heard it talked about in coffee shops, tourist boutiques, and under thatched, restaurant umbrella tables at the beach. Despite our initial misgivings about Sayulita, we began to get drawn into the feeding frenzy and, even though we were seeing starting prices higher than the eighty thousand dollars we'd budgeted for a purchase, we began touring around with a realtor, looking for something affordable to chomp on. Day three, we came close to making an impulse offer on a tiny view lot with a half-finished foundation. As it turned out, some issues caused us to take a pass. The issues—mostly involving the lack of clear title—revealed other, more substantial challenges to buying property in Mexico. Coming to our senses, we realized that snapping up the first place we were interested in, so early in the trip, wasn't such a great idea anyway. Enthusiasm waning, we decided that we'd move on the following day.

January 2 - 4, 2006

On our way out of town, we feel exhausted from surfing the waves of Sayulita's real estate chatter. Like all beginning surfers, we realize the learning curve is going to be steeper than we imagined.

Heading north along the coast with Amy (head out the window to help us navigate), we begin striking out from the main coastal route, Highway 200, a two-lane snake of a road that rises and falls along the vagaries of the Sierra Occidental mountain range where it meets the Pacific. Following patchy dirt roads to desolate beach towns carved out of the jungle, we steadily check off places of little or no potential interest from our trusty Nelles map.

One stop we make, in Lo de Marcos, seems to have possibilities. Nice arcing beach. Pretty, flowing estuary. Long string of thatched, palapa restaurants. Decent-looking RV campground right on the beach. All good signs despite it also having a slightly abandoned, ghostly atmosphere. Or maybe it's because it's a gray day.

At the south end of the playa (beach), we see a hand-scrawled 'Se Vende' (for sale) sign and follow a steep footpath leading up the hill. Perched near the top of the trail, overlooking the beach and estuary, is a majestic house, nearly finished but showing signs of ongoing construction.

Yelling out, "Hola! Hello!" we see a middle-aged white guy step out onto the balcony. "This the place for sale?" we call to him.

"Um, yeah, sure it is," the guy answers, seeming confused by our presence. "Come on up."

We climb the steps and he greets us at the landing that joins an expansive terrace with stunning views.

"Hank," the man says, sticking out his hand.

Over the next hour, we tour the house and hear of Hank's problems. The house seems well built and has a workable floor plan, although the emphasis on security—including a genuine "safe room" tucked in the back —is somewhat disconcerting. Hank, in what seems to be an odd, reverse-psychology attempt to sell the place, describes in detail all the problems he's had with permits and construction. He caps off his tale of woe by telling us that the work has been halted for more than a year due to a property-line dispute with his abutting neighbor.

"He says he had a survey done," Hank informs us, "and claims his property line runs right through my living room! I'll prevail, but legal challenges here can take a lifetime. Fucking Mexico," he spits. "I can make you a great price, all things considered," he adds after an awkward pause. "Say, a hundred-and-fifty thousand, furnishings and appliances included."

Thanking him for the tour, we accept the packet of document copies about the property he offers for our inspection and let him know we'll have to think it over.

As we drive back out toward the highway, our heads are once again spinning with the possibilities.

"Amazing view," I say to Holly. "We'll never find a better deal."

"I know, I know," she says, "and it's nearly finished. I like the floor plan…"

"Yeah, even with the weird safe room. And the price? Can you imagine what that place would be in the States?"

"Yeah, well into the millions," Holly says.

"Kinda creepy though, the whole situation. And Hank seems like he's hanging by a thread. Must be going crazy there, all alone in his dream turned nightmare," I say.

"Actually, now that you mention it, the whole beach seems kind of desolate, don't you think? Can't quite put my finger on it, but…"

"Yeah, I was feeling the same," I admit.

"Oh well, guess it wasn't meant to be," says Holly. "Chalk up another near miss for the home team." She pauses. "I wonder what this next place, Chacala, is like?" she says, back to studying the map.

✷ ✷ ✷ ✷ ✷ ✷ ✷

By the end of the first week, we'd bumped and jolted down every pot-holed road leading to the beach between Vallarta and the next city up the coast, Tepic. San Pancho, Chacala, and Rincon de Guayabitos a bit further north are other "almost" towns we visited. However, nothing quite clicked, so we decided to keep moving.

Finally, heads swimming in a real estate whirlpool, we circled back to Vallarta to take a break for a few days.

2 - Disaster Averted

January 5, 2006

Heading south out of Vallarta this time, our next stop is El Tuito, a classic Mexican village in the mountains. On the way to El Tuito, we pass a giant sculpted iguana marking the location where 'Night of The Iguana', the classic John Huston movie with Richard Burton and Eva Gardner that first put Vallarta on the map back in the '50s, was filmed.

Over lunch and maps in El Tuito, we see that the route we're on, Highway 200, bypasses a large cape, Cabo Corrientes, that juts thirty miles out into the Pacific. We see from the map there are only a couple of roads into this remote-looking peninsula. Instead of continuing on the more-traveled route south as planned, we decide to turn right and explore.

After an hour of poking our way along rough, unmarked dirt roads, we start having second thoughts. Asking one old timer, "Que lejos a la playa?" (How far to the beach?), we're given a serious answer of half a day, mas o menos (more or less). "But it can't be more than an hour!" we reply, incredulous, while checking our map.

"Sí, posible menos, como dos horas, si se tenga un caballo," he replies. (Yes, possibly less time, like, say, two hours, if one happens to have a horse).

It takes a gringo second for us to get what he means. He's on foot, so of course it would take a full half day! Thanking him for his help, we drive on.

Further along, the road gives way to a rough single track, full of ruts and potholes and getting worse. We pull over to ask another crusty old campesino, "Is it possible to drive all the way to the playa?"

The man takes a half step back from the car and scratches his head. "Está rentado?" he asks, scrutinizing the car.

"Sí," I reply, and then continue in my broken Spanish, "it's a rental from Vallarta."

"Well, in that case," the man responds, in what little we can make out of his country-speak, "no hay problema. You can make it if it's a rental car."

Again, it takes us a gringo second to get this guy's humor.

Laughing, he smacks the car on the hood and waves us on.

Still cracking up about it a couple of rutted miles on, Holly recalls having read in one of our guidebooks about a saying here in Mexico: "Bad roads, good people. Good Roads, bad people."

"Well, if the saying holds true," I reply, "there must be some awesome people up ahead!"

An hour later, the dirt track we've followed down out of the mountains levels off into a broad coastal plain of cactus and scrub. The air becomes warm and thick. Passing alongside a plantation of coco palms, the road finally peters out to nothing at the edge of a large lagoon. Locking up the car and joking about crocodiles, we wade through hip-deep water to a low rise of dunes on the other side. We can hear the ocean just over the dunes, but we can't yet see it.

Spooked by our intrusion while crossing the lagoon, thousands of birds take flight, wing a lap, and then resettle. Among them are spectacular Roseate Spoonbills—leggy pink birds that look like flamingos, but which have a strange, flat, prehistoric-looking beak. Cresting the long, low dunes between estuary and ocean, we're stunned. The beach we've stumbled onto is a perfect golden crescent, completely undeveloped, stretching out to the horizon.

"Oh my god," Holly, gasps. "What have we done this time?"

Walking down to the water's edge, we dive in, splashing and laughing. Standing up to our waists in liquid heaven, we babble excitedly about our find. The day is perfect. We're in bliss.

Then, suddenly, while yakkity-yakking with our backs to the sea, the first of several huge rollers hits us, knocking us down, burying us both in an avalanche of powerful water.

Thrown into survival mode, I'm suddenly gasping and struggling to find air. I break surface for the briefest second and then wham, another wave has me tumbling and churning like a rag tossed in a giant washing machine. Short gasps of air are all I'm afforded as the panic sets in. Life in the balance surges and flashes—a chaos of foam, spray, sun shards, and water. In seconds—although it seems like hours—a million thought fragments flash across my consciousness. "Is this it? Will I die here? Got to get standing. Got to get head above water. Holly. Where's Holly? Tumbling. Falling. Out of control. Help! Air. Light. I'm getting a breath now. No, shit, it's gone. Too short. Not enough. I'm going to drown. I'm drowning, really! How can this be? Please. No. No-o-o-o! Upside down, head and shoulder smashed hard against the sand. The pull. Can't fight it. A let-up. Breaking surface. Quick breath, barely. Not enough again. Water everywhere. I don't want to... Crap, another one. Tumbling. Swirling. I can't make it. I have to make it! Have to. HAVE TO! Have to survive! Is Holly surviving this? How long? Breaking surface again. Gasping. Air. More light. Glittering beads of light, beautiful light, then gone again. Stripped away. Going under. Going down. How long this time? Flipping over backwards. Water in nose. Chest full of water—or is that fear? Do I care about dying? Should I just let go? No. Don't let go. Can't let go! Terrible this. It has to end! HAS TO END! Tumbling force. Liquid weight. Can't fight it any longer. Must fight it. Must find surface. Must find up!"

Finally, there's a let-up and I'm able to make headway, gaining a foothold and struggling onto the beach. "How long has it been? Half a minute? Five? And crap, where's Holly? More panic. Has she managed to survive this? Crap, crap, crap. Where is she, WHERE IS SHE?"

Rolling over, I see her. "Oh my God, YOU'RE ALIVE!" I call out to her bedraggled form crawling out onto the sand—a mix of fear and incomprehension on her face.

Afterward, we sit there hugging each other on the sand, trembling and absorbing the magnitude of the unholy baptism we've just been through, unaware that some significant part of our old lives is being washed away this day—not just by the waves but by all that's unfolding.

One thing is certain: with our neglect this time forgiven by great, knowing Nature, neither of us will ever again take the Pacific for granted.

3 - Land Ho!

January 5, 2006 (continued)

Driving back from the beach, still shaken from our near disaster, we come to a larger gravel road heading south along the coast. Not long after, we encounter a fork with yet another side road and a funny little hand-lettered sign for Hotel Mayto.

"A hotel way out here?" says Holly, incredulous.

Our composure regained, we both laugh at the prospect and decide to go check it out. Half an hour later, we're pulling up beside a manicured, white-washed hotel with a swimming pool and palapa restaurant situated at the far southern end of the beach—the same beach that had given us our BIG LESSON. Aside from a nice-looking house on the other side of the road, there's nothing else in sight. The hotel—dreamlike and abandoned-looking—appears to be an oasis for ethereal travelers recently drowned in the surf and gone on to playa heaven. To the left, a couple hundred yards distant, the beach gives way to a large, green, rocky headland jutting out into the ocean. Lounge chairs and palapa-umbrella tables are spaced along the beach in front completing the empty but otherwise picture-perfect scene.

"Well, this works," says Holly.

Taking our seats at one of the empty restaurant tables, a fresh-faced, high-school-age waitress appears from the back and takes our order.

We begin to deconstruct the experience we've just had. Yakkity-yakking again—but this time from the safety of the palapa restaurant—we share our versions of the episode with each other and then with the wait-ress.

"Está bien nadar aquí en frente del hotel, pero definitivamente no está allí" (It's fine to swim here in front of the hotel, but definitely not that way), replies the waitress, pointing up the beach in the direction we'd come from after hearing of our near disaster.

Despite the trauma of getting here, we sip cold drinks and marvel anew at the unspoiled beach we've stumbled upon. Another gringo family has arrived and is having lunch, and several other people that have come in are chatting at the bar. Overhearing the family talking about buying prop-erty, Holly and I can't help introducing ourselves and joining in. The par-ents, we learn, have recently purchased in Boca de Tomatlán, a nice little Bay this side of Vallarta where we'd stopped and looked briefly on our way here. The couple have recently quit their corporate lives and now sell boiled corn at country fairs in the summer months and take the rest of the year off to come to Mexico to play.

"We buy the corn at five cents an ear, and sell it for two-fifty," the man tells us. "We have people throwing fivers at us all day long in the summer months. Pure cash. Once we did a fair or two, we were ruined for the corporate life. Now we have a fifth-wheel RV to live in on the road and tons of friends we make the summer circuit with."

As a financial planner, Holly is always fascinated to hear of people reinventing themselves and creating alternate economic realities for themselves.

Going to the bar to pay our bill, I stand shoulder to shoulder with a wiry, crusty-looking guy of indeterminate origins. Speaking to the waitress in pitch-perfect Spanish, I assume he's Mexican until, turning to me, he offers up, "Are you looking for land?" in flawless English, "I heard your wife talking to those folks over there about buying."

"Um, sure," I answer. "Do you know of anything available around here?"

"Actually, I do," he replies. "Name's Steven, by the way," he continues, sticking out his hand. "Everyone here calls me Esteban. And yes, I've got some property that I'm thinking of selling. I'm just here picking up a to-go order. I've been gone several months. You're lucky you caught me. If you wait a few minutes, I can take you to see the place, if you'd like."

"Uh, sure," I answer back, still processing and disoriented as the day's events continue to unfold at a heady pace.

Soon Holly and I are following Esteban's tiny white clown car, even smaller than our own, through a gate back up the road, about three hundred yards from the beach and the hotel. We follow him up a winding dirt track that leads further back into the property, and then up, around, and behind a small hill, finally pulling up in front of a very basic-looking, cement-block hovel of a house. Despite the grim-looking shack, the yard is tidy and pleasant enough with planting beds, an asparagus patch, and a few scattered vines of blooming bougainvillea.

Out of his car now, Esteban beckons us into the yard, grinning. "Bienvenidos a mi casa (welcome to my house). Let me show you around!" A giant German Shepherd watches us warily while a second mongrel slinks about in the shadows.

"Oh, them," Esteban says, seeing us eyeing the dogs, and the dogs eyeing us. "Afuerate, Puppies!" (out of here, Puppies!). He scolds the slinking dog while putting his hand out to soothe the more noble-looking shepherd at his side. "Watch that one," he says, motioning toward the slinker. "That's Puppies. He'll sneak up behind you and take a bite if you're not paying attention. Ha!"

Holly and I share a glance. Is this a joke, or do we really need to be on our guard?

The three of us sit at a table in the shade, Esteban tucking into his takeaway lunch while describing his situation and giving us some background.

"My folks were immigrant Italian," he explains, "so Spanish has always been easy for me. I've been teaching English in the schools here. That and chess," he adds. "The kids here love it, and I love them!"

Intelligent and articulate, Esteban explains how he and his wife, Camille, were the first gringo settlers in Mayto, arriving nearly ten years ago. They moved here from their goat-herding homestead in rural New Mexico. He explains that over time Camille had drifted off to Vallarta, and even back to the States, more and more, until finally, their marriage was no longer tenable for him. He explains that with the split, Camille got the beach house they'd built next to the hotel, and he'd taken the raw land above the beach where we are sitting now.

"We're still close friends, Camille and me, but she's moved on, and so have I."

His plan now, he informs us, is to sell one of the two contiguous parcels he owns and, using the proceeds, travel more and paint.

"After all this time, and now with Camille gone, I'm just plain lonely here," Esteban continues. "It was fine when we were a couple, but now that that's over, I need to stretch my wings and fly a bit."

Esteban goes on to tell us that he's an artist looking to expand his career, and he's just gotten back from three months in San Pancho (near Sayulita), where he's been making gallery contacts and beginning to have a new life. He goes on to say that while he's enjoying the change of scenery, he still loves Mayto for it's BIG NATURE and tranquility and intends to keep it as his home base between stints to other places.

In turn, we tell Esteban a bit about ourselves and our quest, and also about our experience with Big Nature earlier that day. Esteban seems less interested in the near drowning or the Roseate Spoonbills we saw than he is about hearing that we waded across the estuary.

"That estuary has a big croc in it! This truly must be your lucky day!" he says with a laugh.

Esteban then goes on to explain the two contiguous parcels he has for sale, one that is sixty acres, and the second which is forty acres with a house on it. His intention, he informs us, is to sell one and keep the other as home base. He's asking two hundred and fifty thousand for the larger parcel or one seventy-five for the smaller one with the house on it.

Digesting all this has Holly's and my hard drives spinning fast. Aside from the fact we've defied death twice today, we're also absorbing that—for about the same price as the postage-stamp-sized house lot we were looking at in Sayulita—we can have land, real land, here. That and a house ready to use if we opt for buying the smaller parcel. Tempting as this is, there's also a crude, isolated feel to the place that's off-putting to me, as I expect it is for Holly.

"Come on," says Esteban, getting up from his lunch and grabbing a machete, "let me show you around!"

Still intrigued, we follow close behind. Esteban pushes "King," the Shepherd, ahead of us through the brush as we follow a trail up a small hill on the ocean side. "Snakes," Esteban says. "The dogs know their job is always to go first."

Then it happens. About thirty steps up the hill and WHAM, we are looking out onto a breathtaking view. Stretching out below is an incomparable vista of low hills and forest backed by infinite ocean with the golden sand beach we'd come along—and which nearly killed us—stretching out and out to a pinpoint horizon. To the right of where the beach curves into the distance, the mountains we came down earlier rise up from the coast like a giant reptile crawling out of the sea.

"Stunning," Holly says, mouth agape.

"Nice place you've got here, but too bad about the view," I say to Esteban, who's staring out to sea and showing no sign of hearing me.

An hour later, Esteban is ushering us back down the drive to the front gate. "Well," he says, grinning, "you know where to find me if you decide you're interested. I'm always up by sunrise. Feel free to stop back anytime, and I'll show you the whole spread!"

We say our goodbyes and drive away, heads dizzy from the day's roller-coaster ride. Driving back to the gravel road that led us here, we turn right at the intersection and head south.

"I don't know," Holly muses as we drive, "it's beautiful and all, but I feel like it might be too isolated here."

"Yeah, I know," I agree. However, inside, I'm buzzing.

A couple of minutes after leaving Esteban and his ranch, we arrive at another intersection with a smaller dirt road and a single sign reading, "Tehua Mixtle," with an arrow to the right.

"Well, here it is, yet another road less traveled," Holly says with a nod to the right, and then adds, "It's getting late. We should start looking for a place to stay. Might as well go ahead and see what this Tehua Mixtle is all about…"

Taking the right, we climb up the gnarly track, pass through a small cut in the hills, and find ourselves looking out at an extraordinary view. The rocky kilometer of headlands that started at the end of Mayto beach, and which we've skirted by road, now gives way to sheer cliffs bathed in sunset orange dropping away into blue-green ocean to the south. Farther in the distance, the beach begins anew, stretching to a vanishing point on the horizon. Below us is a picturesque fishing village hugging the natural harbor, a dozen small, panga fishing boats bobbing up and down with the rhythm of the sea.

"Whoa," we gasp in unison. It's been a day to remember, and apparently it isn't over yet!

Driving down a steep, sandy, access road into the town, we feel as though we've been transported to the Mediterranean. Rolling through the one narrow main street toward the quay, mere feet from doorways and storefronts, dogs and children chase each other while adults lounge about in hammocks and on front steps, nonchalantly checking out the gringos passing by. The entire world—or at least this one small slice of it—feels at peace.

We pull up to a mariscos (seafood) restaurant beside the central pier, a half-dozen mariachis—dressed to the nines in pink ruffled outfits, spit-shined cowboy boots, and grande charro hats—wander out, joking and laughing. Seeing Holly, they surround the car and begin crooning a capella style, hats to hearts and arms outstretched in chivalrous, operatic fashion. After the song, they bow their gentlemanly goodbyes and drift off.

"Hmmm, I suppose that could be taken as a sign from the cosmos," Holly notes joking, but clearly moved.

After a terrific harbor-side meal of garlic-drenched, grilled red snapper, we find our way to a small hotel situated on the water on the other side of the pier. Settling in for the night, we're both exhausted but also giddy and drunk on the uncorked, effervescent bottle of possibility that's been opened before us.

Too restless to lie down, I go out on the balcony overlooking the harbor. Out there with me is a gringa woman from the room next to ours. Ignoring me at first, she is drawing on a cigarette while watching the rising moon turn the harbor to silver. Below us on the beach, a group of children play in the shimmering plasma of the water's edge, and, farther out, bobbing pangas tug at their tethers in a gentle, rhythmic dance.

"Hey, so you've found paradise too," the woman eventually says, snubbing out her cigarette.

"Yah," I respond. "Nice for us that the guidebooks missed this one. How did you find it?"

"My husband and I live up in San Pancho. We met a funky artist dude who has land for sale."

My heart stops, but she continues...

"For the last month, we've been listening to this guy Esteban talking up his place. We thought we'd come down and check it out. If it's as great as he says, we may end up buying it. We're planning to go find him after breakfast tomorrow."

Quickly I say goodnight and am back inside our room.

"Who was that?" Holly asks.

"Sh-h-h-h-h," I whisper. "Holy crap, you'll never believe it!"

Telling her what I've learned, the two of us are in immediate panic mode. Had we come this far only to have such an incredible opportunity snatched away from us? Are we even sure this is our spot? It seems that a decision is now somehow making itself. This new situation is stimulating our competitive hunting instincts, something we both have in excess.

"We've got to get up at the butt crack of dawn!" Holly whispers. "We know Esteban will be up. We'll get him to show us the entire property. We'll have him take us out back where this couple from San Pancho will never find him!"

Setting our alarms, we collapse, exhausted, into a restless, fitful sleep.

4 - All In

January 6, 2006

We're up with the alarm before sunrise, packing the car and then hightailing it to Esteban's. Rolling through the gate at first light, we tell him we want to see every inch of the property.

Glad to have us back, Esteban wants to make us coffee and have us sit and chat. Trying not to seem pushy, but anxious to get him out to the back forty before the couple from San Pancho come looking, we do our best to nudge him toward action. Soon enough, machetes in hand, the three of us are heading out through the back of the goat corral, up and over the first big hill, and away from the house.

A network of trails created by Esteban's eighty goats runs throughout the property. It's along these trails that we explore. It turns out to be a memorable day as Esteban, dogs in the lead, guides us through arid woodlands of papalillo, palo santo, wild plum, and guamuchil trees. One grove we pass through looks like a Monet painting—dappled forest shade accented with wispy, vertical brush strokes of Spanish Moss. In other areas, we cross tracts of spiky wild pineapple; traverse rugged, rock-strewn ravines; and climb to hilltop vistas of magnificent Mayto beach stretching its arms to embrace the distant mountains. On one of the most substantial hills is a stand of forty-foot-high, hundred-year-old organ pipe cactuses. Toward the back of the property, we come across Esteban's herd of goats, which crowd around us, nibbling our clothes as we pet them and laugh.

During the tour, Holly and I learn more about the two abutting parcelas that comprise the property. The first parcela with the house on it, closer to the main road, is the smaller of the two. Aside from the one structure, and a series of dirt tracks that Esteban has cleared to access several hilltop ocean-views, the rest of the property is raw, rugged, undeveloped land. Esteban reminds us that we have the option of choosing one parcel rather than the whole thing if we'd prefer.

Following Esteban we arrive at vista after hilltop vista and begin to get our heads around the idea of owning such a large property. Clearly, this is nothing like the picture we've had in our minds. But our imaginations are now taking over and filling in the blanks. By early afternoon, Holly and I are smitten and decide to make an offer. Telling Esteban this, the three of us return to the house to begin a serious discussion of how buying the property might be possible.

Arriving back in Esteban's front yard, he finds a note from the San Pancho couple saying they were sorry to have missed him.

Making a quick huddle, Holly and I inform Esteban that we want to buy the smaller, front parcel with the house, but that we'd also like to secure the right-of-first-refusal for the larger back parcel should he ever decide to sell that piece.

* * * * * * *

Throughout the subsequent days, we were puppy dogs at Esteban's heels, meeting local folks, listening to his stories, and getting a welcoming feel for the place. Far from our first impression of it being too isolated, Mayto, a village of about a hundred, began to project a fun vibe, with smiles and waves greeting us everywhere we went.

One new character we met during this time was the manager of Camille's guest house, Casa Jardín (pronounced "har-deen," meaning Garden House), Efren Romero. Fleshy-faced, with pelo chino (curly hair) and an infectious grin, Holly and I like Efren right away, despite Esteban's prior warnings that Efren is a "lazy sack of shit and not to be trusted." Reading between the lines, we could only guess at the contempt Esteban must have held for Efren, Efren having become Esteban's replacement as Camille's confidant and general go-to guy after Esteban and Camille's divorce. It was clear to us that Casa Jardín, which Esteban built—and which Efren now managed for Camille—was the hub of an awkward, three-spoked wheel that represented both pride and sorrow for Esteban.

Despite Esteban's admonitions, Efren and his family became Holly's and my closest friends in those early days. After we decided to rent Casa Jardín, Efren—with his pretty wife, Estella, and their three children in tow —showed up with big smiles each day, ready to water the sprawling gardens, hack down coconuts for us, and bring us fresh fish or Estella's famous flan for dessert. Together with the family, Efren kept the place spotless and the gardens magnificent.

Afternoons, after finishing his work, Efren and I would continue a friendly chess rivalry we'd started. During the games, he taught me bits of Spanish and the local campo-speak such as "la revancha" (meaning revenge or grudge match), "no hay bronco" (no problem), and "purale, güay!" (focus, dude!). In turn, I taught him useful gringo expressions such as "spill the beans" and "shoot the breeze." Sometimes we understood each other well, but most of the time it was marginal. Even Efren's name ended up being a running linguistic misunderstanding—for over a year, we thought everyone was calling him 'a friend' because of his smiley good nature.

And so, in a mosh pit of mangled Spanglish, Efren and I laughed away the afternoons and forged a goofy etymologic camaraderie.

Another family that was to become a significant part of our Mayto experience lived next door to Camille's beach house. This Mexican-American family had recently moved to town after twenty years working and saving in California. Now they were beginning to build their dream—El Rinconci-

to ("the little hidden nook")—a family-run guest house on the playa. To the north of Camille's place and Hotel Mayto ran a small estuary and beyond that a university-sponsored turtle research station. 'The Turtle Camp', as it was called, was destined to become a very successful and lucrative draw for travelers to the area, but its founder would also go through a bitter land fight that would last many years and tear at the social fabric of the otherwise peaceful little town.

During that first visit with Esteban, we also learned of a fabulous mansion built into the cliffs nearby that was owned by several partners from Los Angeles. The place was the brain child of one of the partners, a successful architectural designer who'd previously designed houses for Bob Dylan and Don Henley. "They're interesting folks. You'll definitely meet them," Esteban assured us. "The mansion's owners, that is," he clarified, "not Dylan and Henley."

With each new facet carved into the rough gemstone of Mayto, a previously hidden glimmer and shine began to emerge. A journal entry from that time sums up the sense of wonder we were feeling:

January 7, 2006

What is this place, Mayto, that we've stumbled onto?

On Google Earth, Mexico appears as a chile-pepper-shaped appendage hanging down from the United States. Even Mexico's two principal mountain chains, the Sierra Madre Occidental and the Sierra Madre Oriental, while grand in their own right, cling to the continental underbody as if subservient afterthoughts to the more magnificent Northern American Rockies.

Zooming down and focusing in on the Pacific Coast, over on the left, you start to see hundreds of beaches, stretching thousands of miles, all strung together by a two-lane coastal highway. Beginning as a blur, then snapping into focus on the computer screen, you begin to make out beaches that run the gamut from hidden coves and fishing villages tucked away down dusty dirt roads to miles of long, palm-fringed, golden virgins. At this magnitude, it's also apparent that many of the beaches have long since been "found" and infected by a rash of high-rise resorts, cruise-ship ports, tacky beach shops, relentless condo salesmen, and all other manner of tourist-borne commerce.

Zooming in closer on the mid-coast—just below where the great long thumb of the Baja Peninsula hangs down to the west, where the divot of the Bay of Banderas holds thriving Puerto Vallarta—you begin to make out Cabo Corrientes, a forgotten lump of land protruding out into the ocean as if it was a rough-hewn pendant, dangling off the leather thong of coastal Highway 200.

Finally, at full magnification, Mayto Beach comes into focus, the last stop on your virtual tour. This is a surprisingly fine gem that you've happened upon, with its pristine, swimmable beach, nearby fishing village, and almost complete lack of commercial development—a pearl among pearls, if there ever was one.

How is it that the development vultures hovering in circles over their maps of the future haven't caught the scent and come rushing here already? Surely, as its name—"Cape of Currents"—suggests, this must be a place of swirling, competing energies to have resisted development this long.

Have we found our spot, we wonder, or has it found us?

✳ ✳ ✳ ✳ ✳ ✳ ✳

Over the next couple of days, we continued our tour of the area. Despite Esteban's eccentric demeanor, it turns out that he's a popular, highly acclimated guy, and we learn that he served on the local water commission, a fact that impressed both Holly and me. (Little could we have imagined then that I, too, would one day become a municipal official here—a dubious honor bestowed upon me a few years later when I was elected Treasurer of the Mayto Beach Commission. Despite the dignified title, I was, in fact, voted in during the first of three total meetings at which—despite much excited talk of new signs and a pedestrian-only zone on the beach— no action was ever taken, and I took fiduciary charge of the daunting sum of zero pesos.)

Over time, we've learned a lot about that—the fact that life here is most often doled out as an even mix of funny and sad. Chistoso y triste.

And ahhhhh, Esteban. Hard to capture a clear image of that guy. For most of those first days that we were with him, he was upbeat bordering on giddy, but there was also a hint of some dark thing lurking. Skinny as a rail. Leathered skin. Stub of filterless cigarette most often used to light the next. Clothes clean but of the cheapest, dime-store quality—his dress an odd combination of flips-flops and button-down shirt tucked into belt-less, uni-size, elastic-waist pants. And, like his clothes, Esteban's moods were random and disparate. Over the next several days we got used to seeing his buoyant, helium balloon highs pop suddenly, only to inflate again almost as quickly.)

January 8, 2006

As we're driving the snake-like dirt road to nearby Villa Del Mar in his tiny white Atos, a mere pimple of a car, Esteban's voice is pitched and laughing above the wind and road noise.

"… and you should have seen the look on his face when I told him his horse was gay!" he exclaims, laughing, smoking, and stick-shift driving, all in one motion.

Suddenly, a pickup truck laden with crates of tomatoes careens around the corner, heading our way. As the driver swerves to avoid us, tomatoes come flying, hitting our roof and splattering the windshield. Instantly Esteban is transformed to a snarling beast: "Ignorant troglodytes," he yells, giving the finger to the rear-view mirror. "This whole damn country can eat shit and die as far as I'm concerned," he growls, muttering a string of invectives under his breath.

For the next few minutes, Esteban's foul mood persists—his anger a menacing shark circling just below the surface until finally swooshing back to the depths as we pull up to a friend's house in the neighboring village.

Despite these mood swings, which we're beginning to get accustomed to, Esteban is known everywhere in Cabo Corrientes and is a popular tour guide. Wiry and wired; lubricated, salt-and-pepper hair; hyper-smart and temperamental, Esteban never hesitates to tell us exactly what he thinks about his neighbors—both the good and the not-so-good.

The first house we stop at belongs to the fisherman Julio, a shirtless barrel of a man. Julio stands in his doorway grinning broadly, one eye closed permanently and several large, leathery scars decorating his ample belly. It is at Julio's house, we see our first tejon—the local name for the coatamundi, an agile, raccoon-like animal with a long, bushy, ringed tail; impressive claws; and a prodigious snout like that of an anteater. With Julio looking on, his three scruffy kids demonstrate the coati's agility to us. Tied to a tree with a rope leash, the coati lunges up into the air for an ear of corn held high; is jolted as the rope reaches full extension; and then flips over backward, lands, circles, and then lunges, again, and again. We all laugh at its playful acrobatics, although I also find the creature's relentless, trapped energy disturbing.

Esteban is in sideshow barker mode now. "Those two scars are bullet wounds," he says pointing to two marks on Julio's oversized belly. "The long one here plus his eye are from a diving accident," he continues, indicating a couple of other deformities. Julio, an affable model, nods, and smiles, proud of his various achievements.

Later that afternoon, as we're sitting atop the hill next to his house and watching the sunset unveil itself, Esteban goes deeper into his backstory. Pulling a magazine out of a well-worn Fed Ex envelope, he shows us the cover. The photo is a striking shot of Esteban and Camille posing on the beach. In an interesting inversion of conventional roles Camille, standing proud and tall is holding the reins of a Chestnut stallion, while Esteban, twenty years more youthful-looking than his current state and twenty pounds more solid, sits rigidly in the saddle. "We were quite a couple," he says, carefully returning the magazine to its protective folder.

Next, Esteban proceeds to tell us a more complete account of the split with Camille and, in embarrassing detail, the depths of his loneliness here on the ranch—his monologue running steady as a rushing arroyo.

"We had some amazing times, Camille and me, but she needed more than what either I or this place had to give her. We're still good friends," he reiterates, pausing for a moment and gazing off into the shifting colors of the sunset. "Her mother was dying and her trips away dealing with that, and other things got longer and more frequent. I felt abandoned, and finally I told her I couldn't continue that way. I love her still, you know (takes a long drag, f-f-z-z-z-t, on his third cigarette), and she wanted to stay married, but I'd had enough. I told her I wasn't willing to live half abandoned like that any longer." Another pause. "But I'm also terribly lonely now. It's to the point where I've started going door-to-door, asking friends for a daughter I can take as a new wife. Some of them laugh at me, you know. They either tell me I'm far too old or else they start talking about sums of money that are absurd, even if—or should I say, when—I do end up having it."

"Hmmm…" Holly and I nod, not knowing quite what to say and taking in the irony of his thinking it's the price the neighbors are asking that's the absurd part of the equation.

"All the girls here want is a TV, makeup, and fancy clothes," he continues as the sky over the ocean gives up the last of its bloody glory. "I can give them that, can't I?"

"Last week I did manage to have a girl here," he continues, "but it only lasted a night. She has a three-year-old boy that she insisted sleep in the bed between us." Long pause and f-z-z-z-t cigarette glow lighting his worn, leathery face in the almost dark. "Imagine that," he continues, incredulous, "her thinking she could move in and use her son as a human shield to avoid ever having to have sex with me!" F-z-z-z-z-t.

January 10, 2006

Waking early at Casa Jardín, which we've rented for the week, Holly and I head out for a sunrise walk on the beach. Juiced by the idea that this might become our new winter home, Holly and I run laughing, dodging waves, splashing each other, and tossing pieces of driftwood into the surf for floppy-eared Amy. Like the glossy breakers rolling ashore, waves of excitement surge across our morning. Beyond the break, a pair of gulls dive for fish in the frothing surf and spray. Everything is perfect, or so we think.

Glancing back toward the point, something catches my attention.

"What do you think that is?" I ask Hol, pointing to a small, dark, fast-moving object on the sand about thirty feet away.

"A crab?" she asks.

We turn and head in that direction to investigate.

"Nah, don't think so," I respond, knowing beach crabs to be much more spindly and sand-colored.

What we find is a tiny, leathery turtle, about three inches long, struggling to get out of the crab hole. Bending forward, we examine the little creature.

"He must have fallen in on his way to the water," Holly suggests.

Reaching down, I try to pick him up, but there's a tug from underneath. Gripping the turtle more firmly, I pull again, extracting it from the hole, only to find it's not alone. Hanging from its back flipper is an ornery sand crab, snapping defiantly with its one free claw. A few light shakes and the crab falls away and then scoots back to its hole, taking a small chunk of turtle fin with it as a consolation prize. Fortunately, other than a nasty scar and harrowing story to tells his buddies, our turtle friend seems fine. Placing him in the wash, tiny flippers flailing, he gets sucked partially out to sea but is then returned by the next wave. The poor little guy is tumbled back and forth across the sand like that several times before finally disappearing into the sea.

Continuing on our walk, Hol and I go few more feet when, grabbing my arm, she cries out "Look!" while pointing ahead. There, scattered across the sand, are more than a dozen black blips like the one we'd just rescued—castaways left behind by a large, retreating wave. "We've got to help them," exclaims Holly, the playful young girl she is when happy now fully engaged. Running back and forth, we scoop up and carry the precious packages to the water, trying to keep ahead of the increasing numbers of baby turtles deposited by each new wave until we see the scope of the challenge—hundreds of black dots bobbing and tumbling on the incoming waves. Stepping back, surf swirling around our feet, we shake our heads.

Then something else happens. One of the two gulls we'd noticed earlier makes a calculated dive right in front of where we're standing.

"Oh, my god, he's got one!" Holly shouts, as the gull, baby turtle in its beak, pumps skyward.

Sure enough, there in its beak is a dark lump of nature's innocence. Then, before we fully realize what's happening, the second gull swoops down with the precision of a fighter jet and scoops up another turtle at the bottom of its inverted arc.

"We've got to do something to help them!" shouts Holly.

Together, we run into the waves, yelling at the gulls, flapping our arms around in comi-tragic parody. Defiantly, the pair of gulls rises and falls, mocking our efforts in darkly choreographed rhythm.

"There's nothing we can do," I shout across the waves to Holly. We retreat to the beach, feeling helpless and beaten.

Then, as abruptly as it had left us, good fortune returns. Within minutes, the feasting gulls have had their fill and lose interest, winging their way up and over the point.

"That was terrible," Hol says as we stand watching the survivors bobbing on the waves. We contemplate what we've seen a while longer, thankful that the dying is over.

Minutes later, we catch sight of the two gulls returning from over the rocky headland. "Oh, crap," Holly moans as the birds wing their way toward us. Then an even darker reality hits. Behind the two lead birds comes one more, then two, then six, then an entire flock of gulls, beating a path in our direction.

We watch the carnage for a minute or two until it becomes too difficult for Holly. As we walk away, I try to assuage her grief with wisdom about the beauty hidden in even the darkest of nature's harsh realities, but I know it's a lame attempt—the joy of the morning having been carried off.

✳ ✳ ✳ ✳ ✳ ✳ ✳

All in all, Mayto seemed wonderful, especially with Esteban giving us the grand tour of the area, introducing us to our future neighbors, and even taking time to play a game or two of chess with me in the shady yard of what would eventually become our house.

Like singles having a great first date, Holly and I, on our first date with Mayto, were excited by all the possibilities.

Before resuming our trip further south, Esteban, Holly, and I scratched out a rough agreement of terms to buy the property on a scrap of paper. We made two copies, all official-like, even though the idea of this being a legal document was absurd. We agreed that we'd sign a more formal purchase and sale agreement in Vallarta once Holly and I had transferred the deposit funds to Mexico, a day or two before our scheduled flight back to the states.

Assuming our scribbled agreement with Esteban to be unenforceable, or at least something we could buy our way out of if necessary, we told ourselves that we should follow through on our planned sojourn further south along the coast. The reality was, however, that we were hapless fish, hooked and landed by the beauty and untapped potential of Mayto, but we continued south anyway to complete the exercise.

One spot we visited, and which captured our imagination, was a beach called Chamela, several hours further south. There we met a vivacious, middle-aged woman named Maria who showed us several unusual properties. Maria owned a small beachfront palapa restaurant near a hidden cove where we made camp for several days. During our stay, Maria showed us a few available properties she knew of, often swinging a machete nearly as long as she was tall to cut through the weedy undergrowth standing guard around the vacant houses. Holly got especially excited about the striking-though-gutted remains of a mansion high up in the cliffs overlooking the ocean. I, in turn, was intrigued by a different property Maria showed us—a rundown wreck of a place in a crocodile-infested mangrove forest, just off a spectacular but deserted, un-swimmable beach.

In the end, these tempting morsels only served to confirm our decision and further whet our appetite for Esteban's property. Returning to Mayto on the way back north, we met with Esteban to re-affirm our intentions.

January 24, 2006

Today, the last day before our departure to head back to the States, Esteban takes us to a local soccer game. With half the village present, the scene is a patchwork of color and activity—jersey'ed players chasing tired-looking ball across threadbare field; tops being snapped off dripping, ice-cold beers; groups of men joking and shouting; clusters of women scolding and laughing; and roaming dogs searching for scraps—the crazy-quilt patches all stitched together by a running thread of raggedy children, darting and weaving, giggling and shrieking. As the only gringos present, Holly and I are self-conscious at first but gradually sync in to the rhythm, accepting beers and sodas, greetings and handshakes, and excited to be introduced to life behind the cultural curtain.

Tomorrow, on our way to the airport, Esteban will accompany us to Vallarta where we'll make a stop at the Notario's office and sign a contract to purchase the property.

* * * * * * *

There was one minor mishap those first days with Esteban—something that would have reverberating karmic echoes in the years ahead. After we received a tour of his fledgling fruit orchard, Holly didn't latch the gate correctly. When we returned from a short excursion, the three of us found the goats happily munching the last remnants of the fruit trees that Esteban had recently planted. With us, the prospective buyers in tow, Esteban made a pretty good act of laughing it off, but it was clear to us that he was seething inside.

Among the myriad other things we didn't know then was how much upheaval the process of buying this property would cause us. Nor could we have known the extent that this trip would find us leveraging all we had and, eventually, cashing out the comfortable, steady lives we'd spent thirty years building back in New England.

But, at that point, we didn't need to know. Our mission accomplished, reconnaissance over, we'd found what we'd come looking for—a place to escape to in winters, and then some!

Section II

Primeros Pasos (First Steps)
Autumn 2006 ~ Spring 2008

"The beginnings and endings of all human undertakings are untidy."
~ John Galsworthy

5 - The Deal Goes Down
(Then Back Up, Again)

There's a tropical disease that the CDC is yet unaware of. It infects anyone that spends too much time in Latin America. The vectors of this disease are still uncertain; however, it's believed to be spread by mosquitos, sand fleas, or possibly excessive alcohol consumption. The disease, once caught, leaves its victims unable to function or be satisfied in their regular lives north of the border.

Holly and I, plodding through what we called our 'wash, rinse, repeat' lives back in predictable old New England while dreaming of Mayto, became so afflicted. Like crewmen being teleported back to the Enterprise during a Klingon attack, we were caught halfway—molecular ghosts in a failing transport beam, stranded in some disembodied nether-place between diverging realities.

Over that summer, we worked at making the dream of Mayto more real by purchasing a massive Dodge 250 Ram with slide-in camper and rigging it out for our next trip back. The camper, outfitted with propane refrigerator and other amenities, was meant to provide all the creature comforts we'd need for our return to Mayto, whether camping at the property or touring around to other parts of the country.

By the autumn of the 2006, the truck and camper were ready to roll, and plans were in full swing for our return to Mayto. Winter was the slow season for my photography business, and my employees would be able to manage for a couple of months without me. Holly's business of managing the finances of eighty families, on the other hand, required her to stay on a shorter tether, and meeting up with me for periods of two to three weeks at a stretch was all that she could manage. Increasingly, we were becoming distracted adolescent lovers lost to an obsession—the dreamy idea of all that land and possibility causing increasing dissatisfaction with our default lives in the states.

Communication with Esteban during this time was excruciatingly sparse. The closest available internet for Esteban was at the high school in Villa Del Mar, the next village down the coast, and that only had service when the cosmos happened to be perfectly aligned. Holly and I would receive random, cryptic messages from him about once a month such as, "We're all set. Everything coming along nicely!" or, "Don't make any dramatic changes yet. The bureaucrats in Guadalajara seem to be playing games with us." These terse emails would either make us fly like a kite or send that same kite of hope crashing to earth.

Other messages, such as, "Papers ready for next step. Please wire $5000 U.S. to my account by the end of the week," would cause Holly and me to scramble to put together the funds, swallow hard, and make the transfers. Throughout this time, we were increasingly nervous because of a bailout clause in the purchase agreement that we'd included and which specified a November deadline—at which point either party could pull out of the deal if the titling process was still unfinished. Having so far ad-

vanced Esteban north of fifty thousand dollars—and knowing it to be unrecoverable if the deal were to fall through (escrow services had yet to arrive in Mexico at that point)—we forged ahead on faith that Esteban would be OK with completing the purchase even if the deadline, which Holly and I had insisted on, were to pass.

Finally, mid-November, a few weeks before I was scheduled to leave and drive the camper rig down to Mayto ahead of Holly and our five adult kids who were to be joining us for Christmas, we received a final, shattering email from Esteban:

"THE DEAL IS OFF!" was all it said.

With no way to reach him, Holly and I were thrown into complete turmoil. In panic mode, we decided that I should leave immediately, and the final two weeks of preparation were compressed into two days.

With the first snow falling in New England the day before Thanksgiving, I called to Amy from the cab of the truck: "Hey, Amy. Wanna go for a ride?" Amy hopped in, thrilled at the prospect, and, with dog as my co-pilot, I gave Holly a kiss and began driving south.

November 21 - November 28, 2006

For the next six days, I'm a rolling worry fest, obsessing my way southward through Pennsylvania, West Virginia, Arkansas, and all the other states in between Maine and Texas, while catching only minimal snatches of sleep in truck-stop parking lots. With music tapes and monotonous Spanish lessons struggling to be heard over the groan of truck tires on pavement, the entire mid-central-south United States blurs into one, long, continuous ribbon of worry.

"Welcome to Missouri!" a passing sign says.

"Ha, welcome to *misery* is right," I snarl back.

"64-oz T-bone Steak, this Exit!"

"T-bone Steak this, you bastard," I say, giving the poor, undeserving billboard the finger—remembering Esteban and the tomatoes.

"The Deal is Off? The F'ing Deal Is Off? Dafuk? He can't just do that! He's got more than fifty thousand dollars of our money. We've got a contract, for Christ's sake! He can't just do that. HE CAN'T JUST DO THAT!" I complain bitterly to Amy, who's snoring on the seat beside me, long since transitioned from doggy-going-for-a-ride-euphoria to deep canine boredom. Possibly even clinical depression.

By the time I reach the border crossing, three days in, I'm coming unhinged.

"Purpose of your trip?" the uniform asks me.

To kill Esteban, I think to myself. Or did I say it? It's hard to tell. Having spent the last 72 hours inside my echo-chamber head, and that inside a rumbling truck cab, and that inside a...

"Sir?" the uniform prompts stiffly.

"Huh, umm, oh, sorry," I mutter, snapping out of it. "Tequila and sunshine?" I manage, forcing a smile.

With three more days of highway food and hundred-times-heard cassette tapes still to go, the narcos, if they're out there, better scatter and hide.

* * * * * * *

Like most good, worry-induced stress, my neurotic obsessing proved all for naught. By the time I arrived in Mayto, I'd gone numb. Rather than unloading on Esteban, which I probably would have done had I encountered him at a rest area back in Texas, I instead greeted him with a smile and a hug. He, too, had returned from whatever dark pit he'd fallen into and, within an hour of arriving, the two of us were sitting at the plastic table in his front yard toasting a renewed pledge to see the deal through. Mildly apologetic, Esteban told me he'd been having a bad day the day he'd emailed that the deal was off. He was sorry, he said, that he hadn't been in touch since, but he'd been busy as hell. I bit my tongue, thinking of the turmoil the early departure has caused Holly back home and of the six thousand miles of angst I'd just endured in getting there.

And that wouldn't be the end of it—the angst—by a long stretch. With more than two-hundred-thousand unsecured dollars on the line by the time we finally got to closing, faulty communications would continue as the deal's central theme, compounding the stress as the quagmire of privatizing the property wore Holly's and my nerves—overstretched bungee cords barely holding their load of precious cargo—to the breaking point.

During one particularly stressful period, Esteban had a Mexican cash buyer offering him double our price to break his contract with us and sell both parcels immediately. Somehow, we managed to talk Esteban out of reneging on our deal, but not before he'd announced that we had one week to exercise our right of first refusal for the second parcel and that he'd raised the combined price of both parcels to slightly more than half a million dollars. In a Hail Mary financial scramble, Holly and I met with bankers, took out second mortgages on our house and a business condo we owned, and continued our rush toward the edge of the cliff, and our headlong financial plunge into uncertain waters.

But that was all still part of an unknown future. At the point of having finally arrived, salvaged the deal, and then sitting there sipping a cold beer in the shade with Esteban, I was feeling nothing but relieved—happy to have my optimism, which had been in critical condition the entire drive down, transferred out of intensive care and recovering nicely.

December 4-21, 2006

With the episode of the deal nearly collapsing behind us, I feel like I'm finally really here at the ranch, which, up until now, has seemed more dreamlike than any sort of actual reality. Over the past week, I've walked the property daily with Esteban, learning about water pumps, ranch gates, and other simple systems he has in place. I also drive around with him running errands, meeting more people, and getting an ever-deeper education about the lay of the land.

In Esteban's ten years of living in Mayto, he has taught English and chess to scores of locals, has run an Internet cafe, has served on the local water commission, and, for a brief period of time, tried to make an entrepreneurial go of selling goat's milk pudding out of a takeout window installed at this house.

"It was going great," he explains about the pudding venture. "I was selling gallons of the stuff. I even bought a case of nice little glass serving cups. But by the end of the first month, the son-of-bitch customers stole every single one of the cups. Fuck 'em, the pricks. Their loss. They didn't deserve my delicious pudding!"

At times, his bitter distrust and dislike for all things Mexican, especially the Catholic church, overwhelms his otherwise gregarious nature. Most days vibrant and outgoing, but other days reclusive and broody, Esteban essence is as hard to catch hold of as a swirling dust devil. Still numb from the six-day drive and a bit shell-shocked from the recent 'The Deal Is Off' disaster, I tag along and make friendly with him the best I can, learning to back off and give him space when his darker moods surface and breathing a big sigh when, toward mid-December, he announces he's leaving. His plan is to move to the mountains, nearer to Guadalajara, so he can better shepherd the privatization paperwork through the muddy quagmire of bureaucracy there. He tells me he's planning to turn the ranch over to Holly and me to use for our time here this winter. With the prospect of the kids and their friends coming to visit in a week—and Holly and I having the run of the ranch for the winter—the murky crystal ball I've been peering into these past months starts taking on a luminous glow.

Up the road, at Rancho Los Naranjos, we meet Enrique, get a tour of his rooster coops, and smoke one of the big joints that Esteban is so fond of. In addition to raising the best fighting cocks around, Enrique is the local narco drug distributor for this area. "Good guy to know, but I try not to get too close and personal" Esteban offers as advice.

A little later in the day, a coconut's throw down the beach, we meet Israel (pronounced Is-rye-al) who appears too young (and handsome) to be a full-on biologist in charge of the University of Guadalajara's turtle research station.

"Smart guy," Esteban advises me. "He's another good person for you to know." Israel gives us a tour of the camp: a collection of makeshift huts, an open-air dining hall, pit toilets, a couple of palm-thatched cabañas, and several large, netted pens where nests of turtle eggs are protected.

"The goal is we keeping the eggs here protect until they make hatch, then getting them to ocean for sunset so they have a full night ahead before seabirds and other animals has them," Israel explains in broken English.

Not exactly a perfect solution, I think, remembering the slaughter Holly and I witnessed our first morning in Mayto.

"…but really, eets as much about the poaching as the natural predators," Israel continues. "We patrolling the beach at nighttime collecting the fresh nests, and we brings them back here to keep the poachers from stealing them."

"Poachers?" I ask, deciding not to make a joke (crack a yoke) about delicious 'poached eggs.'

"Yes, some of the local peeples here still eat them. Some mens still thinks the eggs makes them more powerful lovers. Our biggest job here is to make them old macho guys more educated. We mostly get Olive Ridleys turtles here, but Mayto is one of the only beaches left on Pacific coastal where we get some Leatherback also. Something to see, those big girls coming ashore to lay their eggs. Especially in the time of when the moon ees full. Looks like Super Bochos (Super Volkswagon Beatles) driving up onto the beach from the ocean! We make save-ed thousands of Ridleys since the past two years we come here, and maybe like two hundred Leatherbacks," Israel informs us proudly.

In the next town, Villa Del Mar, we meet Casi Miro, another smart, bilingual local who spent eight years in the States working as an auto mechanic in Oklahoma and, later, as a ranch hand in California. Weighing in at about 120 pounds, Casi's well-worn cowboy boots and plate-size silver belt buckle describe a borrowed image out of sync with his diminutive frame and timid demeanor. Dogs in the yard scratch and flies buzz as Casi Miro gives us a tour of the scrapyard in front of his house. Mixed in with engine blocks and disembodied transmissions are various inventions that Casi has been working on.

"This one I make-ed from a chainsaw and an old bicycle," Casi says, showing off the rusty remains of a child-size go-cart. A couple of water jugs mounted on tractor suspension springs make for excellent bull riding practice for his two young sons. Atop a post is an experimental wind generator fashioned from tractor fan blades and a Volkswagen alternator. A rusty Mad Max-inspired dune buggy parked alongside the scrap heap is Casi's main transportation around town.

Esteban and I head back to Hotel Mayto. We have dinner together under the outdoor palapa as the heat of the day loses its force, softening and blending into the glow of sunset. There I hear the story of the hotel's owner, David Soto senior, a wealthy opera singer from Guadalajara who created Hotel Mayto, this modest oasis of civilization in the middle of nowhere.

"He's been a true benefactor for the whole town," Esteban tells me. "The Patrón of many here. He doesn't need to make a peso off this operation. He really just created it as a getaway place for his family to play."

Esteban also introduces me to his most loyal friend, Luzano, the hotel manager. "He's the only guy here, other than David Soto, that I can really trust," Esteban informs me.

* * * * * * *

Years later, after Esteban is gone, Luzano, having lost his job at the hotel, will become, for a time, the butt of the town humor mill. Driving daily out to Piedras Azules, an exposed outcropping of rock a few miles up a nearby arroyo, Luzano will pound away with hammer and chisel trying to break apart several van-sized chunks of granite. The spirits, Luzano will tell everyone, visit him in his dreams each night and instruct him about where a vast treasure of gold is buried. Several years after that, the fantasmas will still be visiting Luzano in his dreams, and he'll still drive out to Piedras Azules occasionally to take a few whacks at his unyielding nemesis. Eventually, however, his stature will be restored when he becomes manager of a big building project for the ex-pro football player, Rulon Jones, who's purchased property a couple of villages north of Mayto along the coast.

During the weeks I was in Mayto, touring around with Esteban and getting acclimated to village life, Holly, who'd been in New England wrapping up all the unfinished business I'd dropped to drive down, was preparing to join me at the ranch just before Christmas. Plans were in place for all of our kids and some of their friends to join us. It was an exciting time once Holly arrived, the two of us getting everything ready for the Christmas holidays.

6 - Eggs at the Gate
(And Other Adventures in Language Land...)

I remember an offbeat Mex-Western movie based on a mix-up over the word caballo, which, in Mexican Spanish, means, specifically, a male horse, but which, in English translation, is generally thought of as any horse, male or female. In the movie, a suspected Mexican horse thief is being interrogated by a gringo posse. Misunderstanding their questioning (in his mind, he definitely hasn't stolen a "male" horse), the Mexican denies their accusations and, in doing so, infuriates the men because of his blatant lying. What ensues is an extended chase scene across the Rio Grande into Mexico.

I always loved the idea of that epic linguistic mistake and other etymological missteps like the tricky false cognate "embarazada" (saying you're pregnant when what you mean to say is that you're embarrassed, which, of course, doubles down on whatever embarrassment you're expressing to start with). Another classic mistake is asking someone if they like huevos (eggs) which, for a Mexican, is automatically assumed to mean that you're asking, "Do you like testicles?"

I loved these bloopers until Holly and I started making some of our own spectacular linguistic blunders.

One of our good ones occurred during our second winter in Mayto.

A bumper sticker we'd found the previous summer had been affixed to our camper rig before we drove it south. The sticker, a ten-inch white diamond, had nothing on it but the name of one of our favorite Mexican Movies: "Y Tu Mamá También".

"I love that movie," I said to Holly when I saw the sticker for sale in a novelty store back in New England.

"Yeah, me too. It'll be great on the back of the camper," she agreed.

With the sticker displaying our sophisticated knowledge of Spanish and Mexican film culture, I drove that rig six thousand miles across the U.S. and Mexico, and all around our new Mayto community for several months.

One day Esteban commented on it. "Oh, by the way," he said nonchalantly "you might want to think about taking that bumper sticker off your truck."

"Oh? What's the matter with it? It's a great movie," I replied.

Chuckling, Esteban responded, "I don't know anything about the movie, but that's a common dicho (saying) down here. It means, 'Fuck you... (pause) ...and your mother, too.' Those are generally considered to be fighting words."

December 22-23, 2006

Holly and I have rented Casa Jardín, where our adult children and their friends will be staying. During our time in the States we'd been talking up Mayto to friends and family. Busily preparing now for everyones' arrival we're anxious to have their first impression be a great one.

Next door to Casa Jardín, El Rinconcito—the fledgling hotel, restaurant, beach bar, and social epicenter for both locals and travelers alike—is a buzz of building activity. Not much for lounging on the beach, I join in the action some days, learning the basics of Mexican construction: laying up block, mixing and pouring cement into crude, wood-plank forms, and using an angle grinder to cut stone and tile.

Mexicans, I've found, love word play. Almost any word can be stretched and contorted like Play-Doh into a variety of forms. Likely as not, a simple 'sí,' as in 'yes,' becomes 'Simón' or even 'Simón Bolívar,' leaving Spanish neophytes like me scratching our domes in confusion.

Having grown up with a 'pun-ishing' father and being a collector of tortured twists of the tongue, I feel an inherent connection with Mexican wordplay, which is generally obscure and even downright weird at times— that is, when I have some clue as to what's actually being said. Trying to walk on wobbly, beginner-Spanish legs while pitching in with the work at El Rinconcito, I struggle to understand the continual joking of the crew but find the language different from anything I've encountered in my books or classes.

"Soy tu chido chilán (I'm your cool worker dude)," I say one day, trying hard to pick up a few of their words and participate by using them to make a little flourish of alliteration.

"Nuestro chido chilán (Our cool laborer dude)," Fernando corrects my accent.

"Nus chilandrón (Our super-cool laborer dude)," someone else kicks in.

"Chilán-chilango (Mexico city-slicker turned laborer)," illiterates another.

"Chilán-chango vestido con chaleco (Worker monkey dressed in a vest)," responds yet another—the train a runaway now.

"Como chillin' chilangos vestido en chido chicanos chula chanclas (Like relaxed Mexico city-slickers dressed in a cool latina's flip flops)," one of the group, who's bilingual, adds, tossing a bit of spicy spanglish into the dish they're serving up.

"Chingón cuñados chupando chelas!" (Super cool cousins sipping micheladas—a popular drink made with beer and lively flavorings), contributed by one of the crew adds still more spice.

'Oh great,' I'm thinking, smiling along like I almost kinda sorta know what

the hell they're all joking about at this point while feeling disappointed that even

this simple exchange has left me totally lost—the few words I tried to play with having run away and left me abandoned on the verbal playground.

"Cállense, carajos! (Shut up, knuckleheads)," Fernando chides the lot of them. "Manos a la obra! (hands to the work)." The labor resumes.

In the evenings, when things would settle down, Holly and I began getting to know Fernando and Maricela better and enjoying a growing kinship with them. Fernando—hard-working, beer-guzzling, always friendly, and sporting a pony tail and compact, pugilist's nose and frame—is impossible not to like. As is Maricela—a generous, loving, buoyant, earth-mama-spirit-being who can also drink and swear, or gossip with the best of the local ladies. I decided to try to learn my street-speak from her.

December 25, 2006

Christmas Day. Our kids and their friends have settled in and the lot of us celebrate by challenging some locals, organized by Efren, to a rousing game of beach soccer in which we promptly get our gringo asses handed to us. The locals' strategy is formidable. Efren's six-year-old daughter Karla takes down our players, who are three times her size, with swift kicks to the shins, while son Freddy, star of the local Mayto team, effortlessly dribbles past any of us left standing.

With friends and family around us, the vacation days float by on waves of laughter and margaritas, and the hook—our growing love affair with Mayto—is set ever deeper.

As is often the case, however, just when things are rolling along most smoothly, reality's pesky side asserts itself.

Later in the afternoon, I'm out front of Casa Jardín cleaning fresh pargo to grill for our Christmas dinner. Inside, Josh, our oldest son, is working on the dinner trimmings while, out on the porch, the rest of the gang is reading, working a jigsaw puzzle, or napping. Suddenly there's an explosion from inside the house: BABOOM! followed by several screams. Holly, up on the porch, is yelling "J-O-S-S-H-H-!" and, followed by the others, she disappears through the screen door into the house.

I bolt up the stairs three at a time.

Inside, everyone is crowded around Josh, who is lying unconscious on the floor.

Holly, once a registered nurse, is kneeling over him gasping, "Josh, Josh, Josh, Josh…."

"Get back!" I command. "Everyone get back and give Holly room."

Within seconds, Josh's eyes are fluttering open. He's beginning to come to.

"What the f—," he mutters, regaining consciousness and looking around.

"The stove!" someone says, pointing across the room to where the oven sits, doorless and off-kilter. In front of the oven is a pair of flip-flops, previously Josh's but now worn by the invisible ghost of someone cooking.

It's clear that Josh, at over six feet tall and a solid 200 pounds, has been blown clean out of his flip-flops all the way across the room.

"I was just lighting the pilot," he explains, still groggy, while Holly, holding him tight, strokes his hair. "But those stupid knobs are all worn and I couldn't see if the gas was on or not. It must have been on since we used it this morning…"

Soon he's up and about, and, despite his new look—devoid of any facial or arm hair—the family is returning to normal:

"Josh, you look like a Mexican hairless!" younger brother Zach points out.

"Homer Simpson Goes to Mexico!" one of the other sibs pipes in.

"How was your first flying lesson, Bro?" another asks.

"Did you shave all your hair off for more speed?" a visiting friend contributes.

"Que pobrecito peloncito," (What a poor little baldy) Efren's wife Estella says, laughing, upon seeing Josh later that afternoon.

December 27, 2006

Two days after the oven incident, Efren comes running into the yard yelling urgently. "Daniel, Daniel, ven acá, ven acá. ¡Hay huevos a tu puerta! ¡HAY HUEVOS A TU PUERTA!" (Daniel, come quickly. There are eggs at your gate. THERE ARE EGGS AT YOUR GATE!)

Up on the porch playing cards, we all look around at each other quizzically.

"Eggs at the gate? What the hell does that mean?" someone asks.

Always the instant authority on everything, I answer, "Oh, it's probably someone selling fresh eggs. That happens a lot here, people showing up selling things…"

As I say that, Efren, out of breath, comes bounding through the door onto the porch, repeating about the eggs but with what seems to us an urgency exceeding the matter at hand.

Efren then grabs me and starts pulling me off the porch, urging me toward the road. Followed by the others and curious as hell, I follow behind as Efren gestures forcefully up the road toward the property. "Mira, Daniel. Mira tu puerta!" (Look, Daniel. Look at your gate!)

In a flash of understanding, I finally get the urgency. There, up the road where our gate should be, is nothing but smoke.

Doing linguistic backflips, my mind tries to put all this together: Huevos a tu puerta. Huevos a tu puer… AHHHH. NO. THAT'S NOT IT AT ALL! What he's been saying is, "¡Fuego a tu puerta! ¡FUEGO A TU PUERTA!" (Fire at your gate, FIRE AT YOUR GATE!). Apparently, someone had tossed a live cigarette butt and the prevailing breeze sent a wall of flames through into the property. The fire is now advancing up the hill toward Esteban's house, where Hol and I have the camper parked.

For the next couple of hours, we, our kids, and a few neighbors who happen by, use rakes, shovels, buckets of water, and anything else we can lay hands on to wrestle the fuming monster into smoky submission.

Along with the language lesson, we also learn that dried cow turds are terrific fuel for keeping one's field burning for as long as possible.

✶ ✶ ✶ ✶ ✶ ✶ ✶

Poor Efren, with his infinite patience for all things 'gringo'.

The next time he was involved in our linguistic mayhem was when, for no good reason, I taught him to say, "What the fuck?", assuming he would know not to use it everywhere. For the next week or two, Efren would pop up out of the bushes, shrug his shoulders, hands outstretched, and say in his adorable Mexican accent, "Daniel, what the fuck?" or, "Holly, what the fuck?"

The problem was that Efren, a proper family man, apparently didn't understand exactly what it was he was saying, and I didn't know that he didn't know. All I can figure is that "what the heck" was what he must have thought it meant, because, one day, when there was a big group of people next door at El Rinconcito, Efren walked into the scene and, seeing me, shouted out above the din, "Daniel, what the fuck?"

The group—our crew, some locals, and a handful of tourists—all turned in his direction, laughing and giving him a big thumbs-up of approval.

Fernando was standing beside Efren, who was smiling along at the phrase he'd used but also looking a little confused by how much reaction it had received. Turning to Efren, Fernando explained what "What the fuck?" meant. Efren, turning as bright a shade of red as it's possible for a Mexican to turn, came running over and tried to strangle me.

A suitable linguistic lashing I received as proper payback for the 'embarazada' moment I'd handed Efren came soon after that.

January 7, 2007

Yesterday evening, Holly and I had dinner over in Tehua Mixtle with a couple of friends from Vallarta. From the upstairs restaurant terrace overlooking the moonlit harbor, we had yet another of what we call our 'vacation moments'—those perfectly ripe slices of vacation fruit. I was especially in my glory, breaking a sweat and guzzling beer to douse the flames of homemade salsa mulata hot sauce I'd smothered my grilled huachinango (red snapper) with.

When the waitress came to the table, I asked her, in my neophyte's Spanish, if she might be able to give us the hot sauce recipe. In what I took to be a joke about her not wanting to give up her sacred recipe, she shook her head "no". Now, three or four beers into the evening, I was certain we had some sort of repartee going and joked back, "Oh, I see. I get it. If you tell me the recipe, you'll have to kill me."

Instantly the waitress stiffened, backed away a step, and curtly asked us if there was anything else we needed before disappearing into the shadows.

"I guess she must not have understood me," I explained to my friends, and then told them the joke I'd attempted to make since they didn't speak as much Spanish as I did.

After that, a rather grumpy older woman from the kitchen came out and finished up serving us. We didn't see the waitress again that evening.

Hours later, drifting off to sleep, I bolted straight upright.

"Crap," I said to Holly.

"What?" she asked, half asleep.

"Oh, man, this is bad."

"WHAT?" she asked again, frustrated.

"I think…Yes, yes, I'm sure of it…."

WH-A-A-A-T-T-T?"

"I told the waitress that if she didn't give me her recipe, *I'd* have to kill *her*!"

"Arghhh," moaned Holly, rolling over. "You're an idiot!"

The following morning, I'm down at El Rinconcito, relating the incident to Fernando and asking him to come with me over to Tehua to help straighten things out.

At the restaurant, Fernando explains my pathetic attempt at a joke. We have a good laugh with the woman from the kitchen, who turns out to be the owner and someone we'll get to know well over the years. Her daughter, Liz, the waitress, is also there. She smiles along, but less enthusiastically.

* * * * * * *

It's taken a few years, but, now and then, when the story gets retold over grilled snapper at the restaurant, Liz laughs, no longer afraid of me.

To this day, Holly and I still struggle to go deeper with our Spanish— that elusive gateway to the kingdom of culture. Though we've attended our language classes, listened to our tapes, done our verb and vocabulary drills, and even dreamt occasional Spanish dreams—and even though I'm what I call "sloppy fluent"—the twinkling fairy of true fluency still alludes me, flittering and flirting, just out of reach. For me, the biggest challenge has been the local "campo speak" dialect, thick as tar, that dominates the countryside. As a visual learner, I can nail a word in just a viewing or two, but that same word, if heard rather than read, becomes a mischievous gremlin that can slip by me twenty-five times before I'm finally able to grab hold and wrestle it into submission. Fortunately we seem to at least be getting past the worst of our self-inflicted 'embarazadaments,' those pregnant, embarrassing moments we all love to hate.

Finishing up our visit that winter, Holly and I do our best to secure the camper and house and say our goodbyes to the new reality we're gradually inhabiting. As I take one last look at the truck before leaving, I catch sight of the slightly less faded spot where the "Y Tu Mama También" sticker had been for all those months and smile.

7 - Return

On our return to Mayto in the autumn of 2007, Holly and I were nervous bundles of anticipation. Our communications with Esteban since leaving the previous winter had been, once again, challenging. Often it would be a month or more in between emails from him, and those continued to be abrupt, cryptic messages such as, "Hit a snag in Guadalajara. But don't worry, I can work it out" or, "Things still moving forward, but funds are getting low".

One day, out of the blue, we received a phone call from the Cabo Corrientes municipal offices. Over staticky line I could just make out that Esteban was needed in El Tuito to sign a document related the sale. Apparently, the office in El Tuito, an hour from the ranch, had our U.S. number on file as the contact of record. We sent an email to Esteban, which he eventually collected from the high school in Villa Del Mar. The following day, he drove to El Tuito and signed the papers, thus completing the multi-week, twelve-thousand-mile, communications loop.

Even though we didn't hold title yet, Esteban had plans to be away and gave us permission to stay at the property and use his house again over the entire coming winter. With our businesses running well and reliable staff holding down the fort at home, Holly was planning to carve out a couple of longer stretches to be in Mayto, though we were reconciled to the fact that I'd be alone there for some of the time.

Once back in Mayto, we begin to settle in. Despite our having gotten acquainted with the place the previous year, everything about it now seemed fresh and exciting. What we missed seeing in the newness of it all, however, was that some deep foundation of perspective was also beginning to shift for both of us. During our time away from Mayto, Holly and I had continued grinding away at our working lives in New England, telling ourselves that things were completely normal. Throughout those months, our bodies plied our respective trades while our heads inhabited another world—a faraway beach in Mexico. It wasn't fair, really. How could working lives of intense obligation and responsibility possibly compete with an imagined, carefree ranch life in a tropical paradise? Once we returned, the imagined future and larger-than-life present joined forces, conspiring to upend our other, more mundane world back in the States. Basically, we were ruined. We just didn't know it yet.

Meanwhile, Esteban continued to pull the strings and grease the wheels of the privatization process. Ours being only the second ejido property in all of the Cabo Corrientes region to go through the bureaucratic minefield of privatization (i.e., removal from being part of an ejido—pronounced eh-he-doh—a communal land holding common throughout Mexico since the land reforms of the '70s). The process was particularly grueling. Early on, Esteban invited all the ejido members (ejiditarios) to a goat roast on the beach, where, after gallons of beer and tequila had been consumed, hands were raised and permission was granted for the property to be removed from the communal land holdings. Due to the contacts he'd been cultivating, lawyers he'd been consulting with, and bribes he'd been paying, Esteban was certain we were only a matter of weeks away from completing the process at both the state and national levels. Little did we know then that we were still more than a year away from holding the title!

November 28 - December 12, 2007

The drive up to the house is, in itself, an adventure. Arriving at the property, we find the quarter-mile-long driveway completely covered in head-high, weedy undergrowth. Gunning the engine of this year's rental sedan, I plow ahead as fast as possible while trying to stay on the road. Slashing a pathway up the hill, the sea of weeds is parted by the hood of the slip-sliding car, sending a rush of noise and blur of green, as good as any Jurassic Park ride at Disney world, rushing past the windshield. Sliding to a stop in front of the house, we get out and inspect the car, which, with hood and grill covered in shredded plant material, has been transformed into a grinning dinosaur, stopping now to enjoy a delicious weedy lunch.

The house, which we'd only actually been inside a few times the previous year, is in even worse shape than we remember it. The solitary bedroom, basic bathroom, and stark, minimalist kitchen are partitioned from each other by walls that try to reach up to the Spanish tile ceiling but don't quite make it, leaving a small gap between ceiling and roof. Rough cement floors and bare, unpainted walls give a grim, desolate feel to the place. This is only to be outdone by the filth Esteban has left in his wake. Amid the dirt and debris in the bedroom, a stained futon mattress is the only furniture.

Our pickup truck and camper, parked beside the house, are intact, but, to our dismay, we find that one of the back windows to the house has been jimmied and a water pump plus a few tools have been stolen. Between the theft and the dismal condition of the place, our sunny flower of optimism is beginning to wilt.

Despite the setbacks, we set to work. Having renovated our house in New England—which was in equally desperate shape when we started, yet ended up on the cover of a prominent New England home-decor magazine—Holly and I are confident that we'll soon have this new challenge whipped into shape. After dragging out the futon, which looks to have served Esteban and his dogs for many years, and replacing it with a basic bed frame and mattress, our little borrowed bungalow begins to look livable.

One of my first projects is to build a wooden framework to hold the slide-in camper currently sitting on the back of the truck. Mounting it on the frame will allow us to use its tiny gas refrigerator and kitchenette (since the kitchen of the house is little more than a sink) while liberating the truck to use for transportation once we return the rental car.

Esteban's sad, jury-rigged solar electric system—consisting of one small solar panel on the roof, wires running down the bedroom wall to a decrepit 12v marine battery, and a string of wires leading to bare, 12v lightbulbs—gives us just enough power to brush our teeth and read a few pages before dimming, flickering, and finally delivering us into darkness each night.

"It's an adventure," Holly and I tell each other.

"Besides, we love candles," Holly adds with a lightness clearly meant to offset the gloom.

Little by little, we even grow accustomed to sharing our space with a Whitman's Sampler of animal brothers and sisters, even though we do, at one point, cold-heartedly evict the family of rats living in the kitchen cupboard.

$$* * * * * * *$$

As is common in relationships, we eventually came to hate many aspects of life here that we loved at first. One of these things was the open, Spanish tile ceiling. It didn't take long to find out that the hundreds of spaces between the overlapping, concave, terra cotta tiles that created a beautiful pattern of dappled light also served as openings thorough which dust, insects, and a constant barrage of tiny, windblown acacia leaves were all free to enter as they wished. Even the dreaded alacránes (scorpions) were free to come and go.

"Oh well," Holly shrugged at one point early on, "we'll just have to give the place a little sweep every day. We'll get a beautiful mosquito net," she added, trying to stay optimistic. "And look at the airy, open Spanish tile ceiling. I've always loved the tropical feel that Spanish tiles give a room."

Our Cocker Spaniel adjusted less well, as the scores of gecko lizards traversing the walls were a constant source of anxiety for her. Like the Spanish tile ceiling, the geckos were another relationship that started as joy but which we grew to despise over time. Initially, we loved their skittish presence, their goofy smooching sounds (the reason the locals call them 'beso de culos'—kiss asses), and their wriggling, spastic, movements. Many times, when opening a cupboard or a window shutter, Holly and I would experience a jolt of fear as a gecko darted out of its hiding place. "Ha, gotcha!" each of us would laugh after the other had jumped back with a gasp. Over time, however, the cute little shits they deposited everywhere got to be tiresome.

As part of the purchase arrangements we'd negotiated with Esteban, we stipulated that the herd of goats would be left behind when the transac-

tion was complete. Esteban, who was now away from the ranch for months at a time, had left his mongrel dog, Puppies, as the resident guard animal and had hired a local boy to feed and check in on them as well. The goats were mostly self-sufficient and could be left alone if given a steady source of water.

On our return, however, we found Esteban had not honored our agreement concerning the goats. Apparently he'd entered the crash-and-burn phase of his departure from the ranch and had posted a "Se Vende Chivas" sign at the front gate and soon sold off the entire herd while Holly and I were away in the States.

Holly and I were disappointed to return the second winter and find the goats gone. We weren't upset enough to make an issue of it, however. Grudgingly, we realized that since we were part-timers who only showed up in the winters, taking care of a herd of goats was impractical. As it turned out, we had our hands full when it came to animals without goats, anyway, and the Spanish tile ceiling let in other things besides the geckos…

December 15, 2007

Holly is sweeping the floor in the kitchen while I lounge outside in the hammock on the porch. Hearing a shriek from inside, I grab a machete and run to investigate the commotion. Inside, I find Holly in full battle mode using the broom to swat at a four-foot-long snake that's wriggling this way and that trying to escape. "It fell out of the goddamn ceiling, right in front of me!" Holly shouts, half hysterical. "Kill it!"

With one quick swing of the machete, it's over. There's a sharp "ping-g-g-g" as the machete slices through sinewy muscle and strikes the cement wall that the serpent is trying to climb. Choreographed with the ping, the head pops up and over the table in a graceful arc and disappears somewhere over in the corner. Laughing but horrified, I grab the still writhing body and carry it outside, leaving a trail of bloody tears. Holly, meanwhile, starts moving chairs about, looking for the missing head.

After tossing the body, I do a quick, post-mortem research in our reptile guide and find that the serpent I've murdered was a harmless boa constrictor. An innocent. Now I feel bad and vow to be more mindful next time. "Oh well, you didn't know," I say to absolve myself, returning to my hammock. Inside, Holly continues her sweeping. Halfway back to sleep, the swoosh of her broom and the buzzing of a fly combine in a drifting duet. The fly, persistent in the way of all flies, is making strategic raids on my mellow.

Suddenly there's another shriek.

"What the fuck is it this time?" I shout, nearly falling out of the hammock and running inside, where, broom in hand, Holly is on the attack again, a second boa writhing about her feet.

"It fucking happened again!" she shouts. "This one fell right on my goddamn head!" More prepared this round, and knowing the snake to be harmless, the two of us corner it and, using a forked stick, manage to pin it down. While Holly keeps it pinned, I grab it behind the head, pick it up, and carry it outside, its sinuous body wrapping and unwrapping around my arm with unnerving strength.

＊＊＊＊＊＊

It was around this same time that we were joined by yet another roommate of the reptilian persuasion. A good-sized black garrobo iguana, which we often heard rattling the roof tiles at night, took up residence on top of the wall between our bedroom and the bathroom. Known to eat a wide variety of insects, including the nasty alacranes (scorpions) we feared, we figured that the old guy wasn't hurting anything and decided to let him stay. At night, he'd shuffle about up above, hunting his prey, and, by morning, he'd be back lounging in his favorite spot on top of the wall, hidden except for his tail which always hung down in the same spot along the wall inside the bathroom.

Poco a poco (little by little) we began making improvements on the house. Classic saltillo floor tiles were laid, and we had a carpenter, Manuel, replace the crappy aluminum front door with a heavy rustic wood one and make cabinet fronts for the bare kitchen shelves. For the finishing touches, we hired Efren's teenage son, Freddy, to come paint the inside.

December 18, 2007

It's the first day of painting, a Sunday. Efren, who's fast becoming our most trusted local friend, stops by in the morning to help Freddy get started. Knowing Freddy to be the star of Mayto's soccer team and an excellent horseman, we feel he'll do as good a job as anyone might. Taking charge, Efren shows us all how to water down the five-gallon bucket of paint half-and-half with water so it will spread farther.

"But Efren," I question him, "doesn't that make it necessary to have more coats of paint? Don't you end up using the same amount but with more work?"

Looking at me with a sympathetic 'You poor gringos don't know anything, do you?' expression, Efren shakes his head. "No, Daniel. In Mexico, we do it this way."

Equipped with various sizes of paintbrushes, rollers, a paint tray, and an extension handle, and fitted with ear buds attached to a cheap cell phone at his waist, Freddy sets to work. Hanging out in the front yard drinking lemonade with Holly and me, Efren gets up and goes inside repeatedly to check on the progress and give instructions. Finally, satisfied that Freddy is well on his way to a brilliant painting career, the three of us leave him to work and head down to El Rinconcito to see what, if anything, is going on there.

The afternoon is a typical one at El Rinconcito. A bunch of both Efren's family, the Romeros, and Fernando's kin, the Herreras, are all hanging out in the shade under the palapas at the beach. As is normal for Sunday get-togethers, several of the women are busy chopping fresh abaojón needle fish, avocados, onions, cilantro, limes, and tomatoes to make heaping plastic bowls of fresh ceviche and guacamole. As the two families laugh and mingle under the palapas, giant, two-liter bottles of Sprite and Coca Cola are introduced to their smaller, more powerful, glass-bottled cousin, tequila, in a family reunion of spirit and kinship. Children—darting here and there, chasing each other laughing, or crying when hit too hard by an older brother—are tolerated until, having kicked a soccer ball too near the food and drink tables, they're hauled off and dunked in the surf by their parents.

By late afternoon, Holly and I are exhausted and head up the road to the house. Freddy, just finishing up, has done an excellent job and, to our surprise, has finished the entire place.

"Wow. Amazing." We congratulate him. Glancing around the rooms, we smile to let him know we're pleased with the job he's done.

As Freddy cleans up, I count out the bills. When I fork over 250 pesos, or about $20 U.S., plus another fifty pesos as tip, Freddy seems thrilled. Happy faces all around.

Early the next morning, I wake to the sound of Holly laughing in the bathroom.

"What's up, Hol?" I call to her, still half conscious. Barely able to talk for the laughing, she says, "You've got to come in here. You've got to see this."

As I stumble to the bathroom, Holly points to the top of the wall above the tub.

"Uhm, OK," I say, noticing the 'painter's holiday.' "So, he missed a spot."

"Look again," Holly says, still sputtering. "Why do you think he missed *that* place in particular?"

"Umm… Hmmm… Wait… Oh my god… You can't be serious!" I say, realizing the little bare patch is the same size and shape as an iguana's tail!

Sure enough, later that afternoon, we see our old pal the iguana out in the yard, the top of his tail the same color as our freshly painted walls.

✳ ✳ ✳ ✳ ✳ ✳ ✳

From then on, the iguana's name was "Stripe," and, even after months of wear and fading, he still looked dashing from the fancy 'detailing' Freddy had given him.

December 24, 2007
Today, Christmas Eve, finds Holly and me picking up the kids and their various friends and partners at the airport in Vallarta. After loading our giant Dodge Ram plus a rental car with supplies, and bringing aboard a parking-lot mongrel that the kids name "El Guapo," we dub ourselves "The Griswalds" and begin this year's family Christmas vacation, hooting and laughing our way back to Mayto.

December 25, 2007
Christmas day is the second annual soccer game on the beach. Our gringo crew, dubbed "Los Tejones" after a common marsupial in the region, is looking for a comeback from last year's devastating defeat, handed to us by "Los Venados (The Deer), the ragtag band of local youth and parents. In theory, we should have Los Venados outgunned, particularly given that we have our daughter Aja and her partner Kim with us, both semi-pro Roller Derby skaters with backgrounds in soccer. El Guapo does his best to help, but the problem is Los Venados are employing the same strategy as last year. Efren's daughter Karla has grown a foot and is ready to dish out even stronger shin-shattering blows. Efren's son "Prieto," budding soccer star and expert house painter, is now an invincible sixteen-year-old who effortlessly lays our pathetic gringo butts to waste.

An hour in, the locals having re-asserted their dominance, the game devolves steadily into player's visits to the sidelines to chug beer or make laughing, splashing tackles in the rolling surf.

December 28, 2007
This year, Holly has arranged with Maricela (Mari) to cook my favorite dish, chile rellenos, for my fiftieth birthday, which is today. With our kids

and their friends staying at Camille's guest house right next door, the makings of a great party are taking shape. Between all the locals hanging out and our own crew, it turns out to be a grand feast followed by everybody, including El Guapo, dancing in the sand until well after midnight.

At one point, a giant beetle lands in the middle of the heaving bodies. Laughing, everybody dances out of the way as our son Josh moves in, taking charge. Standing over the huge bug and using the breadth of his traveler's Spanish, he invokes the crowd to decide the insect's fate.

"Sí?" he yells out to everyone, sticking his thumb high in the air "Or No-o-o-o?" He surveys the crowd with dramatic flair, thumb turned down now. "NO-O-O-O-O-O!" everyone shouts. And with that, Josh's size-eleven flip flop—the same flip flop from which Josh was launched when the oven exploded last year—comes down hard, flattening the insect to much laughing as the party continues.

I can only imagine the looks on all the other flips flops faces when they hear Josh's flip flops tell about the vacations Mexico they've been having.

✳ ✳ ✳ ✳ ✳ ✳ ✳

In the end, El Guapo, a golden stud of a specimen, turned out to be quite the rogue. Disappearing each night, then reappearing the following morning, bedraggled, smelling horrible, sporting a shredded ear or flesh, or limping gimpily. By the end of their vacation, our daughters Jessica and Hillary, who'd originally planned to take El Guapo back to the States, had cooled on the idea of trying to get him his green card, and they ended up passing him along to a family we met on a trip to Sayulita the week after Christmas. The family we gave him to was certain Guapo was their recently deceased uncle reincarnate. As much as we'd been enjoying El Guapo, we were all relieved to be rid of him.

Returning to Mayto the following year, Holly and I were amused to find all of Mayto populated with dogs of similar appearance and dubious character to that of El Guapo. Still later, Holly and I received a random email from someone saying, "You don't know us, but we were given El Guapo by the family you gave him to last year in Sayulita. We just wanted to let you know that he's alive and well, and living in L.A.!"

Receiving that email, we could picture El Guapo wearing cool shades and an ascot, and driving a Lexus convertible down Hollywood Boulevard.

Vacation over and all of our visitors gone, Holly and I returned to the process of securing our title, though communications with Esteban, our main link in the process, continued to be difficult. The village in the mountains he'd moved to had no real Internet access, and communication services in Mayto were still a stumbling toddler—more down than up for most of the time. The previous summer, I'd pre-ordered the very first iPhone, and the week the devices arrived in stores in June 2007, I had one. Wandering around with my shiny new smartphone, I soon found two or three spots around Mayto that had cell reception. One was a big tree by the main road on the other side of town. Passing that tree, one would often see people standing around or sitting in parked cars (often ours), making calls or receiving simple text messages. With my futuristic smartphone, I could even download an occasional email.

Later, I found that by climbing the highest tree on the highest hill on the property behind our house, and holding the iPhone up over my head, I could get a couple of bars and, on a good day, email almost as fast as I'd been able to do with the old dial-up service in the '90s back in the States. Up in my tree, hand held in high salute to technology, I felt like I was starring in a ridiculous Mexican sequel to 'The Gods Must Be Crazy.' I eventually nailed steps, a seat, and a board for a desk onto the tree and held office hours like any average Joe.

By mid-January of 2008, communications from Esteban picked up as title approvals were being given and final closing documents drafted. Despite the rush, receiving PDF documents from the top of a tree in rural Mexico with a first-generation iPhone was far from being a quick process. More than once I'd have my arm up for forty-five minutes, with a download 95% complete, when the battery would go dead. Descending from my perch, I'd hike back down the trail, charge up the phone for an hour at the house, and begin the process all over again.

With our deal to buy Mayto swinging like Tarzan from vine to vine, and me playing my own absurd role up here in my tree, we continued our adventure through the perilous bureaucratic jungle. Then, on one of my trips up to the tree, I received yet another confidence-crushing bombshell from Esteban...

January 20, 2008

"R-r-r-r-i-i-i-n-g-g. R-r-r-r-i-i-i-n-g-g." (I have my ringtone set to the classic, old-timey telephone sound, and here, up in my office, is the first time I'd heard it ring in Mexico!)

"Hello? ssz-c-z-c-r-a-t=ch... sz-c-z-c-r-a-t-ch... Hello, Daniel?

"Yes, who is this?"

"It's Esteban...ssz-c-z-c-r-a-t=ch. I'm calling from Mascota. The title is complete, but I think... I think I've had a heart...ssz-c-z-c-r-a-t=ch..."

"What? I didn't catch that last part. What did you say?"

"I think..ssz-c-z-c-r-a-t=ch...had a heart attack."

"Oh my god. Are you in the hospital?"

"No, I won't let those pinc...ssz-c-z-c-r-a-t=ch touch me. I'm here in my... you...ssz-c-z-c-r-a-t=ch. Can you he..ssz-c-z-c-r-a-t=ch me?"

It continues like this for half an hour. Apparently, Esteban was up late painting the previous night when thunder exploded in his chest and he was knocked to the floor unconscious. Now, at ten o'clock the following morning, he's regained consciousness and is calling for help. Unable to convince him to seek medical help, I'm at least able to talk him into taking some aspirin and tell him to hold tight. That we're on our way.

Six hours later, Holly and I are at his rented hovel in Mascota. Looking like a wax museum figure, Esteban is up and about, making coffee. Having a cigarette.

For several hours, Holly and I do our best to persuade Esteban to see a doctor, but we might as well be trying to open a coconut with a plastic spoon. The most we're able to do is talk him into turning over all the privatization paperwork he's been dealing with before we say our goodbyes.

✱ ✱ ✱ ✱ ✱ ✱ ✱

Taking the packet, Holly and I hired a law firm in Vallarta and, one month later, we were at the closing table with Esteban, who, though still weak, was looking better.

One of the last steps in the process, after the state and national work in Guadalajara, was a required final sign-off by the local ejido. The law firm assigned a specialist in ejido matters to accompany me back to Mayto for the signing. Gathering up the local ejido's Mesa Directiva (Board of Directors) took all afternoon as local kids were sent off to find fathers and uncles at work in their parcelas. By dusk, we were all assembled, an informal 'junta' (meeting) at the side of the road in the middle of town. As onlookers gawked and pickup trucks rolled past sending up clouds of dust, the Vallarta lawyer, a crusty old relic, hand wrote the final document. Because the lawyer had forgotten his folio, the document was written on the only thing we could find—the back of an old file folder I'd scavenged out of our car. We still have that priceless piece of personal history, complete with signatures of Ejido Del Mar's most important politicos, as testament to the harrowing two-year process we'd been through.

Paranoid to begin with, Esteban now had hundreds of thousands of dollars in his bank account. True to what he'd been telling us for months, he left for the drive south to the Guatemalan border immediately after closing, and was never heard from again. I stalked him on the Internet for a time and found he'd settled in Belize and was writing for a local online rag there. As he promised, he refused communication with anyone from Mexico, even Camille. After the second year of his departure, all signs of him vanished.

Despite the challenges of dealing with Esteban's lousy communication and wild mood swings for nearly three years, we remain forever grateful for his integrity in following through on our agreements. We are also appreciative of all the goodwill that he and Camille, Mayto's first gringo "settlers", brought to the community. Their excellent relations paved the way for all the others, like Holly and I, who have followed.

For us, the closing was just another step in the process of owning, with many more months of nerve-wracking legal gyrations ahead for forming a Mexican corporation and then, finally getting the deeds registered.

In the interim, Holly and I, still feeling restless to know more of Mexico, decided to spend time in Guanajuato, a colonial city in the central highlands where we took Spanish classes and made many new ex-pat friends. Returning to the coast mid-March, we paid Mayto one last visit before catching the flight back to our 'real' lives in New England.

8 - Central Casting, Part 1
(El Rinconcito)

There was a popular TV sitcom back in the '80s, Hill Street Blues. The show, set in an unnamed urban police headquarters, was an odd mix of lifelike, dramatic situations and completely outrageous minor plot lines played by bit-part character actors. Against a backdrop of a dingy precinct headquarters, the show's regulars swapped snappy, fast-paced banter while bumbling through moral and ethical dilemmas, having affairs, testifying in court, and, sometimes, fighting crime. Despite being formulaic, what set the show apart (it ran 146 episodes and earned a record-setting 98 Emmy award nominations) was the weekly introduction of one or two bizarre, character-driven sub-plots. The casting director must have had a blast sifting through mountains of aspiring actors for quirky, comic characters on a par with the likes of Seinfeld's Kramer or Mash's Klinger.

Now, if you take that basic format, strip away the precinct setting, and bring all those wacky character actors onto the set of Gilligan's Island, you'd have a pretty good approximation of the local beach hangout, El Rinconcito. Destined to become the social epicenter of Mayto, El Rinconcito was, for our first several winters here, little more than a basic guest house with half dozen guest rooms plus Maricela, Fernando, and their two children's personal quarters. Set back a hundred yards from the beach, El Rinconcito was often abuzz. This was largely due to many of Fernando's ten brothers and sisters living nearby plus all of their relations visiting from all around Mexico and the United States.

Group dinners were the rule at Rinconcito and, beginning early in the afternoon, everybody would pitch in—pressing tortillas, chopping fish for ceviche, uncapping cervezas, or giving plenty of unnecessary instruction. For us, and any other gringo tourists that found their way down the tortuous rag of a road from El Tuito, the introduction to Mexican family life was a joy. After dinner, the long row of plastic tables would be separated for games—poker or other peso-an-ante gambling games for the adults and the classic Mexican picture card game, Lotoria, for the kids—while the drunk or restless wandered from table to table joking and causing trouble along with the laughing, shrieking jumble of children, dogs, and crawling babies.

By the time we finally took full possession of the ranch in the winter of 2008—a full two years after starting the process—the demographic of El Rinconcito had begun to change. Parts of the road down from Tuito had been paved, and the development buzz was starting to infect the air with its unpleasant odor. Rumors of a huge land deal down the beach past the turtle camp were circulating, and the tourist-to-local mix at El Rinconcito was becoming whiter.

Fernando, a tireless improver (man after my own heart!), was constantly expanding the Gilligan's Island stage set. Crude signs carved into chunks of wood give instructions like: 'Smile. Relax. Be Happy,' 'Sit Here,' 'Sunset Spot,' or, the helpful, bilingual instructions painted over the urinal:

"Atentale—Aim Here!" An assortment of blocky, rustic, parota-wood fur-niture was added, and the sculpture garden—a rambling mélange of drift-wood, sea shells, animal bones, washed-ashore plastic toys, creepy baby dolls, and other random flotsam—was becoming a destination all its own. The collection of cow skulls was growing, and 'Joe's Bar,' a stand-alone cantina run by Fernando and Maricela's son Joel—a.k.a. Joe—who'd re-cently graduated from bartending school, got moved from place to place depending on Fernando's mood. Completing the assemblage was a small store, Todo en Poquito, that sold everything from fishing gear and suntan lotion, to women's clothes, tools, snacks, and BB guns. The store was set up in one of the building's ground-floor openings, while upstairs new rooms were being added at a steady clip. El Rinconcito, place where everyone is welcome, and everyone feels like they've just found their new home.

February 8, 2008

Many of the the ex-pat guests that find their way to El Rinconcito are tire-some drunks, but a decent mix of more interesting personalities also touches down. Afternoons, after having my swim or a run on the beach, I often make a swing through the Rincon like a birding enthusiast on the lookout for unusual species.

This afternoon, one of these sightings is Preacher George. I learn that Preacher George, previously a Pentecostal preacher, has turned away from the church and is now a proselytizing maverick, railing against organized religion's false prophets and profits. Preacher George bears striking re-semblance to Burl Ives, particularly when singing and playing his guitar. Unlike Ives, however, his songs are pure, outrageous sacrilege, sung in a deep southern drawl with lyrics like:

"God sent me packin'. Think I'll have to give him a whackin'. Gonna give the good book the real thumping it deserves…"

or

"My accounts are in tatters, my life is a bust. Gonna put my faith in Jesus, 'cause he saves at First National Trust. Yes, Dear Lord, Jesus Saves, Jesus Saves, and he's getting a pretty good rate. Jesus is one fart smella', he saves at First National Trust…"

Preacher George—folk-singing rebel missionary, out to save the real heathens of the world.

Talking to Preacher George about his blasphemous sermons between songs is a trip. Having been a Pentecostal, Preacher George has spent a lifetime wrestling the big questions the way Crocodile Dundee wrestles alligators. After suffering a personal trauma that brought his confusion to a head—and having now won back his soul and left the church—Preacher

George jokingly refers to himself as 'the pastor of the dark side' with an online ministry of thousands of unrepentant sinners like himself.

"It's been one hell of an amazing trip!" Preacher George says, eyes twinkling. "I used to stand in the pulpit, preaching my Pentecostal pecker off, week after week, to maybe a hundred people, two hundred tops. I was trying to be a true believer—giving it every damn thing I had. I wanted to bathe in devotion, to swim in the light of consecration, but, in the end, I realized it was all a total load of crap! Now I'm gaining like a thousand new souls a month! Damn, son, I've even got more n' a hundred ex-ministers like myself who've seen the dark and are now followin' my work!"

"Well, what do you preach if you're not preachin' Jesús?" I ask. "The devil?"

"Nah, man. Nah. Nothin' like that. I just tell it like it is, you know. I tell 'em how the church—all churches—are a motherfucking racket. Pure, un-holy, un-Godly cults, all of 'em. All about power n' money. Power n' Money! 'If ya gotta believe,' I tell my followers, 'believe in Love, man. That's all that's important!' That, good music, good sex, and maybe a shot of rye whiskey and a joint now and then. Ha!" he exclaims, laughing and raising his bottle in salute.

As he breaks into another song, I wander off to the moonlit beach, shaking my head at the marvel of it all.

* * * * * * *

During this time, Fernando and I are getting to be good friends, playing handball in the afternoons in one of the empty cement rooms under construction, running the beach and swimming at sunset, and washing it all down with ice-cold beers.

That same winter, several other interesting people drop from the sky and appear at Rinconcito like transported aliens—or, perhaps, fallen angels.

One of these aliens came in the form of a certain Joe Torres. A mystery at first, it soon became known that Joe had been left at El Rinconcito by a mutual friend of Fernando's because of The Rincon's relative obscurity. Joe was on the run from both the Mexican mafia and the U.S. taxing authorities. A clean-cut Mexican-American who looked more like a high school gym teacher than a gangster and who spoke practically no Spanish, Joe hardly embodied the part of 'mobster on the run.' Despite the ominous rumors, everyone around the Rincon liked Joe immediately. Everyone except Maricela, that is. Maricela, unnerved by the stories, kept complaining to Fernando, "He's gotta go before someone shows up here looking for him. Please, Fernando. He's gotta go!"

But Fernando, never one to turn away a paying customer, managed to hold Maricela off with well-practiced stalling tactics. By month's end, the mutual friend had come to shuttle Joe Torres off to some other hideaway.

I can't say I've ever met a happier guy than Joe. I realized this when having my sunset swim one day. I was all alone and pretty far out, farther than usual, a good hundred yards or so, when I heard what seemed to be singing coming from even farther out. With quick little flourishes of paddling to rise up out of the water, I looked to see who or what the singing was coming from. Sure enough, there was good ol' Joe Torres, silhouetted against the glowing horizon, swimming and singing. Singing and swimming.

Another memorable actor to take the Rinconcito stage that season was Bilbo, a shaggy, scrawny, cartoonish-looking guy who tells me straight away that he wasn't christened Bilbo but legally changed his name after reading The Lord of The Rings *trilogy a record-shattering seven times! Bilbo is a wiry guy with too-tight, cut-off jeans shorts; scraggly, grey-blond hair; and skin that's seen more sun than the Sahara. Nice enough guy, probably bucking seventy years old, Bilbo is poignantly optimistic about the things in life he still wants to do such as sailing the west coast in a catamaran, something he admits he'll need to find a way to make happen 'pretty soon.'*

February 17, 2008

Tonight, I'm one of the restless ones at The Rincon. I pull up a chair with a couple of guys I know from Tehua Mixtle. A fisherman, Alfredo, and I get into an interesting discussion. Alfredo, I learn, believes the world is flat. Laughing at first, thinking he's joking, I soon see that he's serious, and we begin our debate. My Spanish is still a bit too limited to express complex principals such as gravity and orbit, so I have to resort to using a couple of pieces of fruit to show him my version of celestial reality—a lime circling an orange becomes the earth circling the sun.

The discussion goes back and forth for a while before Alfredo finally says, "I know, I know, Daniel. I know that's what they say. I watch the Discovery Channel all the time. But they're wrong, I assure you!"

Alfredo's belief system is reconfirmed on his boat each day. The land, rather than shrinking timidly below the horizon as it would do if the world was round, instead climbs nobly out of the water the farther out to sea Alfredo ventures.

"If anything, the sea gets higher as you go out," Alfredo tells me assuredly.

Trumped by the irrefutable, I concede the discussion and buy him another beer.

February 24, 2008

This afternoon, I'm out on the beach under a palapa in front of Rinconcito talking with Fernando's aunt who's visiting from Vallarta. Luisa is a joyful woman in her sixties or seventies. Beside her, her husband Pedro, who has no legs, is snoozing peacefully in his wheelchair where several of the brothers have carried and left him.

"We were so excited, Pedro and I," Luisa is telling me. "Our Griselda got married and moved out last month. Since we have extra room now, we decided to make a store in the front room. It's getting harder for Pedro to work, you know (with this she reaches over and pats Pedro lovingly on one of his stumps), so we figured a store would give us some extra income. We spent all last month getting it nice and buying all the things we were planning to sell. Opening day, we were so excited! Pedro went to work at seven in the morning as usual, and when he came home and saw the store almost completely empty, he was thrilled. 'How much did we make?' he asked, all excited like a little boy. I had to remind him, 'Pedro, mi amor, remember, we have nine children and twenty-seven grandchildren, most of them here in the barrio. I don't think we made anything!' " she says, laughing.

And that's the thing I'm coming to realize about Mexicans. One rarely sees them upset about anything.

Later in the evening, Fernando is on one of his boisterous rolls, playing guitar and entertaining the guests, each song ratcheting up the volume of his showmanship. Now he's singing 'Cielito Lindo,' that most classic of Mexican folk songs that demands every suffering soul to 'canto, no llores'—sing, don't cry. Even though his guitar is wildly out of tune and the beer-driven, operatic delivery is breaking through barely listenable sound barriers, it's still a gorgeous song, the nylon strings singing and crying, all of it perfectly representing the essence of what it is to be Mexican—a sweet, joyful song, sung in the face of great suffering.

Yet another memorable night at Rinconcito, an itinerant troupe of fire dancers trades Fernando camping for a live performance. There, under swaying, moonlit palms, a small group of us are treated to a surreal ballet—balls of fire, hoops of flame, thumping trance rhythms, and tanned, youthful bodies, all fused together in a flowing, molten, glow. Great combination that—fire and flesh!

March 2-3, 2008

Yesterday, the most recent guest star of this season—Season Three—a dangerous, dark, evil smudge of a man with all the loving energy of a hired assassin, arrived at The Rincon. (Holly and I have started calling each winter in Mayto Season One, Season Two, etc. because of the obvious reality-TV show qualities). Wheeling around the access road leading into The Rincon and shattering the calm came a huge, black pickup truck, motor racing, music blaring.

Up until this bit of gringo nastiness showed up with his druggie-looking blonde wife, two young boys, and several rough-looking Mexicans in tow, the day had been a standard, mellow Sunday afternoon at El Rinconcito.

Jumping down from the truck, the driver, all sinewy muscle and tattoos, surveyed the place and barked out to no one in particular, "How's the beer in this dump? Nice n' cold, I hope. I'm dry as my granny's twat. Does this place serve any food or what?"

With a movie villain's swagger, the badass strode across the sand to one of the tables, pulled up a chair, and motioned for his entourage to follow. "Waiter, oh waiter," he called to Fernando, who looking as shocked as if he'd seen the grandmother's part in question.

As the rest of us shrank into the shadows, the show continued. His gravelly smoker's voice audible fifty feet away, the man leaned back in his chair, took great sucking drags off his cigarette, and joked with his buddies in flawless grosero (uncouth) Spanish.

Slinking off set, I headed back to the ranch.

This morning starts off with a hideous racket of motocross dirt bikes zooming up and down the road, out on the beach, and along the dirt road that runs past our gate, doing donuts and shattering the peace. I wander down to the road to investigate the commotion, I see one, then two, then a third and fourth motorcycle screaming by the front gate. Feeling my gut tighten, I realize it's the vile guy encountered at The Rincon yesterday and his brood, now re-announcing their presence with hideous plumes of noise and dust.

Immediately the local gossip mavens—more efficient than any high-tech, first-world communication network—kicks into action and, by day's end, it's known that the new bad-guy ladrón in town is named Ryan, and he's a friend of the town's least noble family, the Mendozas, whose broad-branched tree has more than its share of overripe fruit. Ryan, it's said, is purchasing a lot from the Mendozas and is planning on moving to Mayto.

According to the lightning-speed chisme (gossip) machine, Ryan met Chaga Mendoza in prison in Texas, where they became fast friends. Recently released, 'Bad Ryan,' as the gossip mongers have already begun to call him, has come to Mayto to take Chaga up on a deal struck in prison to sell him some land.

March 4, 2008

Three days into Bad Ryan's siege, I go for my swim and then swing by El Rincon. There I hear a huge racket coming from the other side of the parking lot in the direction of the smaller Playa Amor (Lover's Beach), about 300 yards to the left. Near the top of a dune, at the entrance to Playa Amor, the beastly black truck is parked, doors wide open, heavy-metal music blaring. Beside the truck, Bad Ryan's bikini-clad wife dances like a club girl, arms swaying akimbo in the air, while the rest of the gang passes a bottle around and looks on.

"They've been there for hours," laments Maricela. "Even for us Mexicans, this is a bit too much."

A bit later, I run into Efren out front of Casa Jardin. "What are we gonna do," I ask him.

"I don't know, Daniel. Not much we can do until he breaks the law. Then we can call El Tutio."

Camille, who's here from the States for a week's visit, is particularly unraveled. "What about school, Efren. Don't the kids have to be in school?"

"They should be, yes," replies Efren, "but we can't make them go."

✶ ✶ ✶ ✶ ✶ ✶ ✶

The next several days pass like this, with gathering storm clouds of foreboding descending upon the town.

March 9, 2008

At El Rincon this afternoon, the usual Sunday cadre is hanging out—Fernando and Maricela, a couple of the brothers with their wives and kids, Camille, Holly, and me. It's almost dinner time when, VAR-O-O-O-O-M, the menacing devil truck roars, spitting sand, into the parking lot with a half dozen Mexicans whooping it up in the back. With unnerving bravado, Ryan and his henchmen hop out and begin rearranging tables.

"We're here for dinner," he announces to Fernando. "Bring us a round of beers. We're thirsty as hell."

Scanning the place, Ryan's eyes lock on Camille, who's sitting with us.

"You!" he roars, pointing at Camille. "You're the cunt trying to tell my kids what to do! Who the fuck do you think you are, some sort of fucking my-shit-doesn't-stink goddess? If I ever find out you've got you're prissy-ass nose up my family's butt again, you'll be lucky to keep it!"

Ashen, Camille gets up from the table and slips discretely out the side yard toward her house.

"What are we gonna do now, Efren?" I ask an hour later. "This could ruin the town…"

Holly, Efren, and I are in Camille's kitchen, Holly with her arm around Camille.

"All I did was ask one of the boys if he was going to school when I saw him in town today," Camille says, sobbing.

"I'll talk to Primitivo," Efren says to us. "He's the Delegado. It'll be up to him to do something about this."

March 10, 2008

At the next meeting we have, a day later, Efren informs us that Primitivo, arguably the town's most alpha male, went with several other Herrera brothers the previous night to the Mendoza house where Ryan is staying.

"The brothers say they've never before seen Primativo intimidated," Efren tells us. "This Ryan person got right in Primitivo's face and told him not to bother him with this kind of bullshit again, or else," Efren says, making a classic finger motion across his own neck.

The storm clouds of Bad Ryan's presence have condensed into an even thicker sludge, coating the town in a palpable gloom.

March 11, 2008

Today, everyone is breathing a huge sigh of relief. Just as suddenly as its arrival, the vile menace has vanished.

"They've gone back to the States to make a drug deal," the rumor mill announces. "They're buying the property and went back for the money."

✳ ✳ ✳ ✳ ✳ ✳ ✳

Despite the respite, a sense of unease lingered until, like most bad news, it eventually faded into the mist of memory.

More than a year later, fresh news of Bad Ryan arrived on the morning breeze. The bad-ass gringo Ryan, it was said, had landed in jail for murder

*up in California. He'd pushed his wife from their moving truck. The boys,
the rumor continued, had been placed in foster homes.*

9 - Soccer Sundays

Saturdays are some of our favorite days here. Like anywhere else, the work stops by mid-day and the already easy pace of village life slows to a crawl. Flies buzz and hammocks swing. Off in the distance, there are hints of dogs barking and banda music playing. By mid-afternoon, when the heat searches out every shadow and there's nowhere left to hide, the people of the village head to the beach to catch whatever breeze the sea might be giving up, sit in the shade of palm-thatched ramadas, drink beer and soda, eat heaps of fresh ceviche from styrofoam plates, and play with their children in the rolling surf.

But Sundays, especially soccer Sundays, are even better. Whichever town around Cabo Corrientes is selected to be the week's home field becomes a buzz of activity starting early in the day. Young girls and women get busy gathering up leña (firewood) and lighting the tinder under their cooking comals. Balls of masa are patted and placed between sheets of thin plastic to be squished with one swift heft of the tortilla press's handle. Others are mixing corn masa filling and stuffing husks to make savory tamales, while still others prepare large glass vats of iced horchata, tamarindo, and other sweet drinks.

For their part, the men of the village are also busy preparing. Plastic tables and chairs are gathered up from all over town and stacked high in the back of pickup trucks (the majority of the tables bearing the ubiquitous Corona beer emblem). The fittest of the town's boys who've been selected to play are on the field working through light drills and trying on each other's hodge-podge assortment of used shoes and shin guards. The older and less fit do their part mowing the patchy, threadbare field and marking it using cut-off plastic Coke bottles to sprinkle lines of bright-white builder's lime. At last, when the game begins, the field is a riot of joyous activity.

April 19, 2008 (Saturday)

Today, Efren stops by late morning to see if I'm up for a game of chess. (One of Esteban's lasting legacies is that many Maytonians know their way around a chess board.)

"Quieres jugar?" Efren calls from outside the fence, holding up his board and grinning that irresistible grin of his.

"Sure, amigo, if you don't mind losing," I tease him as required while motioning him into the shade of the yard.

"Ha, Daniel," he replies, "I don't mind losing, but that's very unlikely to happen, you know."

We're both competitive people and a very even match, so these friendly Saturday games inevitably end up an intense duel of concentration and will, obligatorily disguised by a flimsy facade of small talk and joking.

As we settle into this morning's play, Holly brings out fresh iced tea and cookies from the kitchen.

Efren waves off the cookies. "No gracias, Holly," he says. "Estoy entrenando (I'm in training) and may be playing in the big game against Ipala tomorrow."

There's only one thing I know Efren to be more serious about than chess, and that's soccer. In his early forties and becoming paunchy, Efren is one of the team's coaches but also likes to practice with the younger players, who are in their teens and twenties. In fact, this past week, he's hauled me along on two or three days to practice with them. Though I'm over fifty—more than twice the age of many of the players—I'm still in good shape and am almost able to keep up. As always, the people of Mayto are gracious about including others, and the young players of Mayto's team seem happy to have a new face, of whatever color or age, joining them.

But, for today, I'm happy to give it a rest and play chess instead. My muscles are aching in places previously forgotten.

April 20, 2008 (soccer Sunday)

Even though it's Sunday, there are still chores to do. Maybe later, if I get everything done, I'll head over to the game, two villages away in Ipala. Unexpectedly, Efren's rickety little silver-grey Toyota pickup truck pulls up to the gate.

"You didn't get enough of a beating yesterday?" I call out as Efren gets out of the truck.

"No, Daniel, I didn't come to embarrass you again," he replies.

I can see he's wearing the Mayto soccer Jersey and, in his hand, he's holding a second one.

"Here," he says, holding it up. "Put this on!"

"Deberia estar bromeando (you must be joking?)," I say, surprised.

"No, Daniel. It's no joke. A bunch of the boys went to the big fiesta in Cruz de Loreto last night and never made it back. We're short-handed, and both of us need to play!"

"But Efren," I say to him, "I'm old enough to be some of these guys' grandfather!"

"Daniel, it's your duty!" he replies. "You'll do fine. We need you!"

I can see it's useless to resist, and, though partly terrified, my inner soccer star is excited by the prospect. "OK," I yield, "but I'm holding you responsible if I drop dead from a heart attack."

"Yes, yes, that's fine, Daniel. Just get your stuff and hurry up!" he motions, looking frantic. "The game is starting. We're going to be late!"

"Have fun. Good luck," Holly says with a half-smiling, half-disapproving, sideways kind of look as I rush around grabbing my things and head out to Efren's revving truck.

Fifteen minutes later, we pull up to the crowded field. The road is lined with beater pickups and decrepit sedans. A few guys mill about in the road, but most of the activity is around the sides of the field where the ball is in play and waves of shouting have already begun.

"Hurry, hurry," Efren pleads, panicked, as we head over to the emptier part of the sidelines where Mayto's other coach is pacing. Seeing Efren, he gestures and yells to Efren. "Get in there, play forward, cabrón. We need you to make a pinche (f'ing) full line!"

Efren is in his glory and goes running onto the field.

"And you?" The coach eyes me with a circumspect look. "Do you want to play?"

"Um, yeah, porque no?" I reply, "si está bien? (why not, if it's ok?)".

"Sí, está bien. En un rato (yes, in a bit)," he replies over his shoulder, his attention turning back to the game. "Prieto, stay on Checho"! he yells. "He's moving around the outside!" But it's already too late. Checho has made his move and a roar goes up from Ipala's side of the field.

"Coach, I need a break." One of the players, Cristian, comes dragging up to the coach as the rest of the team reassembles, dejected, at our end of the field. It's clear that with half the team absent and no second string for relief, it's going to be ugly. Mayto should have forfeited.

"OK," the coach says to Christian, frustration in his voice. Turning to me, he says, "You're in, Señor Daniel. Let's see what you can do. Take Cristian's place. Right forward."

I'm terrified but thrilled. Right forward is the position I played in junior high. Muscles stiff from the week's practice, I realize as I go jogging onto the field that I haven't even warmed up yet. No matter. I'm in the shit now…

We're lined up for the kickoff. Sensing a rout, the crowd on Ipala's side is going wild with hooting and yelling

"Twe-e-e-e-t!" goes the whistle. The ball is in play. Freddy, the center, has lobbed it downfield to Toni at the wing position over to the left. Things are moving fast. Half in a dreamscape, I run full tilt, trying to keep up. Toni dribbles past one and then another of Ipala's defenders and gives the pelota a good, centering kick. I'm right in front of the goal now and whoa, what's this? The ball is here, right in front of me! I strike out blindly and, holy shit, there it goes, flying through the air toward the net!

Now everything slows to a near stop. The goalie, agile and strong, is suspended sideways in the air, arms outstretched, heading for the intercept, his trajectory perfect. And there's the ball, also suspended, but on a course that will put it mere centimeters out of reach. On the periphery, I see the forms of running players, frozen in space. Even the noise from the side-lines has slowed and stretched into a long, low growl.

Then, just as suddenly as the scene had slowed, it zaps back to full speed, motion, and sound. Bulging out in the back, the net reverberates from the ball having tried to punch through it. For the briefest of seconds, there's a vacuum of stunned silence before the shouting and yelling, even louder now, erupts from all sides.

Now I truly must be dreaming. Prieto, Efren, and several of the others are running toward me, yelling and smiling. Mixed in with all the other sounds coming at me, I can hear 'gringo, gringo, gringo' pulsing through the crowd. Hugs and high fives come at me from all sides.

Turning back toward center field, something else happens. Without warning, a stabbing pain shoots through my right thigh. "Ah-h-g-g!" I let out a yelp. Limping forward, another jet of pain stabs at me, this time in my left leg. "AH-H-H-G-G!" I whimper anew. Bent over in pain, I signal to the coach. He waves me in.

Limping to the sidelines, the yelling subsides, and the rest of the play-ers find their way back to center field. Through it all, I keep hearing the distinctive murmur of 'gringo, gringo, gringo' hanging wondrous on the air.

For several weeks following the game, I'm greeted with smiles, high fives, and good-natured nicknames of endearment such as "Daniel Ortega, Daniel Travieso (Dennis the Menace here in Mexico), or Daniel Osorno, the Mexican soccer star. "Como va tus desgares (how are your pulled mus-cles)?" they all ask, seeing me limping.

It'll be several months before I'm fully recovered, but 'vale la pena (worth the pain),' I remind myself, playing and replaying the fifteen sec-onds of fame over and over again on the little, Sunday soccer field movie set of my mind.

✷ ✷ ✷ ✷ ✷ ✷ ✷

It was on that high note, nugget of notoriety in pocket, that we began pack-ing up the house and getting ready, once again, to head back to our grind-ing, drudging lives in Maine. OK, OK, I admit it. I tend to exaggerate. It wasn't that our lives in the States were that bad. Far from it, actually. Feeling increasingly connected to the crude but vibrant life here, every day feeling like some bit of adventure, the other had lost its luster and had started to feel dull and lifeless by comparison.

As our flight back to the States approached, the news and pressure from back home was ramping up to a steady crescendo. Rumblings in the stock market had Holly's clients more on edge than ever, and my employees were having trouble holding off customers anxious to have me photograph their new 2008 ad campaigns. Wanting to stay here in Mayto, and dreading the work ahead, we set about preparing to depart. We were a little nervous about leaving the house and our camper, which was well out of sight of the road and unattended, but Efren and son Freddy promised to check in on it from time to time.

It was around this time that a new notion began creeping into Holly's and my conversations with one another. "What would it be like," we mused, "to sell our businesses and move down here full time?" Taking little nibbles of this tempting fruit, we left for the States and, little did we know then, our last full year of being residents there.

Previously, we'd moved our camper and set it on a wood-frame platform on top of the view hill in front of the house. Often we would stay up there for the view and breeze rather than using the house. Lying in the bunk of the camper sipping coffee and gazing out at the view one morning a few days before leaving, Holly said dreamily, "You know, I think this is the happiest I've ever been. If we sold our business, paid off our mortgages, and retired early, we could live like this for peanuts."

This, coming from a dedicated financial planner, was the blasphemous, life-altering equivalent of a devout Catholic considering becoming a Protestant or a Jew.

Not long after returning to the States, Holly and I read an article in AARP Magazine *about a couple from New England who'd cashed out their corporate lives and were now five years into traveling the world accepting light-duty house-sitting assignments in exotic locations to offset their expenses. The article started coming up regularly in our discussions about the future. Between Holly's brilliance as a certified financial planner and my love of spreadsheets, we were able to roll out various scenarios for a bailout plan. Based largely on the sale of her business, which was worth quite bit more than mine, the idea of early retirement and escape from our frenetic lives in the U.S. began seriously taking shape.*

Of course, spreadsheets and financial plans are often out of sync with reality, and ours were no exception. "People plan," as the saying goes, "and the gods laugh." Throughout that summer, the gods were laughing.

Section III

Los Principantes (The Beginners)
Summer 2008 ~ Spring 2012

"Be willing to be a beginner every single morning."
— *Meister Eckhart*

10 - Toward Sustainability, Part 1
(Baby Solar Steps)

By the summer of '08, our life back in the States was starting to get a bit too complicated.

The constant negative news about the stock market was causing Holly untold anxiety. Many times during the previous winter, Holly had to leave the ranch abruptly for Vallarta and park herself at an Internet cafe for days. The stress of those times was compound by being away from her office and not even having decent Internet connectivity for weeks on end. The prospect of leaving again for Mayto the following winter while continuing to manage the life savings of eighty nervous families in the U.S. from a technology-less hovel in Mexico was already weighing on her. Despite having an excellent staff and the addition of a licensed assistant who could make stock trades in her absence, the idea of having to manage the office remotely again was making her feel as though she was signing on to manage the Apollo 13 mission.

Holly and I were also personally feeling the financial pinch, juggling multiple mortgages and now second mortgages in order to liberate the cash needed to start paying down the debt we'd taken on for Mexico. A rental property we had needed to be sold immediately, plus yet another refinancing had to be done on our house in Maine as well as the sale of Holly's business condo, which we owned.

As an interesting counterpoint, our little community in Mayto during this period had been completely unaffected by the gathering storm roiling the seas of world financial markets. It's doubtful that any of our two hundred or so neighbors owned a single investment 'instrument' and, aside from news headlines that had all the relevance of weather reports from Mars, the rural Mexicans we knew were blissfully independent of the troubled world outside. Holly and I, shuttling between worlds, found it marvelous that the stock market could completely tank and the heartbeat of life in Mayto would hardly skip a beat. For this and other reasons, we took to calling our life in Mayto 'the bubble.' "It's time to get back to the bubble," we'd often say after some new spate of bad news popped up on our computer screens.

September 17, 2008 (*From Holly's journal at the time*):
How bad will this get? We've lost 20% in our own portfolio. Dan's income is down 40%—over 100K. My income is down at least 10% before today. We have debt out the ass. Cannot believe I just bought this car (Mercedes). Just spent another 40K renovating the Portsmouth property, 16K more gone to Mexico, haven't funded our IRAs, stopped our Health Savings Account, housekeeper, trainer, gym! Time to tighten the belt, big time. Clients are freaked. So am I. Could this be a depression? I don't know!

✱ ✱ ✱ ✱ ✱ ✱ ✱

Despite our belt tightening intentions, we were still our crazy selves, bouncing like ping pong balls between the two disparate cross-border lives while also squeezing in considerable other world travel on top of the Mexico trips. Like the classic routine from the Ed Sullivan show—the guy who kept all the plates spinning—we were a whirlwind of motion, running back and forth, catching and spinning but also watching some of the plates fall and shatter.

Piled on top of the changes and challenges we were facing, I was busy acquiring a new identity. Prompted by a book about the looming climate change crisis I'd read, Plan B 2.0 *by Lester Brown, I'd launched and now chaired a Municipal Energy Commission charged with auditing the town's energy profile and recommending energy savings initiatives.*

Reading more and digging in deeper, I started seeing all modern human activity, and the resulting environmental problems, as a simple matter of energy mismanagement. OCD tendencies locked in on target, I was off on a vigilante crusade that would also give shape to our Mexico experience.

With the constant daydreaming of Mexico as backdrop to all of this, I also began thinking about projects at the ranch that Holly and I were considering—the first and most obvious being electricity at the house. With the help of online chat groups and a local solar photovoltaics engineer, I began designing the electronics side of the solar photovoltaic setup for our house there. Over the summer, in tandem with the Spanish instructional tapes I was listening to constantly, my vocabulary and understanding of solar arrays, charge controllers, deep-cell batteries, and power inverters grew. By fall, I'd assembled the electronics to take back to Mayto and had a schematic ready to put to the test.

At the same time, we'd also begun planning a campground at the ranch. Reasoning that we'd always met simpatico, adventurous people at campgrounds while traveling in Mexico, and realizing that our social life in Mayto was still a too-thin mix, we decided a campground would be a good way to attract the social stimulation we'd otherwise be lacking. Since we were planning a campground anyway, we decided to put an environmental spin on the construction, building with local, natural materials as much as possible.

Even though words like 'sustainability' and 'eco-tourism' were new to our lips, we were off and running on our new eco-adventure!

December 15, 2008

Scratch. Scratch. Scratch…

What's that sound?

It's barely light out, and Holly and I are barely awake. Lying in our cozy bed in Mayto, we look over at one another, confused.

Whistling then, in rhythm with the scratching.

"What the… ?"

"Hola," I call out, sitting up. "Quien es?"

"Soy yo, Juanito," comes a voice back. "I'm raking your yard. Daniel, what's the matter? Are you going to sleep all day?"

Juanito, Fernando and Maricela's son-in-law, is increasingly our best friend in Mayto. Affable and upbeat, Juanito is always happy to lend a hand.

"I dunno, Juanito. I might just do that—sleep all day. I thought you Mexicans were supposed be 'tranquilo.' Why are you here so damn early?" I ask, leaning on the windowsill, watching him move leaves and dirt around.

"Todays's the day we're going make electricity, right?" he asks.

"Oh, that," I say, understanding now.

Juanito is really excited to start putting the new solar PV system together. Last week, when he heard I was thinking about buying solar panels, he took me to a ranch out in the puckerbrush where he'd heard a distant relative of his had some panels for sale. Disbelieving, I humored him, and we left in the truck. When we got to the ranch, a desolate patch of scrub, I was even more skeptical. After a brief conversation the woman of the house sent a young boy out to the fields, leaving Juanito and me to sit waiting. Half an hour later a leathery looking campesino entered the yard.

"Tío, mío, como has estado? (Uncle, how have you been?)" Juanito shouted out, laughing as the two hugged in greeting. "I heard you have some solar panels you're trying to sell. Is that true?"

"Sí, sí, I have panels," the uncle answered. "Over here…" he said, turning and leading us to a dilapidated shed.

Pulling aside a sheet of tin covering the door, we went inside. Sure enough, there, leaning against the wall, was a stack of 175-watt panels nearly as tall as I was and looking handsome despite layers of grime and their randomly cut cables—an indication of their dubious origins. Settling on a price—which was about a quarter of the ones I'd been pricing out in Vallarta—Juanito and I loaded a half-dozen panels into the truck.

"You see, Daniel," Juanito said as we pulled away, "you stick with me. I'm going to take really good care of you!"

Now, a week later, Juanito is crawling out of his skin to get started. That's Juanito in a nutshell—enthusiastic, resourceful, and always up for anything. Recently, I'd made the mistake of telling Juanito we were trying to think of names for the ranch and since then it's been a nonstop barrage of ranch-name ideas.

"Daniel, I've got it," Juanito blurts out every five minutes or so. "How about Rancho Alegre (Happy Ranch)? Or Rancho Lizardo Flojo (Lazy Lizard Ranch). That's a good one, don't you think?"

"Sounds good, Juanito. We'll consider it."

"Daniel, here's a good one: Rancho Misterio (Mystery Ranch)," he says with great seriousness two minutes later. "Or how about Rancho Rediculo (Ridiculous Ranch)," he adds, cracking himself up this time.

A tsunami of names is inundating the shoreline now, and Holly and I are starting to drown in them. Nonetheless, Juanito's enthusiasm is as infectious as it is undeniable.

"Daniel, I know!" he starts in again this morning. "You can call it Rancho Luz de Solar (Solar Powered Ranch)! Let's get started, we're burning daylight!"

"I haven't had my coffee yet. Rake a bit more and then we'll get started," I reply, still talking to him through the open window.

"Yeesh," I whisper to Holly, "what kind of monster have we created this time?" But really, we're loving the ridiculousness of it.

For the rest of the day, Juanito and I climb up and down from the roof, running cables, mounting panels, and attaching batteries, but the fact is, on the inside I'm a mess of second-guessing and worry. I know it shouldn't be such a big thing, but the tangle of ground connections, circuit breakers, and occasional sparks flying off battery terminals has me questioning and overthinking everything. Away from any source of internet or phone, there's no one to turn to now when the inverter-installation manual indicates connections different from the design plans I'd made back in Maine. At 24v volts DC, and hundreds of potential amps, a shorted battery can knock a man down, start a fire, or even cause a heart attack.

Through it all, Juanito proves to be an able student and excellent problem solver. Also great with cement, he makes a nice battery box in a fraction of the time it would have taken me to do it alone.

Closing in on sunset, we tighten up the last of the bolts, double check everything, and are ready to throw the switch.

Flipping the breaker, there's a big, fat nothing. But then, wait, there it is! With a click and a buzz, a light appears on the charge controller. Flipping another switch, the inverter kicks on with an audible hum. Then, plugging it in, another click and hum, and Yes! This is it! The new refrigerator, a modest apartment-size model, gives a little shudder and then hums to life.

Oh my god, we did it. "WE DID IT!" I shout, high five'ing Juan and Holly, who've been looking on. Dancing around the kitchen, the three of us do a jig and are transported to photon heaven.

Hyperbole aside, seeing the green light come on, hearing the hum of the refrigerator, and realizing that we're now sucking energy right out of the sky—and not just a little lightbulb or two's worth but real energy, 120-volts of electricity, enough to power a refrigerator and more—I feel as though I'm experiencing a bona fide miracle!

And, not unlike seeing my first latent image appear in the dim orange light of my father's darkroom as a kid—an experience that set the course of my life for decades to follow—I feel this event to be a revelation loaded with implications. Instantly, I'm hooked on this solar thing and find it to be one of the most empowering feelings I can remember, especially in the context of the larger energy work I'd been getting involved with back in the States. Of course, I'd understood alternative energy and its implications before this, but everything previously had been academic, like studying auto mechanics without ever opening the hood. Now I'm inside the wondrous guts of the thing. *And just imagine,* I think to myself, *this is only one minuscule array I have here!* The potential, I see now, is as unlimited as the sky!

"Daniel, how about Rancho Energia Magico (Rancho Magic Energy)," Juanito blurts out, collapsing my bubble of solar reverie, but giving the three of us a good laugh.

"Yeah, Juanito, that's a good one. We'll consider it…"

11 - Animal Tails, Part 1
(Got Goats?)

Besides all the reptilian encounters, goats have been a constant source of entertainment for us over the years. Usually, when Holly is around goats and other animals, the stressed-out woman recedes and a joyous young girl emerges. At other times, however, the animals have given both of us some our most devastating experiences.

You'll remember that Esteban sold his herd of goats during our summer absence. But now, it was our third winter in Mayto, the year the deal was completed, and we were to finally become full owners. I arrived around Thanksgiving, a full month ahead of Holly. As the holidays drew near, I secretly bought her a herd of ten milkers as a surprise Christmas gift.

December 22 - 29, 2008

Hopping into the pickup with Juanito, we head over to Villa del Mar where, this time, he knows someone with goats for sale. Turning off the main dirt road that runs between the villages along the coast, we head inland several kilometers following a secondary dirt track alongside a broad, dry arroyo on our right. To the left, parcel after parcel of cultivated crops —chiles, corn, and papas—stretch out to the hills in a giant green patchwork. Arriving at a road cut, we take a right and drop down onto the sandy, gravel-strewn arroyo and then cross over to the other side where another cut leads up the embankment and onto yet another parcel. Passing through a gate, we come to a shack set in a thicket. Outside the house, several bored-looking guys sit around on pieces of a cut-up tree or lie, stretched out, in a couple of tattered hammocks. An old wrecked car, grunting pigs, and a large pile of irrigation tubing complete the scene.

When Juanito explains our quest to the group, the owner of the property, Armando, nods thoughtfully and motions to a corral off to the side. After a bit of joking that I don't understand, the group rouses itself, and we set off across the field. There we find a ragtag bunch of ruminants milling about and scratching at the dirt for any bit of sustenance. Far from the plump, uniform specimens Holly and I had seen at various farms we'd visited in the States, this motley crew ran the gamut from speckled grey and with no horns to chocolate brown with horns to dirty white with floppy ears.

"They look kind of thin," I say to Juanito.

"No, Daniel, don't worry. It's the time of year. They'll fatten up soon enough."

After Juanito leads the negotiation, a price is settled and, for a few thousand pesos (about two hundred dollars), the herd of ten embras (females) is now mine—well, hopefully Holly's, if she'll have them.

"You're gonna need a macho," the owner Armando advises, and the other guys nod in agreement.

"How come?" I ask him.

Everyone laughs.

Armando, evidently feeling sorry for me, tosses a large, hornless, macho buck into the deal for free.

Rolling in a couple of days before Christmas and receiving her gift, Holly seems happy with her present but in a reserved sort of way, like a mother receiving a frog as a gift from her son.

"Oh, wow," she says, "I guess we're going to have goats then, after all."

As an added bonus, the day after Christmas, a twelfth goat appears out of nowhere and joins the herd. The strong, all-black embra is an instant leader, and all we can figure is that she'd been part of Esteban's original herd and must have gone into hiding when the others were sold off the previous summer.

Now in charge of her own manada (herd), this renegade doe is a force to be reckoned with. From the beginning, this black beauty proves smart enough to open almost any gate. She also has an epic appetite and can anticipate a handout well ahead of the rest. Because she's not only strong but also smart, we name her Oprah.

* * * * * * *

As Holly warmed to the goats that winter, she became particularly close to the hornless macho, whom she named Chewbaca. Of all the hundreds of goats we've had over the years since, there's never been another one quite like him. Immediately, Chewbaca gained a reputation among our ranch help and local friends as a jugatón (pronounced who-ga-tone), which translates roughly into "big mischief maker." A large guy, close to ten feet tall when standing on his hind legs, Chewbaca could defy most fences and was a constant menace to anything we planted. To top it off, Chewbaca, when excited, sounded like a real live Wookie.

Chewbaca loved Holly and followed here everywhere. Holly and Chewbaca developed one neat trick together where Hol would run down the little hill from the view palapa and then, stopping short at the bottom, she'd turn and throw her hands in the air like a circus trainer. Chewbaca, leaping off the last little ledge, would twist his head and torso sideways in a joyful, airborne arc of shape and form. An impressive maneuver by any measure.

Sometimes, Holly could be seen sitting in a chair reading up on the view hill under the palapa with Chewbaca standing behind her with his head on her shoulder, reading along with her. Or the two of them would be together like that, just watching the sunset.

To pretty much everyone other than Holly, however, Chewbaca was a full-on menace.

February 20, 2009

Today, our carpenter, Manuel, is installing some doors in the house, replacing the crappy aluminum slider with a beautiful, heavy, wooden one. Manuel, I should say, isn't an average guy. Jehovah's Witness and solid family man, he always looks as fresh and perfect as a bouquet of flowers. He has jet black hair, well-coifed mustache, and, no matter the temperature, looks as tidy as if he's just gotten out of a fifteen-minute shower.

In keeping with his looks, Manuel's work is also perfect. Every door latches with exact precision. Every window closes with an airtight 'clunk.'

Yet another hallmark of Manuel is his beautiful 'libretto' notebook. In perfect handwriting and with crisp, clear sketches, all of Manuel's jobs, past and future, are fully documented—from initial-concept sketches, notes, quotes, and measurements all the way through to final billing.

Well, sadly, this morning Manuel set his notebook on a low stone wall off to the side. Returning to review his notes an hour later, he found Chewbaca finishing up the tasty snack.

* * * * * * *

Yet another Chewbaca incident occurred a few weeks later when the wild plum (ciruela) trees we had around the property were bursting into their annual harvest of bright red fruit. One of the crew of workers we had on a building project, Junior, was particularly fond of ciruelas and had spent his lunch break collecting several five-gallon buckets full. At the end of the day, ready to head home with his bounty, Junior found Chewbaca with his head in one of the buckets, finishing up the last of the fruit. Although normally mild-mannered, Junior was furious. The rest of the crew had to talk him out of taking a machete to Chewbaca. When I finally found poor Chewbaca, he was tied tight by the neck to the ciruela tree, whimpering a pathetic Wookie whimper of protest.

As hard as I tried to appreciate Chewbaca for the unique specimen he was, our relationship was tumultuous. The tumult reached its zenith one day when I was finishing a thorough cleanup of our Honda CRV. I left the door open for a second to get something out of the back, and wily Chewbaca jumped inside, all two hundred pounds of him filling both the driver's and front passenger's seats. When I came around to the front of the car to find his ass sticking out the door, I was furious.

"You goddamn piece of shit!" I yelled. "I just finished cleaning the entire car! Get the motherfucking fuck outta there, you son of a bitch!" Grabbing Chewbaca by the tail, I gave it a yank with everything I had.

"Moor-a-w-w-w-h-h!" Chewable screamed and threw his head into the air—well, what should have been air. With a mighty crack, Chewbaca's iron skull shattered the CRV's windshield.

When Holly tells the story, she never leaves out the last part—the part where she's in the kitchen and hears me yell at the top of my lungs, "Somebody get me my goddamn machete!"

Funny thing was, even Chewbaca's progeny had it in for that poor car. A fine, strong brood, Chewbaca's kids were our first experience with baby goats, and we were in our joy. Every morning, Holly would be out in the goat pen at first light, sipping her coffee and letting the babies climb all over her, nuzzling her face and chewing her hair. As the babies got older, they were always scouting for something to climb on. With a kick and a twist like miniature Chewbacas, they'd jump into the air with the sheer exuberance of being alive.

At three months old, when the kids were entering adolescence, Molly, one of the ringleaders of the young tribe, discovered that with one mighty leap she could summit the hood of the CRV. Following her lead, the rest of the gang soon joined her on the hood, pushing and shoving, leaping off, back on, and then off again. After a few hours of this play, Molly, never one to settle for mediocrity, made her way up to the roof. As the rest followed, our car was covered in goat kids. Holly and I were laughing and loving their unbearable cuteness.

The next morning, sun low over the back hill, I noticed hundreds of adorable little hoof prints all over the hood. Optimistically, I dragged out the hose, got a rag, and started washing off the marks.

'Good, they're coming off,' I told myself.

Once dry, however, I saw the prints were actually dents—little denty remnants of Chewbaca's mischievous brood.

By the end of the day, I'd constructed a fenced-in car port to protect what was left of the CRV.

* * * * * * *

Green at everything ranch-like in those early days, Holly and I began teaching ourselves animal husbandry—mostly by our mistakes. Having known Esteban's mongrel, Puppies, and reading more about guard animals, we acquired a young female burro, Lupita, to help watch over the herd.

Lupita was a wonder and would become soul mates with the Australian cattle dog Chanchito (little piglet) we found abandoned in a nearby village. Lupita had infinite tolerance for Chanchito's nipping and jumping. The two of them would spend hours chasing each other around the corral.

From the beginning we'd let Chewbaca frolic with the lady goats to his heart's content. As a result, bellies started swelling with alarming frequency.

"Look, I think Gail's uterus is swollen," one of us would say.

"Are you sure that's her uterus?" the other would respond, joking. "I think it might be her uvula."

"I think that one is having a contraction," we'd say to each other excitedly.

Crouching down to get in close, the two of us would watch as a plump, ripe goat would go into a sort of squatting position. Then—splash, plop, splash—out would come a barrage of chocolate pellets and a gush of bright yellow lemonade.

"Oops, no, guess not." We'd laugh at our pathetic inexperience.

We were prepared by the time the babies finally did start arriving. With clean towels, an ear syringe in case we had to aspirate, iodine for use after cutting the umbilical cord, and baby bottles, we waited. In reality, goats don't need any help with their birthing, but, as with many animal husbandry experiences, we enjoyed the illusion that the animals needed us. We cleaned off slimy placentas, dried and fluffed the adorable newborns, and settled each new arrival into the fine, multi-room nursery we created for them to better bond with their mothers. Laughing and taking videos, and were transported to kidding heaven.

Several years on our goat husbandry would suffer a horrible setback but, at this point, everything about having goats was a still a bouncy delight.

The first crop of kiddlings came pretty close together. We were free-ranging the herd at the time, letting them roam the entire 100-acre property. When the first doe didn't show up at the corral for dinner, we figured she'd probably dropped her kids out in the bush. We spent hours tracking her down with flashlights and returning her and her two girls to the safety of the corral. After that, we locked everybody up in the corral for several weeks until they'd all finished kidding.

After that first round the timing of births became much more random, and we'd never know for sure when a kid would pop out. Throughout that next year, there were many times when a pregnant doe would turn up missing at the end of the day, and we'd begin our search. Like jungle commandos armed with walkie-talkies and machetes, we'd fan out, Holly and I, along with our first young caretaker couple, Liz and Riley, searching the steep, prickly, gnarly terrain, often until well after dark.

One time, an embra (female) we'd been expecting to 'drop' kids any time came back at dusk as usual, but she was noticeably deflated and oozing an afterbirth.

"Oh, man. Shit," I called to Holly. "This one left her damn kids out in the bush!"

With all hands on deck, we launched a search-and-rescue mission, walkie-talkies crackling out locations and instructions to each other in the gathering darkness.

"I just went up the ravine by the second hill," Riley called out. "Nothing there. Where do you want me to go next?"

"Try over on the other side, down toward the arroyo," Holly responded. "They like to hang out over there a lot. Liz, where are you at? Are you doing OK?" And so on.

Finally, about when it was getting too treacherous to continue in the failing light, Holly called out excitedly, "You just won't believe this. I saw Lupita over on the beach side of the second hill. She wouldn't come when I called and was pacing back and forth. When I went over to her, there they were. The babies are here. Two of them. They're beautiful! Lupita was protecting them!"

With the babies came milk. Juanito, who often hung out at the ranch and helped with odd jobs, taught Holly and I how to convince chichis (udders) to squirt milk. He also taught me how to throw a lasso, thus beginning my new career and accompanying title 'Goat Wrangler'.

Holly began making cheese thus earning her own new title—Artisan Cheese Maker. Never one for wearing out hammocks, she had taken the first of two summer cheese-making courses at the University of Vermont and was producing excellent chevres, fetas, jacks, and yogurt. Connecting with a yoga studio in Vallarta, she had a ready market for anything she produced. Not stopping there, the idea of creating a local women's cooperative began to sneak in to our conversations.

Often those mornings, I'd wake to the sound of talking coming from the corral. Tuning in, I'd hear that it was Holly out alone with the goats.

"All right, ladies, listen up," I'd hear her saying. "Production's been falling off the last couple of weeks. Gail, pay attention. You too, Frida. All of you, ears forward! If you want rations of the good grain, the Super Potro from El Tuito, to continue, you're gonna have to pick up the pace. You're an elite manada, the best in Cabo Corrientes, so I don't want to hear any lame excuses about how it's too hot or you're not in the mood. Oprah, stop eating and pay attention!"

After years of seeing Holly chronically stressed with her work in New England, I began to see ranch life and this new animal connection as an essential relief valve that she'd been missing—one that we'd both been missing, actually.

Frida, an adventurous and smart goat baby, figured out that by waiting for Lupita to walk by a small knoll, she could leap onto the burra's back and catch a ride (Check out the video, "Riding Lupita" at the Rancho Sol y Mar YouTube Channel). At first, Lupita liked the attention and would actually back up to the knoll to let Frida hop on board. Then one or two others took up the sport. After several days of giving rides, Lupita decided she'd had enough of being their beast of burden and promptly put an end to their capricious shenanigans.

March 2, 2009

It's become clear that Lupita needs romance in her life, so Holly and I have begun searching for a boyfriend for her whenever we're driving somewhere—our country version of Match Dot Com. After passing on several mangy-looking, roadside burros, today we finally find a handsome fellow tethered in someone's yard in Llano Grande, halfway to El Tuito. Pulling up to the house, we call out to an elderly woman sitting on the porch. "Can we rent your handsome burro?"

"What?"

"Can we rent your burro? We want to mate it with our burra."

"No, I'm sorry."

"We will pay well to be able to rent him."

"No, it's not possible. He doesn't go with burras."

Holly and I are now looking at each other blankly. Did we hear right? He doesn't go with lady burros? Is he gay, we wonder?

"Excuse us, ma'am. We don't mean to be pushy, but we don't understand. Why doesn't he go with burras?"

"Go ask your people in Mayto," the woman replies, acting irritated now.

We drive away, disappointed and confused.

March 3, 2009

Still amused and confused by yesterday's burro episode, Holly and I keep saying to each other over coffee, "No, I'm sorry. My burro doesn't go with burras. What? You don't understand? Go ask your people in Mayto. Good day to you then…"

And how the hell did she even know we were from Mayto, we wonder?

When one of our workers shows up for the day, we ask him what he makes of the exchange.

"Daniél," he says, laughing, "most people keep their burros away from girl burras so that they'll mate with horses and make mulas (mules). Mulas around here are much more valuable."

It takes a gringo moment to fully understand.

"Ah, now I see," Holly says, in hysterics. "Once you go burra, you never go furtha!"

✷ ✷ ✷ ✷ ✷ ✷ ✷

One of the most ridiculous goat incidents was when The Flower Lady came to visit. We often got visitors like the flower lady—itinerate vendors showing up randomly, night or day, trucks loaded with whatever items they happened to specialize in, from hammocks and furniture to fruit, meat, roast chicken, fish, housewares, mattresses, or even live animals.

<u>March 10, 2009</u>

This afternoon, a vendor we'd never seen before comes wheeling up the drive. It's a lone woman driving a pickup truck loaded to the gunnels with lush, verdant garden offerings—an entire nursery on wheels pulling up to the house, and Holly is ecstatic. Spilling out over the sides, back, and platform over the cab is a traveling jungle—all of it for sale! Hopping out of the cab, The Flower Lady gives Holly a tour. Palms, papayas, bougainvilleas, limes, copa de oro, guava, and guanabana bushes—you name it, The Flower Lady has it. With a separate section for ornamentals and another for fruit-bearing varieties, the truck is a rolling botanical wonder.

As Holly, ooh's and ahh's over what to buy, I hear Oprah and her tinkling bell crest the hill, returning from the day's forage with the rest of the manada. Enjoying the show here at the flower truck, (way better than shopping with Holly back in the States—waiting uselessly in a store while she agonizes over which shoes to buy), the sound of Oprah's bell barely registers in my consciousness. It's the height of the dry season, with nothing much green around, and, spotting,the truck loaded with verdant foliage, the goats have decided that they'll do a little shopping too.

Oprah, followed by her brigade, comes charging down the hill. Before any of the three of us realize what's happening, the rampaging goat patrol has the truck surrounded and are attacking from all sides. Shrieking, The Flower Lady runs for the cab and jumps in while great mouthfuls of mango, bougainvillea, banana, and pasiflora are stripped away from their tender stalks. Revving the engine and gunning the vehicle down the road, The Flower Lady disappears in a cloud of dust with the ravenous goat army in full pursuit.

We've never seen or heard from The Flower Lady since.

✳ ✳ ✳ ✳ ✳ ✳ ✳

Layered on top of all the animal insanity are the more practical things we began to learn: how to massage a blocked udder (i.e., how to 'treat a teat'), trim goat hooves and duck wings, sequester sick chicks, inject vaccines and medicines, use a microscope to determine parasite loading in goat and equine poo, give milk-of-magnesia and cooking oil to bloaty goats (or, in extreme cases, puncture their abdomens with a 14-gauge needle to let off the foul-smelling gas), and many other useful skills.

Some of this new knowledge we gain from our neighbors or from the occasional times we manage to get a vet to drive the three hours round trip from Tomatlán. Despite being inexperienced and eager to learn the Mexican way, we also recognize a lot of local lore is bunk and take much of what we're told here with a lick of salt. One neighbor, Jorge, for instance, keeps asking if he can borrow our macho goat to mate with the pet deer his family keeps tied to a tree in their front yard.

"Jorge, it's impossible. They're a completely different species. He might be able to do the dirty, but you'll never get a viable fetus," I say, trying to reason with him.

"No, Daniel, you're wrong. I have a friend that's done it before. It looks like a goat but is much faster and taller," Jorge responds.

Other skills we've learned by attending classes at a country fair in Maine when we're back there.

Much of the learning comes from our own research plus trial and error. We attend seminars when back in the States, bring resource books from the U.S., and, as Internet gradually makes its way into our lives over the years, we come to rely on this new YouTube phenomenon where people post instructional videos of pretty much everything. Between chat forums, our reference books, and all these other resources, we gradually learn to become our own country veterinarians, diagnosing and treating the majority of ailments and emergencies. The learning curve is steep, however, and more than once we've lost an animal that could have been saved with a little more knowledge or experience. A few years down the camino, Holly and I will learn one of our harshest lessons.

Michael, a wonderful and experienced volunteer who stayed with us one winter gave us the following sage advice on this matter: "If you've got livestock," he'd often say, "You've got deadstock."

Truer words, I believe, have never been 'uddered.'

12 - Toward Sustainability, Part 2
(Smuggling Solar)

Disclaimer: _The following act of 'eco-terrorism' did not happen. I realize that in the Preface I said that all events in the book actually occurred, but I've changed my mind. This one didn't. If you choose to believe that it did, well, that's up to you, but I cannot admit to nor condone any such illegal activity!_

Throughout the rest of the winter of 2009, Holly and I were busy marking out new internal roads and campsites and planning our first construction project. We decided that the community building, as we started calling it, would house bathrooms and showers, a communal kitchen, a tool bodega, and a laundry and storage room, and was to be built with classic adobe block that we'd make ourselves.

As our annual summer migration back to the States drew near, we were enthusiastic about the possibilities and, although we hadn't even left yet, we were already anxious to be getting back to the ranch in the Fall.

Realizing we were going to need help watching over the place while away, especially now that we had animals, solar equipment, and numerous other investments to protect, we considered Juanito and offered him a job caretaking. Juanito, however, was in the process of splitting from his wife and in-laws at Rinconcito and had accepted a job in Tomatlán.

Getting desperate, we searched the Internet, unaware then that coverage for the ranch and animals would become one of our most intractable issues—one that would influence the direction of the ranch for years to come. This first year of looking, we're lucky, though, and soon land a terrific young couple, Liz and Riley. In their early twenties and just out of college, Liz and Riley are young and enthusiastic. Riley, a gregarious, lanky, dreadlocked mandolin player, is the perfect complement to Liz's petite, blonde, demure presence. At least we thought she was demure—until we heard her sing, that is. Man-o-man, could that girl pack a musical wallop! An instant hit at El Rinconcito, Liz and Riley became a wonderful addition to the local community.

Liz and Riley arrived behind schedule when their Jeep died just inside the Mexican border. It had to be towed back the other way through customs, after which further delays meant I couldn't be on hand to greet them when they arrived. They started their tour of duty with nothing but a pile of sticky notes on how to run the entire ranch! Somehow they managed. With chutzpah and charm they settled into the ranch, and into our hearts, in a big way.

Solar energy? Natural building? Eco-tourism? Community living? Our world, it seemed, was being pulled irrevocably in new directions.

Back home again in Maine for the summer, the solar plot began to thicken.

Always the entrepreneurs, we decided that the campground construction would be ecological and Holly joined me in committing to it being 100% solar powered as well. We did a web search that turned up nothing like it and so we began visualizing having the ranch be the first solar-powered campground in North America—or, possibly, the world!

Rancho Sol y Mar, we finally decide to call it—Rancho Sun and Sea.

Realizing that I needed to know more before taking on such a huge solar project, I enrolled in a NABSEP photovoltaics certification course and begin designing a system large enough to power RV camper connections as well as the community building we were planning.

In addition to all of this, our plans for early retirement were in full swing. My employees and I had agreed to a modest buy-out plan for my business, and Holly, with the help of a broker, had an offer for her firm that would provide enough of a cash deposit to pay off our mortgages and make our escape to Mayto possible. The contract she'd signed required that she maintain a presence in the business for several years, but the sale, we thought, would lift the burden she'd been under and free up months at a time for her to be at the ranch.

Oh, how the gods were entertaining themselves!

Following up on our solar plans for the new building, we purchased a used pop-up camper and I began reconfiguring the inside to transport thousands of dollars' worth of hidden electronics and solar panels back to Mexico in the Fall. (Ironically, the panels we end up buying were manufactured in Mexico, so it'll be a homecoming for them). We realized that the plan to smuggle the gear could prove foolhardy at best, but acquiring the equipment in Mexico would be cost prohibitive, even if available at all, and so we proceeded.

On Thanksgiving, axles straining, I took the little box camper—towed behind our aging, sliver Honda CRV—for a test drive around the block and then made one final inspection of everything before leaving. After the demands and stresses of the past six months, I found myself really looking forward to the monotonous haul to the border. Holly, who was planning to fly to San Antonio and meet me halfway in a few days' time, gave me a kiss and, calling to Amy (yes, Amy has selflessly volunteered to do the drive with me again this year), I set off.

November 30, 2009

So far so good. I picked up Holly in San Antonio yesterday and, though definitely overloaded, the car and camper are behaving well. Now the part I've been dreading for months. The Border.

At the check station, camper loaded with contraband, we receive the dreaded red light, which means a search of the vehicle is obligatory. Having already checked the nothing-to-declare box on the customs form, our little act of eco-smuggling has now crossed the line of no return.

While Holly waits with Amy in the shade of the customs building, I'm engaged in my favorite activity—dealing with uniformed authority figures.

When asked to open the pop-up, I tell the official that it will be impossible because I've lost the crank handle that opens it up—the line I've been rehearsing for thousands of miles. Saying this sets a chain reaction in motion, and I'm instructed to pull into a separate holding area.

Now there's a small squadron of soldiers and inspectors surrounding the car. With two armed guards holding straining Shepherds on leashes, another four soldiers are directed to lift the top of the pop-up by hand. Giving it their husky best, the soldiers manage to raise the camper top a foot or so while the jefe in charge pokes about trying to see into the slit of an opening with a flashlight.

Even though I know they're looking for guns and might not even care that much about a pile of solar panels and electronics, I'm still crapping my shorts and swearing at myself for ever having hatched such a harebrained scheme.

For more than two hours, the inspectors poke and prod. Emptying the CRV of its piles of junk—bags of used clothes for the village, used tools, kitchenware, and a set of spare quad-bike tires—the inspectors eventually lose interest and call off the search before reaching the good stuff—some of the pricey solar electronics, crammed into the rear-passenger-seat foot wells at the bottom of the heap. During their search of the car, I find myself imagining the stack of two-hundred-watt solar panels sweating with fear in the pop-up like cartoon characters hiding from Judge Doom and the weasel police in 'Who Killed Roger Rabbit.'

"What will happen if they catch us?" one panel whispers to another

"I've heard it's pure hell," responds the other. "They'll throw us in prison with a bunch of Chinese knock-offs, and I've heard they only let you out for fifteen minutes of sunlight a day!"

"Sh-h-h-h," hushes a third. "Do you want them to hear us?"

Finally, drunk on a noxious cocktail of sweat and nerves, Holly and I are released without incident. Pulling out of customs, rattled but safe for now, we continue the drive south, exhausted and relieved.

Looking in the guidebook to start planning the stretch ahead, Holly gasps. "Oh shit!"

"What now?" I ask.

"Be prepared for a secondary customs inspection, twenty-one kilometers south," she reads from the book, "where you'll receive another opportunity to get a red or green light."

"Ahhhh, crap," I say. I really don't think I can take any more stress.

Pulling up to the inspection station—this one a lost outpost in the middle of bumfu_ _ cactus nowhere—I can feel my blood pressure rising, and my head becoming an overinflated balloon.

The humorless agent reviews our declaration form from the first inspection station. "They inspected the camper?" she asks, nodding toward the back.

"Yes, yes, everything is all set," I respond.

"OK, push the button," the official commands another agent.

Deep breath, and then, Green! We got the green!

"Thank you, officer. Have a nice day."

Driving on, we high five and laugh. "Yes!" we shout to each other. "Green equals Go! Green-Go! Gringo! We're gringos, ha,ha,ha, and we're through! We made it! Yeah, yeah, yeah!"

✴ ✴ ✴ ✴ ✴ ✴ ✴

The rest of that winter was relatively calm. Excited by the idea of the eco-campground, and with nothing else pressing to pull them away, Liz and Riley decided that they'd stick around, live with us, and help manifest our growing vision. Our first building project—the community building, which would include a kitchen and workshop plus bathrooms and showers for the campground—got underway. Convinced that natural building was the way to go, we began learning to make our own adobe blocks but opted to hire a local abañil (general contractor) to manage the bulk of the project.

Years later, driving through Sinaloa, we stayed overnight at a lovely inn run by an American couple. Somehow, the story of our smuggling came up and we heard the first-hand story of a fellow eco-terrorists who weren't so lucky.

"You guys are lucky" the couple told us. We tried that a couple of years ago and got caught. Not only did they take our solar panels, but they impounded our car. We never got any of it back!"

13 - Fear Factor, Part 1
(Kidnapping and Other Misdemeanors)

I'd like to start off this chapter by stating that Mexico is not, generally, a scary place, despite the U.S. news media's best efforts to paint it as such. (Holly and I have our own, conspiracy theory about the reasons behind this media bias—a media bought and paid for by a corporate America that wants, at all cost, to have Mexico portrayed as anything other than a warm, friendly, welcoming place that the massive Baby Boomer bubble of wannabe retirees can potentially exodus to en masse for a fraction of the cost of staying put in the U.S. Corporatocracy and being held captive by all its overpriced retiree services.)

Yes, of course, it is, statistically, a violent country. However, the bulk of the violence is limited to specific geographic regions or isolated demographic populations—i.e. narco traficantes and the law enforcement trying to stop them. For the rest of us, however—the majority of Mexicans and their northern visitors—life SOB (south of the border) is generally as relaxed and friendly a place as can be imagined. In addition to this pet theory of ours, it's clear that outright racism is also involved in the perpetration of the largely false image people from the States have of this beautiful, generally relaxed country.

That said, Mexico does still have a wild, untamed side. Although infrequent, Holly and I, spending more and more time here on the rougher, outer edge of an increasingly first-world Mexico, have had our share of fear —some of it imagined, some of it real. While constantly assessing the risks and trends, particularly in relation to our level of investment, we both get frustrated with the distorted picture of Mexico that our northern brethren have. Interestingly, this isn't the case with Canadians, who seem to get much more balanced news reporting.

Looking at the U.S. from the outside, the level and randomness of violence in our native country is staggering. Chicago, Miami, Baltimore, New Orleans—nearly every state and city seem to get their share. When we go back to visit friends and family, the degree of homelessness compared to all but the poorest parts of Mexico is shocking to us. In addition, a sense of crime hangs heavier in the air than what we're used to here in Mexico. In the village of Mayto—and even in nearby Puerto Vallarta, a city of over a quarter million—random violent crime is practically unheard of. Children are still safe to roam the streets unattended, women walk home alone at night, and tourists and ex-pats rarely have issues.

So, it's with some degree of reticence that I share some of the scarier moments we've had here. These, we're certain, are exceptional, 'one-off' situations induced, in part, by our somewhat 'edgy' existence and, though out of the norm, are a part of our story.

December 3-10, 2010

Arriving alone this year, and hearing about an attempted kidnapping yesterday, I'm freaked.

Since closing on the ranch, there have been rumors of a large development project on the beach, out past the Turtle Camp. Holly and I have felt a huge ambivalence about this. On the one hand, we're happy for our Mexican friends and neighbors, who'll be lifted from near poverty by the rising tide of development. On the other, we're worried that the other, more idyllic aspects of life here will disappear. While life in many parts of Mexico is difficult economically, there is, conversely, a quality of existence throughout the country that's unrivaled anywhere else we've ever been.

Despite its hard-won, hardscrabble history, there's a gentle friendliness we find compelling. People wave to one another when driving by, and it's difficult to go anywhere without people wanting to strike up a conversation. All day, every day, people across Mexico spend hours sitting on stoops, swinging in hammocks, or gathered down by the local aborrotes tienda (variety store) hanging out, playing games, catching up on the recent chisme (gossip), and enjoying one another. Several afternoons a week during the summer months, friends and neighbors—from babies to grandparents—gather down at the beach, fishing, swimming, playing soccer, drinking beer, and cooking up communal meals together.

This morning's news of the attempted kidnapping throws this innocence into sharp relief, however. Along with developers, the other world, so violent and raw, has apparently come knocking at Mayto's door.

According to the rumors making the rounds, a couple of ladrones (bad guys), young machos from out of town, had been seen driving back and forth by Victor's workplace earlier in the day. Victor is the son of don Ariola, ex-president of the communal ejido and owner of about a fifth of the total beachfront acreage being sold to a developer for a whopping twelve million dollars—a considerable pile of pesos for a dusty little back-country Mexican town to wrap its collective head around. That makes Victor, and the rest of Ariola family, a target for any would-be 'sequestradores' (kidnappers) from as far away as such news might travel. When Victor got off work yesterday, the machos tried to stop his car at the crossroads to Tehua Mixtle, a mere two hundred yards from our back gate.

On seeing the ladrones pointing a gun at his approaching car, Victor stepped on the gas and sped on past, his beat-up Buick LaSabre leaving the scene in a cloud of dust. Thoroughly shaken, Victor only stopped to look back when he got to Villa del Mar, the closest town, five miles south along the coast. Within minutes, the town delegado, Mexico's equivalent of the local constable, was called into action.

The one thing besides Victor's lead foot that the machos hadn't counted on was that Cabo Corrientes has only one road in and one road out. A couple of calls by the delegado to the federal police and the would-be kidnappers became captured animals. Within hours, the rumor mills were circulating the new news—word of the arrests. Following a few swift beatings, two other accomplices (supposedly the organizers of the failed attempt) had been captured as well.

Until today, Maytonians haven't worried about being a target of the crime plaguing other parts of Mexico. Such things seemed as remote as their own dusty village. As of this morning, however, that changed.

Now, I'm a worrier by nature, an inheritance from my father's fine lineage of worriers. "I'm a worrier, not a warrior," I like to say when telling others of my affliction. With all this newness—moving to a foreign country, taking on a new language, different weather, different culture, different rhythm—settling in here has tapped into my predilection for fearfulness. And, ay caramba, now this!

Within a day, my initial, visceral reaction to the kidnapping news has settled down somewhat. However, I'm still deeply shaken. As much as anything, I find myself worried about what Holly's reaction will be when she finds out. At the back of my mind, there's always been the fear that one good jolt to the fragile foothold we're carving out here—like, say, a bad scorpion bite, fall from a horse, or one of any number of other possible catastrophes—would sour her perspective and cause the entire dream to come crashing down.

A week later, I receive another jolt.

December 16, 2010

I'm lying in bed, drifting toward sleep, when suddenly gunshots at close range shatter the night.

"Good Christ!" I say to myself, sitting bolt upright. "That was just over the hill!"

Armed with nothing but a flashlight and keeping my head down, I climb the small hill in front of the house toward the sound of the shots. At the crest of the hill, I'm literally crawling on all fours. Peeking over the top, I see lights coming from the house on the adjacent hill to the right, a few hundred yards distant. More shots. Crap, they've seen me! Dropping down with heart pounding into the dirt, I hear—what is it? War whoops? Laughing? Yes, that's it. Definitely laughing. More shots. What the fuck... are they? Yes, I'm sure. They're drunk. My motherfucking neighbors are partying and shooting off pistols! Jesús Christ. Is this how it's going to be, always having to wonder if it's a party next door or if I'm under attack? Well, at least they're not shooting *at* me. That's something to be grateful for.

Severely bummed, with heart still racing, I head down to the house. Back in bed, in a restless dream state, I'm caught in a crossfire, surrounded by wolves and hyenas laughing demonically as they shoot at each other with cartoon firearms.

Early the next day, I head down to Casa Jardín, where I find Efren watering the bougainvilleas.

"Efren," I implore, "did you hear the war going on last night?"

"Oh, you mean Vera?" Efren responds nonchalantly while stooping to untangle a length of hose. "Yeah, he gets drunk now and then and shoots his pistol," he says. "Nothing to worry about. Just keep your head down," he adds, grinning.

✳ ✳ ✳ ✳ ✳ ✳ ✳

Finally, just as I'm getting back into the groove and feeling good about being back, yet another incident has me foundering in a tarpit of fear... again.

December 20, 2010

News today that there's been yet another fucked-up happening at the crossroads, right near our back gate. Rumors are swirling, but the story emerging is that the ice delivery truck that makes the rounds of Cabo Corrientes every few days has been robbed at gunpoint. What the hell is going on? Has the whole idea of buying this place been a massive mistake? Should we bail now, before it's too late? I feel like I've been punched in the stomach, like it's hard to even breath. Even Efren, who delivered the news today and who's normally light-hearted and fazed by nothing, seems thrown off balance by the rash of aggressive crimes our little paradise is having.

"I don't know, Daniel," Efren said after telling me about it today. "I've never seen anything like it. It's really not normal. I doubt it will continue. Do you have a gun? You should have a gun..."

The night is a long one, and I wake several times, the sheets soaked with sweat.

* * * * * * *

By the time Holly arrives a couple of days later, I've regained my cool and am accepting the general conclusion that the recent incidents are a bizarre anomaly and unlikely to continue. Still, I'm terribly worried about what Holly's reaction will be. To my relief, when I pluck up the courage to tell her a few days after her arrival, all she says is, "Well, we can't let fear get in the way of our lives." Fabulous! That Holly. What a gal!

Taking her lead, I decide that, at least for now, I'll also send fear back to where it belongs—the future.

With those pronouncements, we continue forward, learning to take adversity—and even the prospect of violence—in stride. Just as Mexicans everywhere have always done.

Like most fear, the kidnapping and ice truck robbery incidents soon fade into the fearless realm of memory. Back to normal, Holly and I resolve to move forward but to also be more vigilant and aware as we do so.

One more fear we faced during this time was the situation with the buyout of Holly's business, which was steadily deteriorating. The sale, which was structured as a buyout over four years, was faithfully following the basic law of physics that governs all such deals that seem too good to be true: A silent partner in the purchasing company turned out to be a corporate raider who was systematically dismantling the company, taking profits, and shunting Holly off to the sidelines in the process. With three years of payouts left to go, and more than half the sale value outstanding, the company filed bankruptcy, leaving the remaining client base, i.e., Holly's collateral, in tatters. For Holly, the loss of goodwill with her beloved clients was as emotionally wrenching as was the loss of our planned retirement savings. Determined to forge ahead with our plans for the ranch, our leap into uncertainty took on a daunting new financial aspect as well.

14 - Animal Tails, Part 2
(Alacran Bites, Lizard Love, and Stinky Sea Life)

OK, it's time to talk about our beloved scorpion brothers, or alacranes (pronounce a-la-kran-es) as they're known as here in Mexico—the prick of which (a quick, needle-like jab from the arched, segmented tail) is known as a bite rather than a sting. Alacranes themselves are completely harmless, I've heard it said. It's the nasty tail that will get you, though.

Let me see. Where to begin?

I don't recall first learning about them, but somewhere in our courtship with Mexico—and Cabo Corrientes in particular—we began hearing about everyone's nemesis, the A-L-A-C-R-A-N.

Now, scorpions are everywhere—all over Mexico, the Southwest U.S., and even China has its share. But the alacranes here in Cabo Corrientes have a reputation that sets them apart. The ones here—which are anywhere from one to four inches long, golden-to-nearly-transparent, and sport thin, longer-than-usual pincher forearms—are reputed to pack the most potent punch of any on the planet.

Never one to accept second-hand knowledge at face value, I was morbidly curious to become acquainted with these devils on a personal level. Note to self: Be careful what you wish for.

When we first toured the property with Esteban, he tried to educate us about alacranes. I remember him turning over piles of bricks and stones trying to find one for us and being surprised when he didn't. Disappointed, I grew ever more anxious to see one.

Finally, during one of our subsequent visits, Esteban found me the literal 'mother' of all alacranes—a large, gruesome-looking female, back covered with hundreds of sesame-seed-sized babies. Taking off his flip-flop and giving the matron a good whack, babies scattered everywhere. Brandishing his lethal rubber trudgeon and laughing, he then finished off the last of the scattering devil spawn.

By the time we took possession of the property, I considered myself something of a professional alacran hunter. I'd seen numerous specimens by then, encountered under rocks, in the scaly bark of old fence posts, and pretty much anywhere else a self-respecting alacran would want to hang out. Having learned that alacranes—like their venomous, ocean-based cousins, the jellyfish—fluoresce under ultraviolet light, and remembering a phenomenal exhibit I'd seen with jellyfish fluorescing in UV-lit tanks at the Monterrey Bay Aquarium, I'd brought down UV lightbulbs and flashlights from the U.S. A one-man vigilante fighting force now, armed with the latest high-tech weaponry, I was confident I'd soon rout Cabo Corrientes of its virulent pestilence.

The hunt was on!

The first night out, I killed three. True, being able to see the critters glowing like radioactive isotopes from fifteen feet away, I had a rather unsportsmanlike advantage, but still, I was pleased with my clever solution

and felt we were well on our way to establishing an alachran-free safe
zone around the house.
That was before they decided to fight back.

March 5, 2011

Several days into my hunting jag now, Holly is up at the house making
cheese while I'm down at the campground going over construction details
with Victor, our contractor, who's installing tiles and pebble flooring in the
soon-to-be-completed community-building facilities. I'm in one of the
bathrooms, reaching down to pick up some saltillo floor tiles, when: Zap!
Zoaow! Holy shit. Yup. I just got it!

Gingerly pulling back the tiles with my other hand, I see it now—a
three-inch-long, golden alacran, as handsome a specimen as I've seen in
all my hunting.

Finger stinging like a mo-fo, I grab one of the tiles and crush the
creepy critter into well-deserved oblivion.

"Hoah, Victor," I call around the corner. "Me picó un alacran! (a scorpion stung me!)"

Seconds later, Victor is scooting me up to the house on the back of his
motorcycle.

At the house, Holly starts buzzing around like an insect herself, in-
structing me to STAY CALM! while scrambling to find our alacran-bite
emergency kit—a random assortment of notes and concoctions for alacran
stings that we've been collecting.

"Suck on limes," one of the notes says.

"Crack open carbon capsules, make a paste of the powder, and apply
paste to site of sting" says another.

"Put a clove of garlic under the tongue," demands a third.

Along with the notes is a small vile of liquid—rattlesnake blood mixed
with alcohol, garlic, and herbs that a local friend had given me previously.

"This will save your life," the friend told me while handing me the vile
more than a year ago. Pinching my nose, I swallow it down, hoping it
doesn't have the reverse affect.

"Above all, stay calm," a final scrap of paper reads. "Becoming hyper-
tensive increases circulation and gives the venom an expedited ride
through the cardiovascular system."

So, I stay calm. Truly, I do. I get in the hammock, suck garlic and
lemon, and, for the first half hour or so, I'm feeling generally smug about
the whole situation.

Until it hits.

At first, the train's arrival is a somewhat vague, far-off notion like an announcement over platform loudspeakers to stand clear when there isn't anything to stand clear from but a distant rumbling in subway tunnel arteries. Then, faster than imagined, one feels a gush of wind being pushed ahead of the fuming engine and the platform is transformed by the headlong rush of noise and energy. The train has arrived. All aboard! ALL ABOARD!

Like a ghost imagined but never believed in, the pulsing venom is suddenly everywhere inside and outside of me, making googly eyes and laughing a mocking, psychotic, supernatural voice: "Ha, ha, ha, you smug, arrogant stooge. Ha, ha, ha. You thought you were good with your purple flashlights and all, didn't you, huh? Thought you were gonna hunt me down like some two-bit crook, didn't you? Well, amigo, guess again. You can start believing now, start seeing what a foolish idea that was, because I've decided that I'm going to take you for a pretty cool ride! Ha, ha, ha. Let's get on with it then, shall we? Come on, amigo, hop aboard! Ha, ha, ha, ha, ha, ha…"

The sting is on my index finger (as is common), and somewhere down there, the simple, easy-to-understand pain of the first encounter has morphed, grown and evolved past the initial throb stage into a complete, full-body experience. What up until now had been a tingling, burning sensation has matured into real PAIN, climbing up my arm like an ice climber wearing crampons. Like Gengis Khan's army, looting and burning, the alacran venom is now extracting its full revenge, taking no prisoners on its unstoppable march.

"OK, OK, I'm cool. I can handle this," I tell the demon.

"Ha, ha, ha, ha," it answers back. "I've seen your kind before. Tuff dude, eh? Stoic. Self-assured. Well, amigo, arrogant is what I call it. You go right on being tough, but pay attention. I'm at your elbow now, heading north. How do you think you're gonna feel when I'm under your eyelids? Eee-e-e-ya, ha ha ha…"

"Uh, hey Victor." (Victor is standing by, waiting to see if I'm going to need an antivenom injection from the town 'nurse,' a woman appointed and trained by the municipality to give them.) "Umm, how about going to see if Rosa can come by and give me a shot?" I ask him.

"Sure, Daniel, I'll go get her right now." He leaves.

There's only a thin veil over Holly's terror at this point. "Are you OK? Can I get you anything?" she asks, looking helpless.

As it so happens, her mom, Grandma Joanne we call her, is here visiting. Hovering around, she echoes Holly's concern. "Are you OK? Can I get you anything?"

To both of them I respond, "No, no, I think it's gonna be, fi-i-i-i-, oh, man, it's starting to…" Sputter, sputter, cough, sputter, hack.

What's happening now is that the advancing army has breached the stronghold of my corpus and is making its assault on my thorax proper. In an obvious attempt to overrun the functioning of my hippocampus, chemical weapons have been deployed, and I'm finding it difficult to breath. On top of this annoyance, everything is starting to hurt. Even my teeth are beginning to hurt. "Holy shit, this is really starting to—" harghhh, hack, cough, cough… "come"…sputter sputter… "on."

Spreading even faster now, the pain is everywhere at once. Like the worst flu ever, even my bones are screaming in pain. Worst of all is what's happening in my throat. What started as an irritating, scratchy feeling has now morphed into a vast, unchecked flood of phlegm and spittle, as if every mucous gland in my respiratory system has shifted into overdrive and is producing its own weight in snotty, slimy, effluent. Holy crap. It feels like I'm going to drown in my own snot!

Th-r-u-m-m-m-m. Sound of a motorcycle. Ah, finally, here comes Victor and Rosa!

When Rosa arrives, the scene has shifted. I'm out of the hammock and have moved into the bedroom. How did I get here? Did I black out? Time itself is slipping…

Lying here, I'm vaguely aware that Victor, Rosa, and Holly are hovering over me, looking anxious. Pleasant-faced and matronly, Rosa is asking questions, but her Spanish is coming though garbled—latent transmissions from a far-off universe. "Como scar-i-i-ium-phile, sc-z-zz-dig-rutz-grabiola, sientes Danielgzt? Puedes simbolinte respiras scampin-dindole (How are you Daniel? Can you breathe)?" she asks. At least, I think I can make that much out.

And somehow, despite the pain and possible death that's upon me, I feel detached, light-headed, and hear myself trying to make a joke with her. "I'm breathing fine, Rosa. It's just that the air is having trouble getting past all the mucus."

She smiles in a way that leaves me unsure whether she gets it. Either way, she's loading up her syringe now, government triage training and years of experience kicking in. A true professional.

Except... except... darn... she's forgotten her glasses. Am I imagining this? No, it's true. She's telling Victor and Holly that she's forgotten her glasses.

I hear myself laughing in snotty, stucco bursts.

From my distorted, far-off place, I ascertain that there's some confusion going on. I get that my life may be hanging in the balance, but, despite the pain—a full-blown hurricane of sensation—I find the scene entertaining and feel myself starting to leave my body. Whoa. So this is it! This is that mystical experience of dying I've heard so much about! Here I go. I'm leaving now!

Floating clear and free, I'm up somewhere near the corner of the room, up by the ceiling, looking down. Below me, Rosa, Holly, and Victor have organized themselves into an amusing triage circus act. Rosa has tied a rubber hose around my arm while Holly, calling up her decades past training as a registered nurse, directs the half-blind Rosa toward my bulging vein with her needle. The only problem is that Rosa and Holly don't understand each other very well, so Victor is filling in as translator.

"A little more to the right," Holly urgently instructs.

"Un poco mas a la derecha," Victor translates to Rosa.

"Aqui?" Rosa asks expectantly, jabbing hole after hole into my mannequin arm.

"No. Shit, you almost had it," Holly moans. "Try again. To the left now. There, there. I think maybe you've got it this time!"

Drifting above the slapstick comedy act, I'm in stitches. The three of them, a cross between Grey's Anatomy and the Three Stooges, are terrific entertainment. The pain in that body down there somewhere is unimportant now.

With the first injection kicking in, I'm called to my body, pulled back like a breath of smoke filmed in reverse. *Damn. Really? Do I have to go back? I was really happy up here!*

Returned, I find the pain is like nothing I've ever felt before. How can it be that my teeth are hurting? They're teeth, for Christ's sake. Pure bone. And then, ooh, ugh, yup, here it comes. Please. Help me. I need to get to the...

Blaaaaat. Baaaaarrrrfff.

Kneeling in front of the toilet, puking out what must be brain matter, every bone in my body is screaming. Still, part of me is on another plain. Even though I'm solidly back, inhabiting my body as I'm supposed to be, I'm also removed. Not caring. Numb and amused.

In between heaves, I look up at Victor standing there watching my Olympic vomit thrusts, and say to him; "Hey, Victor, this floor is ugly, don't you think?" The saltillo floor tiles here in the bathroom were terribly installed, and, in my demented state, it's yet another one of my lame attempts at a joke. I'm sure Victor must get the humor; however, he looks confused. It doesn't matter. To me, it's hysterical, and that's more important. That and trying to breathe. The choking, asphyxiating, gurgling phlegm sounds and attempted throat clearing keep playing over and over, disconnected from but also part of me.

Oops. There it is. Another call coming in on the big white telephone: Blaaaat. Baaaarf. My guts, meanwhile, just down the street from my respiratory system, are also having their own lively party. Fun stuff.

Back in bed, I find that Rosa, Victor, and Holly have evolved into an efficient medical SWAT team. "A little to the left. There, you've got it," instructs Holly. "Un poco mas a la izquierda. Ya, la tiene. Asi es," Victor translates, as a second and then third injection is given.

Within minutes of the third shot, the symptoms begin to subside. I'm weak and numb but back from my journey and among the living. Rosa's impressed. She's only had to give three injections only one other time.

✳ ✳ ✳ ✳ ✳ ✳ ✳

A week later, and I still couldn't feel my index finger. Two weeks on I started to get some sensation back. The only reminder of the incident after a month was a mild numbness at the site of the sting. Week five, I was back to normal.

Fortunately, not all alacran stings are this dramatic. A second 'bite' I had about two years later was nothing worse than a bad bee sting. While folk treatments like the rattlesnake concoction I tried still abound, the reality is that 50% of the stings we've seen here at the ranch over the years have been minor incidents that don't require any special treatment or injections. I have a personal theory that the worst of the reactions to alacran stings is an allergic response that can be quelled with antihistamines. Since my great ride, we've kept liquid Benadryl on hand and have had consistent success using it to treat alacran-sting victims—except with our poor chickens, which get stung on a regular basis. They're our advance guard, on patrol around the premises daily searching out alacran, spiders, and other nuisance bugs. However, in so doing, they risk their paltry, poultry lives to protect us. About half the time, when stung, the chickens succumb, often because they're out in the bushes somewhere and, having 'taken one for the team,' they simply lie down to die. When we do find them in time, however, we're generally able to save them by putting them in a dark box or bucket, keeping them calm, giving them an Avapena tab, and letting them recover for a day or so. Ducks, on the other hand, with their longer bills, are less susceptible to being stung. Whenever the subject of ducks comes up with a local, I notice they consider them first as alacran protection—ahead of their value in providing meat or eggs.

Another thing we've learned is that the local nurses aren't always stocked with alacran antivenom. Though expensive, we now keep our own antivenom on hand. That and plenty of liquid Benadryl.

One night, a year or so after my first sting, Holly and I woke to the sound of one of our strongest macho goats, Coco, bellowing and crying out. Scrambling out of bed, flashlights blazing, we found Coco crying and in distress. It was clear by the snot pouring out of his mouth and nostrils that he was suffering from an alacran sting. Panicked, we decide to dose him up with one of our hundred-dollar-a-pop injections. By morning, he'd completely recovered, snorting and stomping and being his usual nuisance to all the ladies.

Now, after years and perspective, we limit animal treatments to the much more economical antihistamine injections. Most recently, our dog, Pirata (Pirate), woke us, crying out with similar symptoms. After administering an intramuscular shot of Histafina, an inexpensive antihistamine similar to Benadryl, he was fine by morning. Our cats have never been stung, to the best of our knowledge, or they may have some sort of natural resistance.

Most of our other animal neighbors here are a lot less threatening, even though they may look the part...

April 6, 2011

This afternoon, lying in the hammock doing some deep, cognitive research, I'm jolted from my work by a familiar scream. Holly, who's been tidying up around the front porch, is standing on a chair and reaching up with both hands extended to where the roof connects to the top of the front wall.

"I've got him!" she shrieks. "I've got the iguana!" (This is a new one that took over after Stripe moved on. He's a restless guy that's been keeping us up at night, so Holly's grabbing him is a great opportunity to give him his eviction notice.) "Quick, help me before he gets a way!"

Clawing and scraping, the iguana, half its body hidden underneath the Spanish roof tiles, is giving his all to escape Holly's grasp.

Jumping into action, I grab a pair of gloves and a second chair, and scootch in next to Holly. Now we're a pair of Lucha Libre wrestlers, and Holly tags out as I grab hold of the prehistoric tail. This guy's a big one. And strong. The harder I pull, the more he redoubles his efforts. It's a battle of wills at this point and far from clear who's going to win. Bracing myself, I give the tail the best yank I've got. With a small "pop," something gives way. Looking up at my hand, still over my head, I see the scaly, writhing, disembodied tail flailing spastically in my grip.

Now a sound is coming from somewhere else. Oh my god, it's me that's letting out a piercing shriek. "Ah-h-h-h-h!" I scream. "Ach-h-h-h," I scream again, flinging the thrashing, satanic life force out into the yard.

At this point, Holly is practically peeing herself from laughing, and the two of us watch in horror as the tail performs a St. Vitus breakdance out in the dirt. One of the creepiest things, we note, is that there isn't any blood. You'd think that any animal, upon losing a body part, would have the self-respect to shed some. But this thing, this sinister soul-less cyborg, is as dry as… well… as dry as a bone.

Finally, the severed appendage tires of dancing and settles in for a nap. Still shaking our heads, grossed out but laughing (is there a word for that? Something so gross that it's funny?), Hol and I retreat to the kitchen for coffee.

Over the next few days, we hear the iguana rustling about up in the ceiling, still very much alive. About the third day after the dismemberment event, Holly spots it running across the yard. Sure enough, it's him. He's shorter but otherwise fine.

"Stubby," Holly declares. "We'll call him Stubby. First we had Stripe, now we've got Stubby!"

★★*★*★*★*★*★*

Stubby was with us for several months after the incident, but, like Stripe and all good iguanas throughout the ages, he eventually moved on to happier hunting grounds.

During the summer of that year, a super-diligent couple we had as caretakers asked if they could bring a local boy, Yamir (pronounced Ya-Meer) on board to help with chores. On returning in the fall, Holly and I found Yamir to be likable and hard-working, and, with our first-choice ranch hand Juanito having moved to Tomatlán, we decided to keep Yamir on. Over time, Yamir started to become something of an adopted son for us. Incredibly bright and fast talking, he was a rambunctious teenager—at times a handful, and always up to something, but also a hard worker and great at arranging deals for goats, construction materials, a slightly used water pump, or whatever was needed at the time. Undoubtedly, he was able to collect a commission on these transactions, but the deals seemed good enough, and he became more and more invaluable to us.

Talking a mile a minute, Yamir would often regale us with local gossip or stories of his youth. Having been a runner for the narcos, Yamir had accidentally shot someone in the face when he was just an adolescent. With the boy hovering near death in the hospital, Yamir was freaked out by the incident and made a pact with himself that if the boy he'd shot recovered, he'd get his act together and leave the narco life behind.

"It wasn't easy, but they let me go," he told me about the experience. "I'm still friends with many of those chavos, though I do my best to keep my distance."

As our infrastructure grew and became more complicated, Yamir and I frequently tackled projects together. In friendly competition, we'd try to out Mac-Gyver each other (pronounced "Mc-Geever" here in Mexico), coming up with unique solutions to engineering problems and the numerous fix-it challenges that rural ranch life entails. Always spirited and laughing, Yamir was usually half a step ahead of whatever I might be thinking or doing.

One more ridiculous reptile visit we had was a classic Yamir episode.

December 7, 2011

Returning from the beach today, a Saturday, several young boys from the village greet Holly and me halfway up the road to our house.

"Daniel, come quick," one of the boys urges. "Yamir has something for you."

"It's a cool present he wants to give you!" another boy chimes in.

Curious, Holly and I pick up the pace, following the ragged, barefoot boys as they run ahead.

At the house, Yamir steps out from the shade of the bougainvilleas. Grinning, he holds out a three-foot-long baby alligator. The alligator's snout, with nasty little fangs sticking out both sides of the mouth, is securely held shut with a bright-pink hair scrunchie.

"Here you go, Daniel and Holly. I want to give you this wonderful gift," Yamir says. "I knew you'd love him. You can keep him in the pond!"

As much as Holly and I hate to disappoint, we make an excuse and decline the offer.

✳ ✳ ✳ ✳ ✳ ✳ ✳

Because we're on the ocean, many of our memorable animal episodes have literally washed up onto the sand and into our lives.

January 18, 2012

This afternoon, I hear shouting and commotion coming from the beach. Walking up our little hill, I look out over the playa to see what's going on. I see lots of people running around, picking up objects from the beach, but I can't imagine what they are. Hopping on the quad bike, I speed down the hill to check it out. I find that a whole school of bonito tuna have beached themselves, probably chased in by a school of something larger. Now, flopping around helpless, the fish are being snatched up by half the village, who've heard the news and come running.

* * * * * * *

Another time, a baby whale, about twenty feet long, beached itself down past the Turtle Camp near the one-kilometer marker. For a week or so, people flocked to the beach from all over the area to experience the thrill of seeing a great leviathan, albeit a dead one, first hand, They posed as loved ones took snaps or arranged themselves for selfies while their kids ran up to the beast, laughing and daring each other to touch it. After week two, however, vultures, coyotes, and other offal enthusiasts started making inroads with the carcass, transforming its once noble countenance into a giant rotting pile of eviscerated gumbo. With the growing aromatic efflu-ence, the eco-tourism surge soon petered out to nothing.

Always curious about things macabre, I kept up my vigil, walking to the site every other day or so to follow the progression. What was most fascinating was that the remaining blubbery bulk literally melted away, day by day, under the blazing sun. By week three, there was nothing left but a rubbery lump of sun-cured skin and, by the end of the month, Nature had hidden all evidence of her ill-fated offspring.

Yet another memorable prize tossed out to us by the sea was 'The Evil Dolphin'...

March 7, 2012

This evening, Holly and I are part of a rambunctious group of about thirty having dinner at El Rinconcito—a large and rowdi gathering of maybe thirty in all. With tequila and beers flowing, Fernando is in rare form, pounding his guitar, singing at the top of his lungs, and entertaining the troops. Only thing is, the odd odor we'd all begun smelling during dinner is getting worse, and it's now unmistakably linked to something from the ocean—large and rotting. Grabbing Fernando in between corridos (bal-lads), I ask him to get a flashlight, and the two of us head out onto the beach to investigate.

It doesn't take long to find the source of the odor. There, tumbling in the waves, is the putrefied carcass of a good-sized, bottlenose dolphin—a solid ten feet long or more. With each surge of a rolling breaker, a fresh waft of stench, each more powerful than the previous, pulses out over the beach, engulfing us in a palpable cloud.

"Christ," Fernando says, "we've got to do something!"

By now, a small group has followed us out to the beach to see what's happening.

"I'll get my truck," someone shouts. "I've got off-road lights, so at least we can see what we're dealing with."

The crowd grows and, for a few minutes, everyone gapes, standing as close to the rolling stench as they can stomach.

"Jesús," one of the drunken reprobates blurts out, "reminds me of an old girlfriend of mine!"

"Fernando, quick, get your fillet knife," some other wiseacre joins in. "There's enough there to feed your guests for a month!"

Fernando and I are out in front of everyone else when the truck with the lights pulls out onto the beach, transforming the whole scene into a Hollywood movie set. Getting our first clear look at the creature, we see something equally as horrifying as the smell. With much of the flesh ripped away, the dolphin, caught in the spotlight and still rolling in and out with the waves, has the most hideous, evil-looking, Tim Burton-inspired grin on its face that one could imagine.

"Who even knew that porpoises have so many teeth?" Fernando mutters.

For a few more moments, everyone stands staring, transfixed by the gruesome sight.

"How about that?" I say to Fernando, pointing to a decent-size log off to the side. "Maybe if use that log and push the dolphin out far enough, it'll drift away."

"Yes, yes," Fernando agrees, snapping out of his trance. "Let's try it!"

Together, holding our breath, we carry the log over to the tumbling body and begin doing our best to find purchase on the creature and give it a proper send-off. Once or twice, we make solid contact and give it good shove before running, gagging and laughing, back toward the others. The crowd is beside themselves, hooting it up and applauding our efforts. Together we all watch expectantly as the little ship we've launched on its maiden voyage bobs around just past the first break.

"Go! Go! Go!" the crowd is chanting.

"Oh, crap," Fernando says, nudging me. "I think it's coming back!"

Sure enough, the timid mariner has had a change of heart, deciding instead to come back to port for another round of grog.

Picking up the log, Fernando and I return to our ridiculous clown game of shuffle board. Once again, we manage to give it a shove. As I stumble back from the waves, I see that Fernando's decided he's going to close the deal. Wading out further with the pole, he tries to push the wretched beast even farther away. Call it bad timing, bad judgment, or bad luck, but, for whatever reason, some sick-humored god chooses just that moment to bring a particularly big swell ashore, sending the vile sea creature crashing headlong into poor Fernando.

"Oh my god, it's attacking him!" one of the onlookers shouts.

Fernando, struggling to gain his footing and scrambling back onto the beach, retches for real this time.

By the next morning, a putrid, evil smog has settled over the entire beach. The odor of death, as much a taste as a smell, sticks to back of our throats. Calls are made, messages sent, and, like an avenging superhero, Nacho, the local backhoe operator, arrives midmorning. Before long, he has the putrid, grinning dolphin entombed ten feet closer to the hell from whence it had come.

From top left: Yamir, jazz swing dance class w/ volunteers, Dan installing solar at community building, kids stuff, Holly and Hillary making cob, Mateo walking the tank, our hippi-lux cob bedroom, Dan, Riley and Angle making adobe block, Dan working on Guest House, Tejones vs Venados annual Christmas soccer game, Holly w/ Paco, Holly swimming Colarín

Section IV

Un Camino Mal (A Bad Road)
Autumn 2012 ~ Spring 2015

"If you're going through hell, keep going." ~ *Winston Churchill*

15 - Toward Sustainability, Part 3
(Who Would Volunteer for This?)

By our seventh winter in Mayto—and our fourth year since gaining title to the property—we'd increasingly begun embracing the idea of pursuing a sustainable lifestyle here at the ranch. We also began realizing that for the ranch to be truly sustainable, we'd need to have other people involved. What's sustainable, we asked ourselves, if, after we die, the project, because it has no financial viability or life of its own, collapses and gets sold off to some unscrupulous developer?

Exploring this notion, we began to envision not just a campground but a whole eco-village forming with pot luck dinners, movie nights, workshops and retreats, people milking goats and growing veggies. Taking ranch products to sell in Vallarta. Doing yoga. Being happy and surrounded by that endless source of hugs—community. "What's not to love about all of that?" we reasoned to each other.

Realizing that to have any sort of community we'd need accommodations, we started making plans to build a guest house. With the experience of having created the community building from traditional adobe under our belts, we'd become hooked on natural building but wanted a process that was more efficient and less grueling than building with adobe involved—particularly the making, drying, stacking, and moving of forty-pound blocks. Our son, Josh had also become interested in natural building and turned us on to CEBs (compressed earth blocks), which were said to stronger and more efficient to work with than adobe. Always the do-er, Holly signed us up for a workshop in Texas to learn how to build with them, and by the winter of 2012/2103, work on our new guest house was underway.

During this time, another changer of the game for us was learning about the volunteer-help circuit. A terrific young couple from the U.K., who'd shown up on their bicycles the previous fall to stay the two free nights' stay we offer to touring bicyclists, were now, six months later, our summer caretakers. The couple enlightened us about work-exchange websites such as Work-Away, Help-X, and WWOOF'ing International, sites that link travelers looking for cheap digs with people needing work help. What we soon learned was that there's a veritable army of itinerate travelers—mostly young people—wandering the globe while stretching their budgets by helping with projects like ours. What we learned over time, however, was that volunteers also come with many challenges.

For the moment, though, we were thrilled. After creating listings and a website describing our project and mission ("To promote healthful, sustainable living, education, and construction practices"), we began receiving stacks of online applications, launching our foray into community living.

Despite all the cutting-edge technological advances we'd made at the house by then (telephone, refrigerator, and lights!), Internet was still a year away. Using the newly installed satellite Internet wifi at Hotel Mayto, we began fielding applications from volunteers. The first to arrive, Josephine, was a shocker. Having billed herself as an experienced, barrel-racing cowgirl and expert horse trainer, we brought her on to help us with one existing, and two new horses that we'd recently bought.

October 11, 2012

Picking up Josephine at the airport in Vallarta, we encounter a six-foot-tall, blonde, super-sized specimen of cornfed, Nebraska-farmgirl stock. Dressed to the nines, wearing a glittering pink cowboy hat, and weighing in at well over two hundred and fifty pounds, the steaming locomotive of a woman turns heads as she strides across the parking lot toward us.

"Dios mío (oh my god), how will she ever get through the door of the camper she'll be staying in?" Holly mutters under her breath, completely serious.

Later that day, we get the answer when we show "Jo" (as she instructs us to call her) the pickup-truck camper that will be her home for the next two months. Jo, looking circumspect, eyes the camper—which was previously removed from the bed of the pickup truck, and now sits perched on a foundation of cement blocks, the minimalist door looking more like an escape hatch than a proper entryway.

"Well this will be interesting," she says matter-of-factly as, turning sideways, she shimmies and squeezes through the undersized opening.

October 21 - 25, 2012

The past few weeks have been a stretch for us all on many levels. For days and days, Jo, using an improvised whip and flagging pole, has been trotting the wilder of the two horses, Canelo, around and around the circular training corral we've built in a process known as "ring work."

Holly and I realize the discipline Jo's giving Canelo is good for him, but having ridden him previously, I know it's not like Jo's having to break him from scratch. Having her accustom all three horses to being ridden daily was the primary reason for inviting Josephine here and something we'd been clear with her about during our online interview process. Now, nearing a month in, she hasn't yet ridden any of them.

"I wonder if she's ever actually ridden?" Holly says to me at breakfast.

"I know, I know. We're going to have to say something. Draw straws?" I ask hopefully.

"You're the one who wanted the horses trained," Holly responds.

"OK. OK. I'll talk to her today."

After breakfast, I head down to the training ring where Jo, already sweating in the day's rising heat, is taking a break off to the side under a huisache tree.

"Jo," I say gently, "when are you planning to actually ride Canelo? That's what you came here to do, right, train the horses and ride them daily?"

At this point, Jo fesses up that because of the 'growth spurt' she's been experiencing recently, she hasn't actually ridden a horse in several years. With a tear in her eye, Jo, who's normally assertive to the point of being brusque, plops right down on the ground in a cross-legged position. Meanwhile, Canelo, looking on, is managing to keep a straight face, but I feel from his energy that he's secretly laughing. Sitting there in the dirt, sniffling softly, Jo apologizes and tells me she's definitely intending to ride Canelo and the other horses—just as soon as she can get him to take a saddle. She also tells me she's losing weight rapidly. She can feel the difference from being here.

"That's OK, Jo," I tell her, trying to sound cheerful. "We're good. I just wanted to make sure you're still planning to ride."

Over the next several days, Jo works on getting Canelo tacked up. Canelo, a real teenage brat—especially after having been left to roam on the property unmolested for more than six months—is having none of it, bucking and snorting whenever Jo goes near him with the saddle. At one point, watching from afar, I'm shocked to see Jo actually haul off and give Canelo a full-on karate kick to the ribs and find myself impressed by both the speed and height of the move.

Finally, the following day, Jo announces she's ready to ride. Holly and I are at the paddock, expectant, as Jo climbs onto the step stool I've rigged up from blocks for the occasion. Canelo is looking nervous and, when Jo takes a small leap up onto his back—struggling at first and then righting herself proudly into a sitting position—Canelo appears to actually sag in the middle. Eyes bugging out, he looks to Holly and me, pleading silently for some sort of horsey forgiveness. 'Get her off my back, and I'll come when called. I'll never try to bite anyone again, I swear it!' Camelo implores us telepathically.

'No way, amigo,' I telepath back to him. 'This is what you get for always 'horsing around'. 'Buck up,' I continue mind-melding to him from across the ring, knowing how much he hates my puns.

With a groan—and one last dirty look at me—he and Jo head out of the corral.

"Well, I'm off," Jo says, quickly finding her groove and expertly reining Canelo out through the open gate.

Holly and I watch in wonder as she trots off down the lane toward the beach.

****

Over time, we've approached the challenge of building community from many angles. Having work-exchange volunteers has brought us tons of affordable help and often a joyful sense of community living but has also produced some of our worst disasters. Never, at that point, could we have imagined what sort of roller-coaster ride we were buying tickets for.

One young woman, for instance, got terribly upset because we wouldn't let her milk the goats. For many reasons, we reserved that privilege for longer-staying participants brought on specifically to work with the animals. This woman, well-liked by the rest of the volunteers, spent much of the two weeks she was with us trying everything imaginable to circumvent our policy. When, near the end of her stay, she realized it simply wasn't happening, she fell into a day-long crying jag that, like a virus, infected many of the other volunteers. Before we knew it, we had a full-on mutiny on our hands, and it took several weeks after her leaving to restore the equilibrium.

Another incident involved an entourage of four. Arriving in two vehicles—a conversion van and a beat-up old Subaru—the group had left Canada convinced that the zombie apocalypse, or something close to it, was about to befall the U.S. and their fair land. Since leaving Canada, bound for a planned eco-village startup a couple of hours south of here, the group had been informed that the village was no longer going to be happening. Deeply discouraged, The Quartet, as we came to call them, was in a tailspin, circling the drain. Taking pity, Holly and I told them they were welcome to stay with us for a while, and that they could help garden or tend to other chores.

Nice enough folks, one of them—who always wore a purple sufi cap with little mirrors embroidered into it—was clearly the group's spiritual leader. Frequently, as they stood together in a huddle, he'd invoke 'The In-Breath' to center their energy, reconnect themselves with the cosmos, and help solve their many earthly problems. Like Moses leading his tribe to the promised land, he and 'The Quartet' as we came to call them, were certain that our ranch was their new holy ground. Adding a nice accent to the ensemble, we also learned that the two couples had recently gone through a partner switch.

By the end of the first week with us, The Quartet summoned Holly and me to a formal meeting. After the requisite hugs at the guest house porch, the meeting began.

November 5, 2012

Sitting together on the porch, Moses, I'll call him, began his pitch:

"Dan, Holly, we'd like to make you an offer. We've severed all ties with our lives in Canada except for a group of others who'll be following us down here once we've established a Center. The collapse of North American society is imminent, and the borders will be closing soon (pauses for a deep In Breath). We have all of our earthly wealth with us—forty-thousand dollars in gold bullion and currency. We'd like to give you and Holly all but a few thousand in exchange for being able to create our own space at the back of the property."

"Uhmm, you have forty-thousand dollars in the van?" I ask him.

"Yes, that's right. In the van and in the car. We went out on the beach last night, had a good cry together, consulted the In Breath, and have all agreed. We want to give it to you and Holly—our wealth in exchange for living here."

I'm in shock, but Holly, former financial planner, is on it. "Well, OK, let's think this through," she replies solemnly. "So, you give us your money and you've got a patch of land to set up shop on. Then what? How will you feed and clothe yourselves?"

"We'll trade our talents with you."

"OK, give us an example. What can you do?" Holly asks.

"Siddhartha and I are professional painters." (For the sake of literary interest, we'll call the other guy Siddhartha).

Siddhartha and the two women nod.

"We can paint anything you'd like."

"And after that? After everything's painted? What will you do for money then?" I continue in earnest, although, frankly, this is beginning to feel like I'm having a conversation with a hookah-smoking caterpillar.

"My words are my fiat currency," Moses replies.

"Uhm, OK. That's fine. Let's say that's true. Let's say that you can give us advice on accessing The In Breath and other spiritual matters. And, in return, I can tell you how to grow food, create electricity, and treat a scorpion bite. In other words, how to stay alive here. Assuming my words have value as fiat currency too, and we trade those currencies, I still don't see how that buys you food or clothes."

"Or how about medical care?" Holly adds. "How will you pay for medical attention if you get sick or hurt?"

"We'll still have some reserves to cover those things." Moses replies, clearly on the defensive now.

"And what if your good friend Siddhartha here gets seriously hurt?" I ask. "Will you use the last of your reserves for his medical care?"

Moses doesn't answer. Eyes closed, he's gone deep into The In Breath. Siddhartha and the girls sit, eyes wide, waiting to see if Moses is willing to pay for the urgent medical treatment that Siddhartha may one day need.

"OK, OK, I say," breaking the impasse. "How about this? We do have some painting we need done. How about if you all stay a week longer in exchange for painting four hours a day? That'll give us all time to think this thing through."

There's a general nodding of heads and lukewarm agreement. It's not the deal they'd been hoping for, but it buys them some time. Standing now, we're all hugging each other, a few tears being emitted by the ladies. Moses seems stiff but is offering us thanks for being such kind and understanding people.

"Oh, and one last thing," Holly says as the quorum is breaking up, "I don't think you should mention the forty thousand dollars to anyone else."

The next morning, we find the campsite they've been occupying vacant.

✷ ✷ ✷ ✷ ✷ ✷ ✷

Some of the volunteer applications we've received over the years have their own story to tell, as witnessed by the following examples (names changed):

Wow! I am blown away at the sheer motivation that seems to have been put forth to create such harmony for humans and nature alike. It would give me immense pleasure to participate in your Eco-Community. I am a fifty-seven-year old, polyamorous, male vegan, poet, and philosopher. I am willing to work hard and help share the bounty you have created. By the way, I am gluten- intolerant, and need to know if the meal program is sufficiently organized to accommodate this. I am also wondering if there is money available to help offset my travel expenses getting to you? I await further instruction with head held high.
In Love & Light,
Tomas.

Or this:

Hi my name is Cosmos. I am on a vision quest of sorts and also on a mission to find my family a new home out of the States.

I feel an urge to travel and root and now it's time to travel again. I have spent the last five years on the big island of Hawaii and the last two living in a permaculture/poly raw food/nonviolent communication community. Missing it so! but due to the fact that the community is having a hard time keeping itself sustainable and very little people who live there are motivated as a whole (would rather lounge than garden) I have moved on.

I have never been to Mexico, but it feels like it's time to visit. I have had garden experience including some aquaponics, small building construction with cob, great deal of horse and livestock fun as I lived on an Alpaca farm for a year in Oklahoma. I feel determined to live and raise my kids in community so we all get our needs met and feel secure, bring opportunities for sharing/teaching/learning. Animal Husbandry is something I want to learn more of. I have raised up dogs, killed my own animals and processed them, milked a goat or two as well as a cow, and would like to only travel by horseback at some point.

I am feeling courageous and ready to put forth energy where needed. I feel desperate in my attempts to gain clarity around my journey. I saw you had opening for someone who spoke Spanish, which is not me. I come with very little money, but with a motivation to cultivate and learn. I am very strong and self-motivated, work well with others, and have fenominal communication skills/mediation. I am even willing to sleep outside the community and come work for free on anything! I plan on coming to Mexico around February 10th and plan to stay for two months. Hope this reaches you soon.

Aloha,
Cosmos

And another:

To Whom it May Concern:
A 73-year-old gentleman from Sweden called Anders is looking for 2-3 weeks volunteer work in 2016. I must stress that his hearing is quite bad but with a hearing aid he can communicate, although it's very individual. Anders doesn't have any specific skills, just a good heart and willing pair of hands.

If he can't find a voluntary organisation or nonprofit willing to accept him, a short-term Spanish course is a viable alternative.

Please get back to us at the earliest opportunity if you can be of any assistance.

Yours faithfully,
Geoffrey Goodman

Or this one with no cover sheet, preamble, or introduction:

I have served as the primary House Manager/Property Caretaker for our family's turn of the century old mini estate (Blithesdale/Worthington Place) (inset); now a thriving B & B. I singularly presided over my grandparents'/ great-grandfather's mini-estate serving as the principal caretaker for approximately 10 yrs., replete with all the blood, sweat and tears (labor of love).

In addition to having traditional high-end formal household experience, I have worked in the capacity as a Personal Assistant; the scope of the principle duties/functions ran the gamut of acting as a House Manager; ensuring the unfettered "flow" and rhythm of the respective Household, typical errand running, travel arrangements, some vendor management, written correspondences, animal pet care/maintenance. The latter is a thumbnail sketch and not completely representative and/ or inclusive of the aggregate duties or pool of skills/talent that I offer. Moreover, I am highly/profoundly responsible and the embodiment of professionalism. I exhibit a very effervescent and affable demeanor with an enviable/unparalleled work ethic.

I possess and embody truly superlative and exemplary communication, client relations, interpersonal skills. Equally, my presentation/interfacing is stellar, refined and impressive. Descriptively and characteristically, I pride myself on being a consummate communicator/facilitator with the ability to interface and comport myself with divergent/disparate audiences'/ clients; with the ability to readily interact and establish sense of rapport/camaraderie.

Because I'm a big proponent of forthrightness; I feel compelled to tell/apprise you that characteristically very all American, conservative sensibilities, self-avowed "straight arrow"/straight laced; the definition of it. Specifically and more pointedly; decidedly a non-smoker/non-drinker.

Enclosed is a copy of my resume outlining my respective qualifications and background.

Thank you.

✷ ✷ ✷ ✷ ✷ ✷ ✷

Another couple we took on gave us an interesting experience.

The application came as an urgent request from Belize. Sabrina, Usef, and their eight-year-old daughter, Sky, were having troubles with the owners of the finca they were currently living at and were looking for a new community right away. Well-written and frank, Sabrina's email described the situation involving an overbearing property owner in detail and seemed reasonable. Despite the urgency and the fact that they were in conflict at their current posting, both Sabrina's and Usef's qualifications seemed solid. Torn, Holly and I held them off, stalling for time while waiting for a response to the due-diligence email I'd sent to the owner of the project, hoping for a reference or at least to hear the owner's side of the story. We were short-handed at that point, so when we hadn't gotten a response by the end of the week, we replied informing them that they could come along.

"This will have to be on a provisional basis, however," I wrote them. "You can do a work-exchange for a couple of weeks, and then we can evaluate the situation."

When they showed up six days later, we marveled at Sabrina's day-glow purple hair and wrote off the family's slightly strange mannerisms as being due to the stress they'd been under and the grueling journey they'd just had—ninety six hours on and off buses.

January 5, 2013

They arrive late afternoon, trudging up the driveway in floppy clothing with a jumble of loose bags. On seeing Holly and me, the child, Sky, drops her little backpack, and, running up to us, draws each of us into a surprisingly powerful embrace.

"She's been so anxious to meet you," Sabrina says. "You have no idea what kind of trip we've had…"

After hugs and introductions, Holly and I get the wayward family settled into the pop-up camper. Tomorrow, we tell them, we'll see them up at our house at eight o'clock for an orientation.

January 6 - 9, 2013

Eight comes, then nine, then ten. Imagining their ordeal, Holly and I shrug it off and go about our chores. Besides, it's a Sunday, and the ragtag collection of other volunteers we have are either sleeping in, or are off at the beach. By noon, having heard or seen nothing of the new arrivals, I go down to the campground to check on them. Finding the camper empty, save for their things, I scratch my head and decide not to worry about it.

Mid-afternoon, the threesome comes wandering up the road. Again, Sky lunges forth and gives Holly and me mighty hugs. "Adorable," we say to Sabrina and Usef...but almost too adorable, I can hear Holly thinking. Having raised five kids, we're on full alert.

Sitting in the shade of our front yard, Holly and I go over the ground rules with them before giving them the tour. Sabrina's shock of close-cropped, purple hair is quite a statement, glowing as it is in the afternoon sun. Sabrina and Usef mention several times their gratitude at having found their 'new home.' They're enthusiastic, to be sure, but there's something jittery and unsettling in their behavior. Sky, meanwhile, sticks close to Holly and me with the fervor of an abandoned puppy. At one point, she climbs onto my lap and starts kissing my face profusely. Glancing at each other with the OMG look, Holly and I finish the tour and deposit the family at the community kitchen.

Walking back up the road, Hol and I laugh it off. "What have we done this time?" Holly asks—a standard line of ours these days.

Meanwhile, we have our hands full with other projects. This week will be a busy one, as we're leaving tomorrow for a trip we'd slated to Guanajuato, a city in the central highlands where we're trying to sell a rental house we'd built there previously. Down at the campground, there are a half-dozen other volunteers, who, along with three or four local workers, are making steady headway stamping out the compressed earth blocks that will be used to build the new guest house. It's grueling, laborious work. The crew breaks into teams each day—two guys mixing the clay-based soil, two loading the hopper and locking the heavy steel lid of the block press into place, and two more offloading the moist, thirty-pound blocks and carefully laying them out to be dried and stacked. I've been putting in a lot of time with this crew the past couple of weeks and, while nervous about leaving, I'm happy I'll be getting a break. The volunteers we have right now are excellent and can manage by themselves, and Yamir will manage the local crew. Holly and I let Usef know he'll be working with the guys making block and that Sabrina will be expected to help the women volunteers with the goats and other animals.

January 10, 2013

We're in Guanajuato, and it's eight-o-five in the morning.

D-r-ra-a-n-n-g, d-r-ra-a-n-n-g. My cell phone squawks and vibrates impatiently from the table.

"Hola? Daniel? It's me, Yamir."

"Hola, Yamir," I respond, feeling anxious as I always do when we're away and an unexpected call from the ranch comes in.

"Daniel, there's a problem."

"OK, Yamir. What's going on?"

"It's the new guy, Uesf. He's not cooperating."

"Well, what's he doing, exactly?"

"He's just playing in the garden or else sleeping all day. He even chopped down a couple of your new planted trees. He said they were in the wrong place. I told him he was supposed to be working with us, but he just laughed at me."

"OK, Yamir. Thanks for letting me know. Just let him alone. I'll be back in a couple of days."

Fifteen minutes later:

D-r-r-a-a-n-n-g. D-r-r-a-a-n-n-g.

"Yes, Yamir, what's happening now?"

"Daniel, the loco is digging up more of your new palm trees. He says these too are in the wrong place!"

"OK, Yamir. Please ask him to stop. Tell him he'll have to leave. No, forget that. Just ask him to stop and I'll take care of him when I get back."

January 10, 2013 (later the same day)

Ping, ping, ping goes the incoming email alert on my phone as I connect to wi-fi at a favorite Guanajuato cafe. It's been a couple of days since I've been online, so the emails are stacked up like planes coming into O'Hare after a winter storm. Halfway through the pile, I come across this one from Rancho Aqua Dulce, the place where Sabrina and Usef were staying in Belize before coming to us.

Dear Daniel Gair,

I apologize for taking so long to return your correspondence regarding Sabrina and Usef. I'm also sorry that I cannot recommend them for the position at your ranch. When they first started with us, nearly a year ago, my husband Mark and I thought they were slightly odd, but we gave them the benefit of the doubt and kept them on. We felt sorry for little Sky and wanted to help her have a good home. It appeared her life had been very unpredictable, and she was nervous and insecure as a result.

In the beginning, Sabrina was very helpful with the housework, and our own daughter Lucy was glad to have a playmate in Sky. Usef was a good worker at times but headstrong and somewhat difficult to manage. The problems began about six months into their being here, when we began to notice that things were missing. At first it was just small things—any type of cheap jewelry, a headlamp, things like that which could have easily been misplaced. After while, it became larger, more important items like cell phones and small power tools. Our other volunteers reported missing things as well. At first, we assumed it was one of the local workers but over time we became more and more suspicious that it might be Usef or Sabrina.

By six months after their arrival, other, even stranger things began happening. Sabrina would be gone for periods without explanation, sometimes even overnight. Knowing her to have a drinking problem, and that she and Usef hadn't been getting along very well, we assumed that she was going somewhere to party. We are known to have some witchcraft practitioners in our region, and rumors began circulating that Sabina was participating.

With all the uncertainty Sabrina and Usef carried with them, we would have cut them loose early on, but we had gotten attached to little Sky and wanted to give her some sort of stability.

About a month ago, my husband Mark set a trap for the thief in our midst and determined, beyond any doubt, that is was Usef. Sabrina's involvement with the local wiccans, or whatever they are, was by then an open secret. Despite being torn about Sky, we told them they would need to move on. The following week was high stress for us all. When I received your email, looking for references, I was stressed to the max and up to my ears in alligators. Then, one night, they vanished. Inspecting their room the next morning for clues, or, hopefully, any of our stolen things, we found, hidden behind the headboard, two super creepy amulets in the form of a man and woman, presumably Mark and I. We believe this because, mixed in with the straw, feathers, twine, and other materials, were locks of hair almost certainly each of ours.

I meant to write you sooner, but, frankly, I was so rattled by the episode that I was afraid of being involved with them one minute longer. Over the past couple of weeks, Mark and I have had continual discussions about it, and, finally decided that you really should be informed.

Again, my apologies for not writing sooner. Good luck if they do head your way.
Sincerely,
Jenny

P.S. Mark and I have looked at your website and love what you're doing. You're welcome to come visit and stay over with us if you ever make it down to Belize. Oh, and one last thought regarding Sabrina and Usef. Please don't let them know that you've been in touch with us.

"Oh, man," I say to Holly, passing her my cell phone. "Read this."

As Holly reads, her eyes get wider and wider. Then, just as she's finishing: D-r-r-a-a-n-n-g, d-r-r-a-a-n-n-g goes the phone in her hand. "Probably Yamir again," she says, handing it to me.

"Yes, Yamir, I know they're super strange. Please tell them to leave…"

"You can't make *him* do it!" Holly, at my side, whispers to me.

"OK, you're right," I reply to her and then say to Yamir; "No, wait, don't say anything. Just let them alone. Let them do what they want. Holly and I will be back on Sunday. We'll take care of the situation then."

January 13, 2013

Arriving at the ranch at dusk, we find it eerily empty of volunteers who'd normally all be lounging around the community kitchen area, cooking, playing cards, or hanging in hammocks. Instead, it's just Sabrina and Usef at the counter, cooking. Sky, who's under the table, bangs her head jumping up to greet us and is now crying pathetically and clinging to my leg.

"How was your trip?" Sabrina asks cheerfully, seemingly oblivious to Sky's distress.

"Ummm, OK," Holly answers.

"Listen, Sabrina, Usef…" I begin, forcing out the lines I've been rehearsing nonstop during the past two days of driving. "We like you guys a lot, but we've realized we're not really equipped here for hosting children." Sky, still attached to my leg and sniveling, has stopped now to listen in. I feel like crap but continue slogging forward into the swampy muck. "We realize you've had a hard go of it, and we'd be happy to compensate you with bus money to your next spot."

Usef stands mute, seeming not to understand, but I can see Sabrina's eyes narrowing and her whole body appears to be tightening into a crouch.

"You two will be sorry for this," she says in a low voice.

"I really think it will be best for Sky if you—"

"Stop!" Sabrina cuts me off. "You know what you've done. Ereshkigal and Persephone will punish you, that I can promise!" she hisses.

With that, Sabrina scoops up Sky, says, "Come on" harshly to the still-catatonic Usef, and heads toward their tent in a flourish of anger.

"Well, that went well, I think," Holly says to me.

✳ ✳ ✳ ✳ ✳ ✳ ✳

Over the years we've hosted hundreds of volunteers and have had several flirtations with people wanting to make the ranch their permanent home. Despite some of the goofier or more challenging ones like those I've mentioned, we've also had some marvelous experiences and continue to greet new arrivals with hopeful, cautious optimism, never knowing what impact, good or bad, each new participant may end up having on our lives.

One exceptional young man who volunteering with us for a while, Joán, arrived, like the Brits, under his own steam by bicycle. Joán had left his home in Switzerland two years earlier with the goal of bicycling to Istanbul. Upon reaching Istanbul, Joán wasn't yet satiated and continued on, following the ancient Silk Road trade route all the way to Beijing. Arriving in Beijing, Joán still had the itch and jumped a tramp steamer to Canada. From Canada he peddled south, eventually finding his way to the ranch. Rolling in the front gate, Joán took one look around and said in a thick, Swiss accent, "I think maybe I stay here for a while!" Eight months later, Joán and another of our volunteers with whom he'd fallen in love rode back out the gate and headed south toward Patagonia. Last time we heard from Joán, he was managing a youth hostel in Ireland and planning to come back to live at the ranch for a while, something we'd be thrilled about.

Overall, the volunteer hosting breaks down roughly into thirds, with a third who are excellent, a third mediocre, and a third who are, at best, complete slackers, or, at worst, manage to derail our train. Because Mayto is such a seasonal, transient place, even the best volunteers are usually ready to move on when the weather starts heating up during the summer months. A few wonderful ones have been back multiple times and consider the ranch their winter home. At its very best, our volunteers gel into a true although transient, joyous community. During a couple of winters, we've hit critical mass with pizza parties, campfires, talent shows, movie nights, skill swaps, and yoga while also accomplishing a huge amount of hard work and helping to move our infrastructure goals ahead. We're forever indebted to the volunteers, apprentices, and other participants who've given so much.

All said, the experience of hosting volunteers and trying to form some sort of ad hoc community has given Holly and me some of our highest highs and lowest lows. Occasionally, while walking on the beach at sunset or gazing out at the ranch and all its exciting projects from the top of the hill, we marvel at how far we've come from the board meetings, fundraisers, and cocktail parties of our former existence. Fortunately, during times of reverie like these, we manage to forget the tougher episodes, and we're blissfully unaware of how much more drama, and even heartbreak, still lies in wait for us...

16 - Faulty Foundations

With four thousand compressed earth blocks made, we were ready to begin construction of the new four-room guest house. Nacho was scheduled to come prep the site but, true to course, he ended up getting delayed by several weeks when the batteries of his backhoe got stolen. Because of the delay, I had to put the mason I'd hired to build the foundation on hold and find busywork for the new cadre of volunteers that had begun arriving to help with the project.

One amusing incident occurred during pre-construction prep work. Reviewing measurements at the site, I was happy to see the big, nine-cubic-meter dump truck of gravel I'd ordered come wheeling in through the gate. As it pulled up, I was shocked to see the massive rig appeared to be a driverless phantom. Then, with airbrakes screeching it to a stop in a cloud of dust, I realized there was a driver, just a tiny one, head barely visible over the dashboard.

Once stopped, the passenger side door popped open, and a small boy, not more than ten years old, climbed down. Striding up to me like he owned the world, he said, "Hola Mister. Where do you want it?" Looking up into the cab through the open door, I saw that the owner of the barely visible head was another boy, a year or two older at best, sitting forward on the edge of the seat, hands up on the big steering wheel, awaiting direction. After I showed the first boy where to put the load, he expertly started giving hand signals, directing his brother, the driver, to the exact right spot. And so another first gets added to the Mayto record books—world's youngest (and smallest) dump truck driver.

January 15, 2013

Finally, Nacho got his backhoe running and came to do the site work. This morning, Pedro, the same mason who'd built the beautiful stone pillars of our front gate, has his crew getting started on the stone foundation. Pedro is a mountain of a man who wears snakeskin cowboy boots and one of those oversized Mexican cowboy hats that look goofy and dwarf most men, but which looks epic on him.

Since Pedro did an excellent, timely job when he built our gate, and his price quote for this new project seemed quite reasonable, I didn't even bother getting other quotes. Pedro's great, and reassures me again this morning that there's no need to worry about the fact that we're behind schedule. He tells me he can make up the lost time and have the job done in a couple of weeks. This is good to hear, because I'll need every minute of the next three and half months to get this project done before heading back to the States in May, ahead of the rains. Being my first time heading up a construction project, I'm already nervous about the looming deadline.

January 29, 2013

Two weeks in, and Pedro's foundation work is lagging behind. The ten volunteers who've come here specifically to help in exchange for learning natural building are all chomping at the bit to get started, so I'm under a good deal of pressure to find work to keep them occupied while waiting for Pedro's crew to finish. Despite his ongoing assurances, it's taking forever, and there's no way he'll be done by the end of this week as promised. Exerting all the pressure I can while still being friendly and accommodating, as is the Mexican way, I do my best to hold him to both the timeline and price quote. Having done this dance before with the crew I hired to work on the community building, I'm actually getting pretty good at it—at least I think I am.

Behind schedule to get started on the next job he's contracted—and probably not making as much profit on this one as he'd hoped—Pedro is starting to cut corners with the work and is giving me pushback about the size and depth of the footings we'd specified while, at the same time, always smiling and telling me not to worry. He'll get the job done, and done correctly, he assures me day after day.

January 31, 2013

Hol and I are up early this morning for a supplies run to Vallarta. Because the foundation work has been going much too s-l-o-o-o-w-w-w-l-y, I'm worried about leaving Pedro and his crew alone for the day. I'm also stressed about leaving the half-dozen volunteers with nothing but busy-work projects for yet another day, but the sealer we need for the tops of the stem walls plus some masonry tools we still need—which I have to pick out personally—make today's trip necessary.

It's the usual marathon day, The Vallarta Shuffle, we call it, and we've had to criss-cross the city going to multiple building-supply stores to search out the specific foundation sealer that I'm looking for.

By the time we finish and make the trek up into the mountains to Tuito and back down the torturous, half-lumpy gravel, half-paved snake of a road to the coast, it's after sunset. Pulling into the ranch, we stop and climb out of the car. While Holly is chatting up one of volunteers (the rest are off at the beach somewhere), I go over and check to see what Pedro has accomplished. Incredibly, he's finished! What I expected to be several days' work he's managed to bang out in one day. I'm thrilled to see it. They've even managed to backfill in all the way around the walls, something I hadn't even counted on them doing. It's just too good to be true!

Then it hits me like a rock. Maybe it *is* too good to be true!

Borrowing a headlamp from one of the volunteers, I grab a pick and shovel and start digging away at the backfill. Soon I find what my instincts had been telling me. To my horror, I see that, instead of standing proud atop a solid foundation footing as it should be, the beautiful stone stem wall has instead been laid on nothing but dirt. As I dig away at the fill, frantic now and getting angry, I find that the entire back wall—completed, miraculously, in one day—is nothing but a facade!

Furious and dripping with sweat, I'm swearing and tearing at the earth —a killer cyborg gone haywire. Lungs heaving as I try to catch a breath, I step back to survey the situation by the light of the headlamp. While one part of my internal dialog is trying to be the reasonable, telling me to calm down, saying that it's not that bad and can be fixed, the other side of my brain, the angry one, is yelling at the top of it's mental lungs: 'No fucking way, you moron! You've been hosed, big time! There's absolutely no way you can leave this or even fix it! It wouldn't be safe. There's no goddamn structure to it at all! You've got to do something! You've got to make that douchebag Pedro make this right!'

'I know, I know, calm down,' says my good-guy self. 'We'll work this out. Maybe we can just have Pedro fill in more rock underneath?'

'Fill in underneath? Are you fucking kidding me, man? There's no way in hell we're gonna let Pedro off the hook like that. Besides, it wouldn't work! We can't build a wall onto this piece-of-shit joke of a foundation! He's got to redo the whole goddamn thing.'

'Well, what should we do then? Tear it all down?' one of my selves asks the other

'Yes, of course, you idiot. It'll have to come down!'

'When? Tomorrow? Won't the cement mortar be too hard by tomor-row?'

'Shit, that's right. There's no way it can wait till then! Motherfucking shit pie! I guess I'm going to have to do it myself! ARG-G-G-G!'

With that, I'm back at it with a sledge hammer, bashing away at the forty-foot-long wall, a powerful wrecking machine fueled by anger. In addition to tearing the entire wall apart, I have to hose everything down to keep the cement from drying and ruining the rocks. I'm at it for hours.

Later, up at the house, I place a call to Pedro. Having expended my anger on the wall, I'm calm enough now to talk to him civilly and am resolved to follow the first rule of disagreement in Mexico—don't show anger in an argument because to do so means you automatically lose. At first, he's belligerent and actually pretending he doesn't understand. Then, shifting gears, he tries to sell me on the idea that the design we had was overbuilt—that all that foundation footing wasn't really necessary. Finally, realizing I'm going to stand much firmer than the wall he built, he assures me he'll make good and will be back first thing in the morning.

January 29, 2013

At eight a.m., Pedro shows up with his crew as agreed. By noon, they've cleaned up and begun clearing away most of the rocks and backfill and are nearly ready to start over again. Piling into their pickup truck to head to town for lunch, they're all smiling and happy. My anger behind me, I'm relieved to have managed to pull this one from the fire and to be getting back on track so quickly. In my relief, I fail to see that Pedro and crew have taken all of their tools with them to lunch. It takes most of the afternoon for me to fully realize they won't be coming back.

✳ ✳ ✳ ✳ ✳ ✳ ✳

Following this disaster, I manage to cajole Fernando's brother, Rotillio, into taking on the mess Pedro had left behind and finish up the foundation project.

The new batch of volunteers we have, plus a couple of excellent long termers, Joán and Mateo, give the project a good head of steam and, by late Spring, we've made up most of the time lost to the initial delays. If all goes well, I'm hoping to have the walls up by Semana Santa and then make a final push to get the roof in place well ahead of the summer rains.

About a year after the incident with Pedro, I run into him at a festival in El Tuito. All smiles as usual, Pedro greets me warmly without the faintest hint of embarrassment or hard feelings. I, too, am friendly and greet him as any old acquaintance would.

17 - The Guy Who Stabbed the Chicken Delivery Guy

March 28, 2013

I feel surprisingly calm, considering…

Yamir's three brothers are all here, ready to swing into action and come to my defense. As agreed to in an emergency planning session a few hours earlier in the day, the brothers arrived promptly at 3:00 pm and are now ready and poised for action, armed with machetes and the big-ass can of bear repellent I'd previously brought down from the States for just such a situation.

They're all acting casual and have taken up positions around the guest house under construction—all within fifty feet or so of where I stand. Holly has insisted on doing her part, too, and has positioned herself over by the quad bike, pretending to talk to Jorge and Christian, senses alert, adrenalin pumping, palming her own can of pepper spray. Even Yamir is ready to swing into action and help me confront the hombre who stabbed the chicken delivery guy, despite the fact that he (Yamir) is still recuperating from having been dragged 100 yards by a horse last weekend.

This whole absurd situation started several weeks ago. With Semana Santa (Easter week) fast approaching and most of the dozen or so volunteers I'd had working on the guest house throughout the winter gone, I've been increasingly short-handed and desperate to get the last of the walls up. With flights booked for May 10th, my drop-dead deadline is looming for having the walls finished and roof on before we leave for the summer and the rains begin. It's become the norm that long after the local crew has put in their ten hours and left for the day and the volunteers are all down at the beach, drinking beers and cavorting in the surf, I'm still at the worksite, checking levels, redoing sloppy work, and cleaning tools. Further behind schedule every day and fueled by worry, I've gradually morphed into an unstoppable, industrial-strength machine made of steel and raw energy, brought to heel only by darkness each evening.

Everything else done, I wet down the compressed earth block walls that are rising steadily, then, climbing up and down off scaffolding and ladders in the failing light, I tuck everything in for the night, covering the walls with tarps to keep the clay mortar from drying too fast in the hot, dry, Mexican wind.

When Angel showed up at the site a week ago looking for work, he seemed nice enough. At five-foot-nine with a smallish frame and boyish looks, he didn't impress me as a strong candidate for hefting thirty-pound earth blocks all day, but I was desperate enough to sign him on. I'd never seen him around town and wasn't expecting great things from him, work-wise, but I needed any extra help I could get. This past week, however, Angel has proved to be a terrific worker—so much so that, this past Friday, after wrapping up and paying the rest of the workers before they took off for the weekend, I was open to considering it when he politely asked if he and his wife could possibly set up camp and live, temporarily, in our campground.

"Where are you from, and where are you staying now?" I asked, hesitantly.

"Marie and I came up from Tenacatita" he replied. "We had a place there by the beach, but everyone got kicked out, and we heard there was work up here."

Like everyone, I'd heard the story about the land grab going on in Tenacatita, a previously chill little beach town about two hours south. Apparently, a rich developer had showed up several months ago, claiming to own the entire bay, and had pulled enough strings to have the whole town evicted. According to the rumors circulating on both the street and the Internet, there was nothing left in Tenacatita now but a miles-long chain-link fence and round-the-clock guards keeping everyone out. Even the small enclave of gringos—who, for years, had been allowed to camp in their RVs at the far northern end of the beach—had unceremoniously been forced to evacuate.

"Mi esposa tiene trabajo en el Hotel Las Brisas, y han estado permitiendonos a camper allí (my wife's working over at Las Brisas Hotel, and they've been letting us camp over there), but they've got a group coming in for Semana Santa and told us we had to leave by this weekend."

All in all, Angel's story seemed solid, so I agreed to let him and his wife move in. I even climbed up to the loft of the community building, dug out a huge old tent we had stored there, and showed him a spot where he could set up camp. Thanking me about eight times, Angel headed out through the gate toward Las Brisas to collect his wife and their belongings. Within an hour, they were back, carrying two large trash bags each and efficiently setting about making camp under a huge, old guamuchile tree.

Now, a week later, everything is different. Angel's work had gone well enough for the previous few days. Increasingly short-handed and behind schedule with the building project, Angel pulled far more weight than I'd been expecting from him. Working tirelessly, he mixed mortar, schlepped block, and cheerfully did whatever was asked. He was consistently pleasant and, on several days, he insisted on staying late to work a few hours after the others had left to help finish up—cleaning tools, covering the day's work with tarps, and helping me wrap up other random chores.

One of the reasons I've been so short-handed is because of pinche Yamir's incident with the horse ("pinche" translates roughly into "fucking" but is used here as a macho guy-style term of endearment). Having lost quite a bit of skin from his hindquarters (Yamir, not the horse), Yamir has been away this entire past week recovering in bed at his mother's house. The story I got from his brothers Jorge, Christian, and Toni was that he'd been over at Rancho Los Conejos helping his buddy Niko get hold of a young, half-wild mare. The two of them had ropes on the yegua, but she reared and bolted, pulling both Niko and Yamir off their feet. In the scramble, Yamir had gotten his foot caught in the rope and was dragged across the road and into the cactus thicket. I'd gone to see Yamir on Monday and had to laugh. Watching TV and sipping Coke, there he was, kneeling on pillows on the floor, the rest of his body sprawled out on his belly on the low bed.

"Oye, amigo, parece como una puta esperando un visitante por la puerta atras (hey, amigo, you look like a hooker waiting for a visitor to show up at your back door)," I ribbed him.

"Sí, Daniel. Porque tardarse tanto? (I know, Daniel. What took you so long?)" he fired back.

Ah, Yamir…

Given all of this, I thought it was strange—and I knew something was up—this morning when Yamir came flying through the gate, full throttle, on his moto and pulled up to the work site in a cloud of dust. At first, I was laughing when he gingerly climbed off the moto, and I realized why he'd come driving in standing up. My smile faded, however, when I saw his urgent seriousness.

"Daniel, I need to talk to you… right away," he all but pleaded in a hushed voice while pulling me off to the side, away from the others.

"That new muchacho you have working…he stabbed the chicken delivery guy in El Tuito and the police are looking for him!"

"Holy crap, Yamir, are you serious?" I asked. Mind racing, I realized it had been a while since we'd seen the young delivery man who usually showed up twice a week on his motorcycle with a cooler full of still-hot, roasted chicken strapped to the back.

"Yeah, and yesterday they fired his wife who was working over at Las Brisas," Yamir continued. "She was stealing! They also say she's the reason the chicken delivery guy got stabbed in the first place. They say she was flirting with the delivery guy, and her muchacho got mad and started a fight with him."

Like the final piece of a jigsaw puzzle, this tidbit of information about her getting fired snaps into place. Yesterday, Angel's wife had shown up at the worksite looking upset and spoke to Angel in whispers off to the side. She's been holed up in their tent since.

"Crap, Yamir, I can't believe it. He's been terrific. One of the best workers I've ever had. I've told him he could stay and work right through Semana Santa if he wanted. What the hell am I gonna do now?"

"You've got to get him out of here right away" Yamir insists. "Why don't you just call the police?"

"Hmmm. I dunno about that," I reply. "What happens if he gets out and comes back looking for revenge?"

Yamir is all keyed up and entering his take-charge mode. "I know, Daniel, I'll get my brothers to come at the end of work today. You tell the muchacho you've changed your mind about him working next week. Tell him you've got guests coming and the place is gonna be full. Tell him anything, man, but you've got to get him outta here!"

"OK, OK, calm down, amigo. Look at you. You can't even sit down, but you're ready to fight? I don't think so. You'd better stay out of it. But yes, yes, definitely, get your brothers to come."

"No way, Daniel. I'm gonna be here too. This is really serious. You need us all covering your back!"

"OK, OK, then. Try to stay calm. Come back with your brothers exactly at 3:00. We'll be ending the work day. I'll tell him then."

For the rest of the day, I'm a mess. Minutes crawl by with brutal slowness. Holly, too, is freaking out but as committed as ever to being part of the showdown.

Now it's 3:15—shootout time at The OK Corral. The other workers have been paid and are gone. As usual, Angel lags behind. One hand in my jeans pocket, palming pepper spray, I've gone from being on the verge of having a panic attack most of the day to suddenly feeling a nearly euphoric sense of calm and resolve. I'm a daring sea Commander now, steering my boat straight into the oncoming storm.

With everyone poised and in position, I call Angel over. "Listen amigo, there's been a change of plans. I've decided to give everyone Semana Santa off. We're not going to be working next week. Thanks so much, amigo. You've been a huge help."

Dark clouds of concern spreads across Angel's face. "I don't mind working, sir. Really. Semana Santa means nothing to me."

"Thank you, Angel. You've been fantastic. Really. One of my best workers ever. I'm giving you a bonus." I start counting out bills and give him double what he's expecting for the week.

"What about after? Will I still have work after Semana Santa?"

"Well, actually, I'm all set after that. I'm sorry, but there's no more work."

The storm clouds in his eyes grow even darker.

"But can my wife and I stay here?" he asks, the tone of his voice hard to read.

Out of the corner of my eye, I see Jorge and Christian. They're moving in closer but still about thirty feet out. Over to the left, their younger brother, Toni, is looking like an actor in a really bad high school play. Machete in hand, conspicuously trying to be inconspicuous, he's pretending to trim around a perfectly trimmed palm tree.

"No, friend, I'm sorry, but that won't be possible. I've got some unexpected guests coming in this weekend. There's a bunch of them, and it's gonna be crowded. But really, you've been so great to have here." I'm fumbling the words now, losing my cool a bit. Starting to sweat.

"Well, sir, when do we need to leave? Can we at least spend the night and leave in the morning?"

Man, this is getting tougher by the second. "No, I'm really sorry. The guests are supposed to be showing up tonight. You're gonna have to pack up and leave right away."

Now we stand just looking at each other. What is it I'm seeing there in that knowing yet innocent-looking face of his? Sadness? Confusion? Anger? Is he ready to cry or explode and attack?

Hands coming out of pockets, he makes his move toward me.

Momentarily I flinch, gripping the pepper spray and pulling it swiftly from my pocket.

But then, wait, what's happening? The vibe is all wrong! I'm confused. What's he doing? Wait, this isn't it. He's not attacking. He's, he's, he's reaching to give me what? A hug? Holy crap, he's hugging me!

Hugging back, eyes popping wide, I look over Angel's shoulder at Yamir, Jorge, Christian, Holly, and Toni, all of whom look as startled as I am, caught in their half stride rush to move in and protect me.

"What the fuck" Yamir seems to be mouthing, arms up in quizzical shrug behind Angel's back.

"Thank you, sir, for all that you've done," Angel says softly, releasing me from his arms.

Stepping back from the hug, he gives me one last unfathomable look before slowly turning and walking away.

Yamir and the others stay on after, hanging out—just in case—talking and stress-relief laughing in low tones as Angel and his wife, over at their tent, pack up their meager belongings. As the two of them finally swing trash bags over their shoulders and head out through the gate, Angel turns and looks in my direction, one last time, and then waves goodbye.

A sudden rush of remorse flops over me like a soggy blanket. "Did he really stab the chicken guy," I wonder, "or has there been some awful mistake?" The chisme (gossip) here runs thicker than road tar, and it's often impossible to keep it from getting one's feet stuck in it. Is that what just happened here? Are Angel and his girl just some sort of sad, collateral chisme wreckage that I've unwittingly helped to perpetrate?

Down at the hotel, amplified music signaling the start of the holidays has started—the Semana Santa celebrations are about to begin. Unfortunately, there probably won't be any of that great roasted chicken from El Tuito this year.

18 - A Very Toxic Water Meeting

After a good summer break visiting friends and family in the U.S., Holly and I returned to the ranch with our batteries recharged. I was particularly anxious to put the finishing touches on the guest house and to start the new season off on a better footing. We also had plans to host a cob-building workshop in February ('cob' being a clay mix similar to adobe but more free-form) and met with Patrick Hennebery, an instructor famous in the natural building world. We'd sold Pat on the idea of coming to the ranch in January to conduct a building workshop that would double as the building of our new 'hippie-lux' dream house on the view hill.

We'd been back at the ranch about a month and things were rolling smoothly for a change.

December 10, 2013

Today, a young boy from town rolls into the ranch on a shiny new, yellow quad bike, pulls a slip of paper from a bundle, and hands it to me. The paper reads:

Noticias: Reunion del Commission de Aqua Potable, Jueves, a las 4:00 horas. Oficina Delagacion, Mayto (Notice: Meeting of the Water Commission, Thursday at 4 pm at the Delegation Office, Mayto).

Oh boy, what's up now? I think to myself. Often in the past, a meeting of the local water commission meant a rise in our water bill.

When Thursday finally rolls around, I finish my day early, shower, change, and head into town on the moto for the meeting. Arriving a half hour early, I settle in with a few other guys at Gerardo's store for a beer and watch a bit of soccer on the T.V. out front.

A short while later, a couple of big white government trucks pull up. They're from the Agricultural Service, and they're loaded with industrial spray-pump equipment and signs announcing the latest mosquito eradication program. My first thought is *Ugh, just what Mexico needs, more chemicals,* but then I also remember the stories of last year's Dengue epidemic and the many accounts of pain and suffering from Chikungunya, the latest mosquito-borne disease making its way into our region. It's not the first time I've had to weigh the ethical pros and cons of the use of toxic chemicals here, and I've decided that, in moderation, chemicals are often the lesser evil.

Sliding down off the porch of the tienda and walking over, I strike up a conversation with the man in charge through the open window of his truck. After I listen to his argument for spraying, I decide that it's the right thing to do and ask him if he can do our place while he's here in Mayto.

"Sure," he tells me, "we can head over to your ranch right now if you want."

Looking down the street, I see that no one's arrived at the water meeting yet, so I head off to the ranch with the chem truck following behind. The big guy in charge and his even larger, gelatinous assistant explain the two options—spot spray or the bigger, general fogger. I opt for spot spraying close by the guest house and a general fogging out around the bushier perimeter. I'm careful to direct them downwind as well as down watershed of the gardens or any fruit-tree plantings. This limits the amount of spraying they can do, but I figure it's the right compromise between the two options—toxic chemicals in select areas or increased potential for us or our participants getting a debilitating disease.

By the time they've finished, it's past the start time for the water meeting. I can feel my blood pressure ticking up a notch, both because of the spraying I've allowed and my gringo aversion to being late for anything. Hopping on the moto, I scoot back into town. Pulling up to the delegation office half an hour after the start time, it's obvious that, if anything, I'm actually still early. The two dozen or so plastic chairs set up in a semi-circle outside the delegation office next to the main road through town are only half occupied, and those in attendance are still in arrival mode, hanging out and shooting the breeze as if the meeting itself may not even happen.

I pull up alongside Jose Juan and start discussing the effect of recent rains on the current tomato crop. Even though I've had ten years of practice, making small talk here is still a struggle for me. Despite my relative fluency and the thrill I get from feeling assimilated, the local country speak—that rapid-fire, spicy, fajita mix of chopped-up slang and double entendres—is still difficult for me to keep up with. This, layered on top of my natural dislike of superficial chit-chat plus my desire to fit in and not seem stupid or make a fool of myself, has me squirming to stay present and appreciate the experience.

Fifteen minutes later, the meeting is finally called to order. Without Robert's Rules to guide the process, everything about the meeting is an ad hoc circus. It starts out mundane enough, with a long, drawn-out accounting of who owes what on past bills. Noé, this year's Commission Chairman, unrolls a three-foot-by-five-foot, hand-drawn chart, done with markers on poster board, showing all the town residents, the months they've paid, and other information such as any new construction projects started. Israel, the Water Commission Treasurer, taps away at a calculator as names are called off, and Blanca, the Commission's Secretary (and past Delegation President), digs through a large plastic bag of ledger books and envelopes looking up names, counting money, and filing everything away in a system as mysterious to me as a tomb of hieroglyphic tablets.

The meeting plods along like this for an hour, with only occasional emotion as one or another resident takes issue with the amount they owe or their record of payment. The tenor of the meeting starts building, however, as the extent of this year's shortfall becomes more and more obvious. As the accounting drudgery wraps up, the weightier issue of the budget shortfall rises fully to the surface, emotions rising with it.

No sooner does the meeting start getting serious, however, than a bread-delivery truck blaring vintage Mexican ranchero music through a tinny rooftop speaker drives slowly by. When it's almost past the group, which has now swelled to more than twenty people, one of the attendees interrupts the meeting.

"Hey, it's the bread truck!" he blurts out, as if no one else had noticed the din of its passing.

"Yeah, let's get some bread!" someone else shouts.

Chairman Noé gives a loud whistle to the truck, which stops and backs up to where the meeting is taking place.

"My treat," Noé says, standing up and pulling out his wallet. People nod, impressed.

At this point, the meeting devolves into a buzz of local gossip until, a few minutes later, Noé returns from the curbside truck with a large, clear plastic bag filled with multi-colored sweet breads and pastries in hand. Now, one of the attendees, José Juan, catches the wave of altruism, stands up, announces, "Ya, me voy para refrescos!" and heads across the street to his tienda to get soft drinks. A minute later and he's back carrying several giant bottles of Coke and Squirt along with plastic cups. Several kids who've been hanging around the meeting are now enlisted to serve, and a delicious sugar party is in full swing.

The meeting, which started with only a handful of attendees, has grown to more than thirty people now. Additional plastic chairs are pulled out to accommodate the crowd while others sit on their motos or scooters or straddle the bicycles they've arrived on. After fifteen minutes of pastries, Coke, and lively chit-chat, the meeting returns to a semblance of order. The issue of Cruz's new cows, and all the water they're drinking, has come up and, with it, the sugar-buzzed meeting is starting to gain some momentum. As the issue of Cruz's cow's drinking problem builds, someone in the crowd blurts out, "What about Fernando? He's been constructing a new room for more than a year now. Just think how much water that must be using!"

"And what about the Hotel the Lamas are building? They're using a crapload of water too!" someone else shouts out.

Bolstering my fledgling bilingual courage, I break into the row to bring up the obvious need for water meters, something I've been trying to generate interest in for a while now. "Without them," I implore, "there will always be finger pointing and accusations of some using more than their share. The whole rest of the world uses meters," I tell the group. "They're not very expensive, and we could begin with just the business owners to get it started. There may even be government money available to support it!"

I sit back down, hoping the idea will get traction.

Kids dodge and weave, mothers coddle babies, and, to my surprise, a spirited debate seems to be starting.

"I think Daniel has a good point," Efren jumps in. "With meters we'd only pay for what we actually use!"

"It's true. If Choriz has rented Toño's parcela to graze his herd, a meter would tell us exactly how much he's using," another pitches in. "We could charge for it, and it would be up to Choriz and Toño to sort out which of them pays. Either way, the extra water the cows drink gets paid for."

The crowd nods collectively in approval. I'm psyched. The idea of meters is really happening!

Then someone stands up and asks what's happening with Hotel Mayto's new water line. "Have they closed off their tap from town yet? (The hotel has its own well now and no longer needs the town water connection.) Have they paid the past six months' bill they owe?"

"I bet they haven't even disconnected yet," someone else joins in.

"Yeah, and they should have been paying more all these years," pipes in yet another.

And, with that, the topic veers off course, and the idea of water meters is already a distant memory.

Feeling deflated, I'm thinking about leaving this Mad Hatter's tea party when I hear a deep audible hum I hadn't noticed before. Looking over, I realize the mosquito spray truck that had followed me to the ranch earlier is now is making its way through the middle of town, coming toward us. Rounding the corner, the ghastly, fuming beast comes into sight. As the hum gets louder and the truck advances, a plume of toxic, oily smoke spews out behind it. The plume, ever expanding, is now a thick fog of mosquito death enveloping the whole town. A woman holding the hand of child runs out of the surreal, grey blanket as two boys of about ten race their bikes through it, laughing.

Nearly upon us, the growl of the fogger is a deafening, high-pitched, mechanical howl.

I'm shifting from self-pity over my first, impotent foray into town politics to a pulse-pounding, fight-or-flight response at the sight of the truck approaching. Holding my ground (well, my chair, actually), I wait to see what everyone else is going to do. With the discussion of the Hotel Mayto water scandal halted because of the noise, the crowd has turned its collective heads to watch the monster and its ominous grey plumage move slowly toward them—or, should I say, toward us. To my horror, everyone, including me, just sits and watches as the seething beast gets closer.

At this point, my mind catapults in a new direction. 'Do I just sit here and take it like… like… like a Mexican?' I ask myself. 'Or should I hold my breath and run for cover, thus alienating myself from the group I'm trying so hard to be a part of?'

The smoke is upon us. It's a taste as much as a smell—a smell-taste at the back of the throat like a precursor to death. Rotting okra. Putrid flesh.

Now my monkey-mind is switching gears again. The theme of my new internal discourse is, which is better, taking one, long, deep breath and holding it, or taking multiple, quick, shallow breaths? I realize that either way, whichever decision I make, I'll end up gasping in one big rush at some point when brain signals to lungs that I'm going to pass out if I don't get a significant infusion of whatever it is—air, poison, ooblek, whatever—NOW!

S-s-z-z-s-i-a-h-h-h-h-h. That's it. I'm sucking in a huge lungful of pure toxin! What will my radioactive, mosquito-repellent death be like, I wonder? A splatter of burst arteries resembling a Jackson Pollack painting? A slow, rasping, sucking, horror-movie gurgle?

Before I know it, the truck and its cloud are past. The people around me are all laughing, waving their hands, and making faces as if to say, "Phew. Boy. Am I'm ever glad that's done. I really, really hate that smell!"

Near dark and, after having resulted in no discernible decisions, the meeting breaks up and we all go home.

★ ★ ★ ★ ★ ★ ★

During the winter of 2014, the Cob Workshop we hosted—with twenty-five students over a period of six weeks—went really well, and the main structure of our house, two, twenty-foot-diameter pods; bedroom; and kitchen separated by an open-air palapa living room, is shaping up nicely.

Looking back now, half a year later, the town mosquito gassing hasn't resulted in any noticeable ill effects to anyone, and it's been one of the calmest mosquito-related disease seasons anyone can remember.

Getting ready to leave for our summer, we're exhausted and excited to be catching a break but also anxious to get back in the fall and continue moving our house project forward.

19 - The Perfect Shit Storm, Part 1
(Stormy Weather Ahead)

*There are, of course, good days and bad days. Good weeks and bad weeks.
Even good years and bad years. The winter of 2014/2015 was one of the
latter—a very bad year. It was the year of "Shit Storm Lillian," as we still
lovingly refer to it.*

*A friend of ours, who started and runs a successful eco-village in
British Columbia, once told us, "Communities like ours are a beautiful
thing—that is, until someone sneaks up behind you and whacks you over
the head with a two-by-four!"*

*We've definitely had our share of lesser head whacks over the years,
but the worst one, Shit Storm Lillian, really packed a wallop and sent us
reeling.*

July 26, 2014

Checking over the endless to-do lists ahead of my departure to the States
for the summer, everything seems to be under control. The roof is finally
on the new guest house, and we're at a good stopping point ahead of the
rainy season. We did have a minor head-whack this past month when the
caretaker we'd hired, a smooth-talking Mexican chavo (young man) by the
name of Chuy, who, despite having checked his references, turned out to
be a druggie and general ladron.

Holly has left for the States ahead of me, and I've now brought a new
caretaker named Ernesto on board. Having spent the past couple of weeks
with him, I find him to be a smart, articulate, charismatic young man
committed to sustainability, permaculture, and education. In short, Ernesto
and I hit it off entirely.

Over a dinner of grilled fish that Ernesto and I cook together, he tells
me how he and his American wife, Jenna, had started an environmental
education program in Panama that they ran for a year before it faltered due
to lack of infrastructure, funding, and differences with the property owner.
Ernesto explains that he's taking a break from his wife and four-year-old
son, as the entire episode in Panama left them penniless and took a toll on
their relationship.

Listening to Ernesto describe the education program they started, I see
the great potential it could have if rebooted in a place like ours. Clearly, it
would be a terrific complement to our growing mission of sustainability
and education!

After conferring with Holly by phone, I propose to Ernesto that he
consider giving the program another go, here, with us. Ernesto, aka Ernie,
is enthusiastic about the idea. We agree to take it slow using the upcoming

three-month caretaker stint as a test of Ernie's affinity for the ranch while simultaneously beginning plans to launch the program upon our return in the fall.

* * * * * * *

During our time in the States, we exchanged numerous emails with Ernie to continue the discussion about launching the program—a mix of permaculture and basic homestead skills such as gardening, natural building, animal care, etc. We dubbed the program EEP (Experiential Education Program), and we were all getting excited about the coming autumn.

About midway through our time away, another friend of the ranch, Lillian, showed up looking to deepen her involvement. A spitfire, dynamic Australian who'd volunteered at the ranch for short stints in the past, Lillian was currently living in Vallarta but wanted to get out into the country. By email and Skype, we discussed the possibility of Lillian moving to the ranch. She and Ernie seemed to get along well, and together they began making plans for sharing the guest house and other ranch resources as she pursued her idea of bringing yoga or other retreats to the ranch and Ernie pursued his desire to recreate his education program. It seemed like a great fit and, after weeks of negotiating a business plan that included both initiatives, we were all excited to start.

The four of us—Ernie, Lillian, Holly and I—hashed out contracts via email to cover the various aspects of having them join the ranch as indefinite, possibly permanent participants. The core agreements we put into place had two parts. Ernie and Lillian could use the facilities to pursue income in exchange for a 'give-back' to the ranch of fifty percent of gross revenues, and the two of them would be able to make their homes at the ranch, rent-free, in exchange for caretaking coverage when we were to be away—particularly for the three-month stretch when we planned to return to the States each summer. While happy about the income to help offset our expenses, Holly and I were most excited about the coverage piece, as our growing infrastructure and animals were making it harder for us to be away.

It seemed that, in Ernie and Lillian, we'd found the ideal participants to join our fledgling community. We were thrilled to have the ranch coming to life, to be moving toward economic viability, and to have the prospect of built-in coverage to help alleviate the feeling of being burdened or trapped by all the growing responsibility of the place.

Throughout the negotiations, Ernie and Lillian showed themselves to be natural salespeople. Lillian, in particular, was nothing short of a force of nature. In the past, we'd had discussions with numerous participants expressing a desire to stay long-term and create some sort of business, but, in the end, they all lacked the entrepreneurial drive needed to manifest their vision. Now we had two self-starters itching to launch their initiatives, and we were thrilled.

Lillian, in particular, was a dynamo. As we prepared to return from the States in mid-October, she was bombarding us with daily email messages and requests for Skype calls to begin moving things ahead. Holly and I were pleased to see so much enthusiasm, but also began asking her to slow things down until our return in a few weeks' time. In crunch mode State-side, we had our hands full wrapping up several projects.

In retrospect, we should have seen the warning signs then. Rather than easing back on the throttle, Lillian kept amping up and needed constant attention.

September 27, 2014

"We need more time to think this over," we'd written her in response to her latest proposal for building a yoga platform. "Packing now. We'll get back to you later in the week once we get on the road."

Lillian's response was immediate: "I hate to keep bugging you two. I know you're in crunch mode with leaving, but I have to let Juan (her boyfriend) know about ordering wood for the new yoga platform. What's the biggest you'd be comfortable having it be? Do you mind if I bring the backhoe in to level the hill over toward the dipping pool for it?"

"Sorry," we'd answer back, "we really are under the gun right now. Please give us a few days to think over this platform idea."

"I know, I'm sorry, too," she'd reply, "but this is the last request I'll make for now. Can you possibly give me an idea of the size I can build, please? And is it OK to hire the backhoe to prep for it?"

✳ ✳ ✳ ✳ ✳ ✳ ✳

And so it would go, back and forth. She just didn't get it and wouldn't slow down. We were starting to feel as though we had a wildcat by the tail, but we were also excited by her enthusiasm and the potential that her energy represented, so we did our best to find the balance of letting her run with some parts while trying to hold her off on the bigger decisions.

When we arrived at the ranch in mid-October and we resumed work on our house, the pressure from Lillian went into hyperdrive. We felt we had a potential storm brewing but didn't know quite what to do about it—her manic, pedal-to-the-metal process was proving to be a bit too much, even for us.

Everything Lillian-related was taking on more complication and urgency. When she told us that an aunt of hers was planning on holding a healing retreat at the ranch mid-winter, a new round of initiatives rose up out of nowhere like a surging flash mob.

Meanwhile, another completely separate and dark reality was lurking...

20 - Fear Factor, Part 2
(Disturbing News)

October 21, 2014

Very disturbing news from El Tuito today. A past president of the municipality, owner of a prominent business in El Tuito and someone we were loosely acquainted with, was gunned down last night. His reputation was of being a straight-up kind of guy and well-liked, so we're shocked and saddened by the news. Once again, I feel a familiar jolt to my confidence, calling into question the safety and, ultimately, the viability of what we're doing here.

The first round of scuttlebutt has it that this person ran afoul of the of the main narco for this "plaza" (area of control for any specific narco group). Later in the day, we run into a friend who tells us he was at an event over the weekend attended by some guys associated with the narco. He tells us the guys were good and drunk, and he overheard them saying the now-murdered guy would "have to go." He also tells us that the narco is a complete crazy who has numerous safe houses here in Cabo Corrientes. He says he's chosen to be here because of its network of back roads that makes it an easy place to hide in and escape from. Finally, our friend assures us that we have nothing to worry about. He says another important regional player keeps the narco in check, and that it's all just "Part of the show."

Thanking the friend for the news, we watch him drive away and are left scratching our heads. Should we be worried about an eruption of violence, or is this one of the semi-dormant volcanos of narco squabbling that erupts with some steam and ash every other year or so, then settles back down?

✶ ✶ ✶ ✶ ✶ ✶ ✶

This is terribly disturbing at first, but, as usual, after a week or two, things have calmed and we barely even think about it. Considering it now, I remember how each of the other incidents of violence that tarnished our paradise over the years (ice truck holdup, the attempted kidnapping of Victor at the crossroads, the narco Day of Insurrection, and the neighbor's random, drunken, nighttime gunshots) all felt terrifying at first, but that the initial rush of fear soon faded.

Reality is that the violence we hear about nearly always involves people actively involved in the drug trade or the upper tiers of political activity. Comparing this to the continuous news reports we receive from the States, where random acts of violence such as school, mall, church, club, and event shootings are becoming practically a daily occurrence. For per-spective, I remind myself that there have been over two thousand shootings resulting in over four hundred murders in Chicago so far this year alone. We simply don't hear about that kind of random violence in Mexico. Lay-ered on this is the sense that people here don't seem nearly as stressed, in general, as Estadounidences (people from the U.S.). The happy, relaxed vibe has its way of mitigating one's fears.

The truth is, the longer we're here, the more this sort of violence seems irrelevant to us. Part of this is knowing more and more people that have only one or two degrees of separation from the head narcos in our region. Knowing these people, and seeing how otherwise normal their lives are gives us perspective. Also knowing the degree to which we receive infor-mation about narco activity in the area gives us confidence that we're not going to get blindsided by some completely unexpected change in the overall dynamic.

The irony is that, over time, incidents like this have tended to diminish rather than exacerbate our sense of fear about living and being so heavily invested here. We try but still we find it nearly impossible to sort out an objective reality regarding Mexico's stability or safety. We'd like to. It's probably the most asked question by people looking to visit or move to Mexico and the subject that garners the most speculation from news rooms to chat rooms to Holly's and my bedroom. Just how safe is it here?

Occasionally, an article surfaces describing Mexico as a failed state. Having traveled thousands of miles across Mexico's highways and byways the past dozen years, it's hard to square that idea with what we've ob-served. Everywhere we look, Mexico is booming with public works in-frastructure projects and private initiatives. Conspicuous consumption, in-country tourism, and wealth spilling out of metropolises like Mexico City, Querétero, Monterrey, Guadalajara, and Cuernavaca is also on the rise. To the casual observer, BMW's and construction cranes represent Mexico's new economic reality.

Just one last bit of inside perspective about everyone's favorite topic— the narcos. We've learned there isn't the clean division between the narcos and the rest of society here that the news media and common stereotype of Mexico would have us believe. That, for the most part, is an overly simplis-tic, journalistic convenience that does a real injustice to Mexico.

What we've found is that virtually everyone in el campo has only one or two degrees separation from the narco world. Cousins, siblings, old schoolmates - everyone knows or is related to narco players. That means that if we go to a wedding or a birthday, we are likely to be 'partying' with narcos, or at the very least, people with direct narco connections. Now that we have a real-time take on who's who, and what's going on, we're able to do a better job of keeping our distance, but we still cross the path of known bad guys, from time to time. It's part and parcel with the life here, and much less scary when you get to know it for what it really is.

It's sad and ironic that the Mexican-Americans Holly and I have met in the U.S. are often terrified of Mexico, and many have never even been to visit, while, by and large, the average Mexican living here has little or no fear of narco activity.

They also don't live in fear of the kind of random violence, or violence from radical extremists that dogs daily life in the United States and much of Europe. Aside from the news reports from distant lands, that kind of violence isn't even part of the collective consciousness here. The fact that Mexicans' north-of-the-border counterparts have such a different perspective demonstrates how powerful the U.S. media machine—and the perception of Mexico it spins—has become.

For the most part, Holly and I have become much more like our neighbors here and consider the prospect of taking a stray bullet or being otherwise involved in random violence to be at least as unlikely as being involved in a mall or event shooting (or explosion!) when visiting the States. Like remembering a movie seen long ago, the fearful image of Mexico we used to have seems more and more distant with every passing year.

Of course, Mexico has huge problems, and narco corruption is a cancer for much of life here, but then so is the institutionalized corruption associated with the fossil fuels-driven corporatocracy, with its byproduct of climate change which is destroying the entire biosphere.

The piece that 'gets our goat,' so to speak, is how badly Mexico has become maligned in the U.S. press. In truth, most Mexicans we know don't give the narco violence any more attention than a passing storm. They're usually much too busy enjoying life!

Meanwhile, speaking of passing storms...

21 - The Perfect Shit Storm, Part 2
(Eye of the Storm)

November 2, 2014

"We've got to have a new casita," Lillian insists. "My aunt needs a private, quiet space in the shade. I'll pay for it and build it. I just need your permission to get it started."

"Umm, OK," we respond reluctantly, "but keep in mind, there will be no way to recoup the expense if this doesn't work out. We could look at spots up the hill behind the last camping ramada, but we're super busy this week. Holly's giving vaccinations to all the goats, and I'm working twelve-hour days to get things ready for the new floor we're putting in the guest house. Can we meet to discuss it this weekend?"

"Well, not really," Lillian responds. "Juan is coming with his crew this weekend. They'll be ready to start first thing Saturday morning."

Feeling a bit bamboozled but not able to come up with a substantial enough reason not to let her go for it, Holly and I acquiesce. Besides, we figure, the casita she wants to build will serve some function and will be good to have, regardless of whether the retreat happens or not.

Walking up to the house, Holly and I shake our heads.

"Wow, she's a force," Holly comments.

"Yeah, she's amazing. If there's anyone with the chutzpah to make a go of it here, Lillian is definitely the one!" I reply.

* * * * * * *

And so it went—Lillian forever pushing and us trying to keep the steam roller of her enthusiasm from running us over. Gradually other layers of complexity began to surface. When Ernie launched his education program, and he began to host occasional students, stress cracks formed in his relationship with Lillian.

November 22, 2014

"Oh, by the way," Lillian starts in, arriving at the house this morning, "I'm having trouble sleeping in the guest house with Ernesto and his students partying until all hours. It's also really not OK with me the way he scoops up all the young girls like they're some sort of toys he can have his way with. I'm thinking about having Juan build me a platform on the sunset hill to the left there where I can pitch my safari tent. He can set me up with a shower and simple outside kitchen. Would that be OK?"

More stammering on our part. "Umm, well, that's a pretty prime spot for us to have you occupy permanently. And what would you do about a toilet and water? Are you sure you're going to want to hike up there every day? You'll need to give us time to make this decision. We'll talk to Ernie and see if we can get him settled down."

"But it's just a tent platform I'm talking about. That and a temporary bathroom and shower. If it doesn't work out, you can tear it all down."

✶ ✶ ✶ ✶ ✶ ✶ ✶

Having raised five kids, Holly and I were adept at the art of stalling for time, but, in Lillian, we'd met our match, masterful as she was at pushing forward her multiple agendas.

When Lillian went off to yoga school for a month, she met a contact she felt could raise the ante significantly for the ranch. The first day back, Lillian was in hyperdrive.

<u>November 23 (the very next day)</u>

"Completely amazing!" Lillian is telling us this morning. "My new BFF at school has a contact, Diego Martinez, a big time yoga retreat promoter from Vancouver who's looking for a place like ours to hold a huge retreat!" she says. "He's talking about bringing down more than a hundred students at a time and splitting the proceeds of the two-thousand-dollar tuition fifty-fifty with us. He's even interested in funding an extensive buildout, and he'll need other facilities like El Rinconcito and Hotel Mayto to house and feed all the students. Imagine the possibilities!" she enthuses. "I'm supposed to have a Skype call with him this week."

"More than a hundred students at a time?" Holly ponders.

"Financing a buildout? You're suggesting we become partners with this guy?" I ask.

"Well, yes and no," Lillian answers. "I could just partner with him, if you don't want to. I'd be fine taking on the responsibility. Imagine the potential income this represents for the ranch!"

"I can appreciate you wanting to have this guy's backing, but we'd have to know him really well before even considering having him finance any infrastructure projects."

Lillian, looking dejected, doesn't seem to comprehend our reticence and tells us so, straight out. "I can't believe you're even hesitating on this," she says. "It puts me in an awkward position. I'm about to land us all the opportunity of a lifetime, with no cost to you, and you're telling me you're not OK with it?"

"There's a lot at stake here," Holly counters. "It's not as cut and dried as you make it out to be. Partnering with someone means losing control of the direction of things. Besides, we've never even met this guy!"

As usual, Lillian isn't having it. "OK, then, let's do it ourselves. One workshop will cover the cost of all the upgrades we'd need to make it happen. Hell, for that matter, I'll find the money and pay for it myself!"

✳ ✳ ✳ ✳ ✳ ✳ ✳

Once again, Holly and I find ourselves off-balance and ambivalent. The prospect of what it will take to get our facilities upgraded for this guy Diego's huge yoga retreats conflicts with our existing plan to get our house livable this winter. On the other hand, the prospect of bringing significant yoga tourism to Mayto is exciting, especially if it could mean displacing the current tourism trend—brainless yahoos arriving in large noisy packs from Vallarta and cruising the beach at top speed in their loud and useless quad bikes and dune buggies. Somehow, we manage to hold Lillian off temporarily while we mull over all the possibilities, good and bad.

Then Lillian also mentions that Juan is thinking about moving to the ranch. A little put off by her announcing this as statement rather than a request, we are, at the same time, excited by the idea knowing Juan is a nice and very competent guy. As usual, we do our best to keep a handle on the spin, letting Lillian know we're open to the idea but would need to discuss the conditions of his living here.

Throughout this time, Holly and I also watch as the volunteer pool we've brought on—a half dozen of some of the best helpers we've ever had —get pulled into the vortex of Lillian's natural charisma and enthusiasm. Instead of pushing forward Holly's and my plans for finishing up our house, the gardens, new composting toilets, and other ongoing infrastructure projects, we turn the volunteers over to Lillian to help her with her various initiatives, mostly urgencies related to her aunt's upcoming retreat. Surprisingly clueless, considering our years of experience raising children and having employees, Holly and I are rapidly losing control of the entire ranch and its volunteers.

Topping all of this off, another young woman, Martha, whom Holly knows and brought on to help market the retreats, also falls under Lillian's spell. Although Martha is being fed and housed by us, she begins working as Lillian's personal assistant. When we learn Martha is working almost exclusively on social media to develop Lillian's stand-alone, independent yoga business—completely unaffiliated with the ranch—we're forced to confront Lillian in the first of what will become a series of skirmishes.

In addition to this stress, Ernie's program is gaining momentum and doing really well (in spite of his emerging wild side), and the turf war between he and Lillian is growing.

"He was so drunk last night that he fell into the fire," Lillian informs us. "His students had to carry him to bed. I really think you should consider getting rid of him."

Despite the growing tension, we maintain a dialog about hosting one of the big retreats and, in early December, Lillian announces that the yoga guru, Diego himself, is planning an inspection visit for the middle of the month.

"This is it!" announces Lillian at one of our weekly meetings. "This is the big, big fish that will put us all on the map!"

With this announcement, the enthusiasm spreads. Giving into it, and truly excited by the potential that Diego represents, Holly and I suspend all of our previous plans for the winter to focus on prepping for his visit. With all of the dozen volunteers assigned to various tasks by Lillian—carrying bricks, shoveling gravel, creating a hundred steps up to the new sunset yoga platform, and even setting to work on Lillian's personal tent platform high up on the other hill—the place is a hive of activity with queen bee Lillian at its epicenter.

By Christmas time, Diego Martinez has come and gone.

"He loved the rustic, authentic feeling of the ranch and guest house," Lillian tells us, feigning enthusiasm, "but he says the other facilities around Mayto aren't quite at the level he had in mind."

Worn out by the effort and disappointed by the results, our little community goes into a funk. Almost immediately, however, Lillian rejuvenates the group, engaging them in preparations for her aunt's retreat that begins in a couple of weeks. At this point, Holly and I have lost any semblance of control of the volunteers we're feeding and housing. Never had we seen a more gifted leader than Lillian—a fact that made the frictions between her and us so difficult to manage.

The tension, already thick, took on a venomous tone after Christmas when one of the core agreements we had with Lillian began to unravel.

December 26, 2014

Lillian shows up all smiles after breakfast and asks if Holly and I would like to go to dinner over in Tehua this evening. "It'll be my treat," she tells us. "I've got something exciting I'd like to talk to you about."

"Umm, sure," we respond. "That will be great."

With this statement, Lillian has us fully engaged. For the rest of the day, we toss out guesses to each other over what the news could be.

"Maybe Diego is coming after all," I offer.

"Or the school in Vallarta wants to start bringing their students here," Holly rejoins.

Over dinner, Lillian drops the bombshell that she's pregnant with Juan's baby.

"Wow. That's terrific. Congratulations!" we tell her with genuine surprise and good wishes. "When are you due? Do you know if it's a boy or a girl?"

"Well, actually, it's coming sooner than you'd think," she responds. "It's a boy, we're almost certain. I'll be having him in June."

When Lillian excuses herself and goes off to the bathroom, Holly speaks up with a note of concern. "Hmm," she says to me, "what do you think this means regarding her agreement to be our caretaker this coming summer?"

"Ah, well, no problem," I respond, playing my role of the optimist as usual. "I'm sure she's still planning to make good on our agreement. Especially now that Juan is moving to the ranch."

When she returns to the table, I broach the subject. "Uh, hey, Lillian, how will having the baby fit in with your agreement to provide caretaker coverage this summer?"

Silence.

I continue dancing delicately. "Hol and I are still planning our time away and need to know our agreement with you is still in place."

"You're kidding, right? You want me to stay here with a newborn?" says Lillian, acting shocked.

"Well, that's why I asked," I say, now on the defensive. "For us, that's one of the most important parts of this whole association we have. That's why we need to know if this new development is going to affect our plans."

"You can't be serious." A new, fire-breathing Lillian emerges. "I announce that I'm pregnant, and all you two care about is yourselves? You really think I'd be staying here with a newborn for the entire summer? I'll be leaving to stay with family and will be away for at least six months, possibly more," she says with a huff.

Not a full-on whack with a two-by-four yet, but we're getting close.

"Whoa, whoa. Let's all calm down," I say. "It's a simple question, nothing more. You've been telling us that Juan is planning to move to the ranch. With the two of you increasingly making the ranch your home, Holly and I assumed you'd you'd want to be here. If not, we can always discuss renegotiating our contract. We're happy about your baby and are sure we can be flexible and accommodate the changes. I'm sure we can work out an equitable arrangement."

"What do you mean, renegotiate? Equitable?" Lillian responds, fuming. "Look at all the work I've done to improve your ranch. Do you think I should have to do all that and be your caretaker too? I feel like you're attacking me for having gotten pregnant!"

"Well," I reply, "summer caretaking coverage is at the core of our agreement. It's super important to us, and our agreement is that it's the basis for you living here rent-free."

"This is outrageous!" Lillian says, nearly shouting. "What about all the business I'm going to be bringing you?"

"The agreement we have has two separate parts," I remind her. "The split on income is your compensation for developing business and using the facilities, and the caretaking responsibility is what you pay, in lieu of rent, for living here. We've been super clear about that from day one," I say, starting to feel a little steamed. "That's our contract. It's what we all agreed to. We've never talked about changing either of those two core parts. If this new situation means you're no longer planning on fulfilling the caretaking piece, then we'll have to discuss some form of rent or other compensation instead."

"This is completely fucked!" Lillian spits, pushing her chair back and standing over us now—an accomplished actress giving us a masterful private performance. Lillian, if nothing else, I realize while watching her, is 'caliente' or 'hot' as a Mexican might describe her—not necessarily sexy hot, but rather hot to the touch, as in 'be careful, amigo, or you might get burned.' Sitting here, watching her, I'm filled with a new appreciation for the word.

"After all the things I've done for the ranch, I can't believe you'd do this to me—that you'd kick me out!"

"W-H-O-A-A, wait a second. No one said anything about kicking you out," I respond. "Yes, it's true you've made some improvements. We appreciate that, but they weren't our initiatives, and we never asked for them. And who knows if the yoga platform will ever even get used now that Diego's not coming."

"Or your tent platform, either," Holly adds. "You may not even end up liking being all the way up that hill, especially once you have the baby. In that case we wouldn't have any use for the platform. Same with the yoga platform. Our fear is they're just going to end up being future maintenance problems. None of these things were our priority and, to a large extent, they were created with the help of the volunteers that we've been feeding and housing. All of these projects intended to launch your business have set our own plans back an entire season."

"Fuck this," Lillian snarls. "I feel completely betrayed!"

In a final dramatic flurry, she storms off into the night.

December 27, 2014

Today breaks hot and dry. Ironically, despite the heat, scorching by noon, we also begin to notice a chill in the air—of the human kind. After going down the hill to get a pipe wrench from the tool bodega at the campground, Yamir comes chugging back up the hill to talk to us.

"Hace mucho calor, no?" he comments. Then, "Los chicos abajo están caliente también! (your crew down below are hot too!)."

"Oh? What do you mean?" I ask, remembering my revelation about the word caliente from last night and knowing Yamir to often cleverly juggle such balls of meaning.

"Haven't you heard?" he asks, surprised. "Everyone's saying you're mad at Lillian because she's pregnant."

"Fucking Christ," I mutter. Then, thanking Yamir for the intel, I go to find Holly.

Still reeling from last night's dinner, we're now dumbfounded by this new development.

"This is horrible," Holly sighs. "Have you ever known anyone to be so manipulative? This totally sucks!"

"She's a handful, for sure," I respond.

"What do you think we should do now?" Holly asks. "If we're not careful, we're gonna have a full-on revolt on our hands!"

As we mull this over, a great sadness seeps in. Overnight, we've been turned, as if by some dark magic, into the evil overlords high on the hill while the serfs in the village below plot revenge and possible overthrow. We're shocked that some of our favorite volunteers—people whom we've come to love deeply—would so readily break ranks and fall into step with her manipulations. But then, when we think of all the time they've had together down there bonding and without having to contend with the downside of her megalo tendencies, we partly understand. Partying together day and night as they are, we can hardly expect to have the same connection to, or loyalty from, the group.

After much talk and thought, we agree that we're not going to engage in a public-relations war. We decide it best to let things calm down on their own without taking any action, having faith instead that the lie being spread will soon blow over.

✳ ✳ ✳ ✳ ✳ ✳ ✳

Assuming this to be the great whack on the head our friend Julie had warned us about, we little imagined how much worse it could get.

A couple of days later we heading out for Vallarta for a planned New Year's Eve celebration leaving the whole smoldering mess at the ranch unattended. At precisely one minute after midnight, we were dancing it up with friends at the big, annual New Year's Eve predominantly shirtless male street rave in Puerto Vallarta when big drops of rain began falling— so unusual for this time of year.

The sweating, gyrating, crowd was loving it as the rain picked up over the next few hours. By morning, the streets were flooding. When we'd picked up a couple of new volunteers at the airport around mid-afternoon and made our way out of town, the main bridge out of El Tuito had washed out, forcing us to take the coastal route to the south. This adding several hours to the trip. At one point, crossing one of many washouts in the road, our trusty CRV sputtered and died. Stranded in a lightning storm late at night in the middle of nowhere, things were looking bleak.

Eventually, we were rescued and towed to the nearest village by a pickup truck loaded with scary drunks. We were exhausted when we finally made it back to the ranch around midnight. The soggy, disgruntled volunteers were all huddled up on the porch of the guest house where they'd moved their tents and other belongings. Soaked and sullen, they barely even greeted us. The year, it seemed, was starting off at an all-time low.

January 4, 2015

Good Christ. Finally, the rain has stopped. It's been a solid three days of deluge—completely bizarre for January. Everyone at the ranch has been hunkered down, enduring the soaker as best they can, but a cold, wet depression has infiltrated everything.

It's a Sunday, and things with Lillian have gone from bad to worse. Her aunt's group is scheduled to arrive this coming Friday, and the preparations are way behind schedule. During the rains, the dark energy cloud we'd hoped would blow over has only intensified. Now, Lillian and her core followers—at least half the group of volunteers—are barely speaking to us. And even though the other half are making a good show of being neutral, it's clear the conflict is taking its toll on everyone.

Holly and I, too, are feeling really down.

"I've half a mind to cancel the retreat and tell everyone that if they don't like us, or the way we're running things, to pack their bags and hit the road," I say to Holly.

"We just have to get through this retreat," she answers. "It wouldn't be fair to the participants for us to cancel it now, and it could also make for problems promoting future retreats."

Only hours later, Holly is on the Internet and finds a listing for the retreat with a price tag many times more than what we'd previously been told by Lillian, and completely out of whack with the income-projection numbers she's been giving us. Doing some quick calculations, Holly and I are shocked to realize that we should be receiving several thousand dollars more for the retreat than the numbers Lillian has been showing us. This is all vastly different than the profit-sharing agreement made clear in our contract.

Fuming now, I head down to guest and volunteer area we call The Lower Hamlet and confront Lillian about the discrepancy. On hearing my complaint, Lillian responds indignantly, "My aunt and the other teacher are getting the rest. That additional money has nothing to do with you or me!"

"Are you crazy? Of course it does!" I say to her. "Our profit-sharing arrangement is clear. You can't divert the bulk of income to your aunt and pretend it doesn't exist!"

"It's for expenses," Lillian counters angrily. "She has to pay the other teacher and lots of other costs. That's not our money to divvy up. It's hers!"

"You left well over half the estimated gross income out of the projections you've been giving us," I counter. "This is nothing like the profit-sharing formula we all agreed to!"

After a few more rounds of this nonsensical argument, I finally say to her, "Listen, Lillian, this relationship is clearly broken. If you have some idea of how to fix it, Holly and I are willing to listen, but, short of that, I don't know what we're going to do or where we can possibly go from here."

"Fine. That's fine!" Lillian is shouting now, aspiring actress ramping up to a grand finale for the small group of volunteers that have gathered off to the side. "I've made other plans. I'll be leaving tomorrow!" she says with a flourish before storming out through the gate and down the road to the beach.

January 6, 2015

Today, Lillian and several others leave the ranch and head to El Rinconcito to set up camp.

As the waves of a new, even darker rumor reach us, we're devastated. Apparently, Lillian is now telling anyone who will listen that we've forcefully evicted her because she's pregnant!

Heartbroken, Holly and I don't even try to disavow the lie or diffuse the mindless gossip machine that's spreading it. A few of our best volunteers continue to be neutral, or seem to be siding with us, but Holly and I are treated like pariahs by the others who stay.

Despite everything that's happened, Holly and I decide it will be best to stick to the high road and honor our commitment to Lillian's aunt to host the retreat. Beyond that decision, however, we're struck catatonic with dismay.

"We're done," Holly laments. "As soon as this groups clears out, we're not taking anyone else on. I don't want to have any more volunteers—ever!"

****

Once the retreat is over, the vile vibe begins to dissipate and some of the volunteers leave. The six or seven core volunteers that stay seem freer to be themselves once the others leave, and we begin to receive an upwelling of support and friendly energy. Like any storm that ravages and then passes, Lilian's turbulent energy seems to have ultimately had a cleansing effect.

Not long after Lillian's departure, the healing begins in earnest with a road trip to The Coming of The Virgin festival in El Tuito...

January 12, 2015

This afternoon, we knock off early, shower, dress, and, together with the volunteers, head up the lumpy serpent road to the annual Coming of the Virgin festival in El Tuito. The town is in vibrant party mode, and we have to jockey for a parking spot on the outskirts with all other exited festival-goers arriving from the surrounding countryside. Downtown there's a crush of people all wandering about in a daze.

The normally solemn zocalo (town square) is transformed into a writhing cacophony of light and sound. Children's carnival rides have been squeezed together—little boats and cartoon characters loaded with screaming, laughing, frightened, or unfazed niños going round in round—along with a humongous, two-story bouncy house now dominate the center of the plaza.

Off to one side, there are small-scale carnival thrill rides for the teens including one that lifts passengers twenty feet into the air, turns them upside down, gives them a shake, and then sets them down again. There's also a twenty-seat cyclone blaring insanely loud banda music while speeding its victims over the single, 'oh-my-god-there-goes-my stomach' hump, around a couple of g-force corners, and then back to the rise. A throng of flirting high schoolers push and laugh while waiting in line. In the center of the plaza, a stage has been set up and is reverberating with the thumping feet of two dozen colorfully dressed folkloric dancers while a small crowd seated in folding chairs gazes on.

Stopping in the food zone, our volunteers load up on giant, 40-ounce Micheladas, grilled corn smothered with fresh cream and chili spice, sickly sweet churros just rescued from a vat of sizzling oil, or sticky fried platano bananas smothered with sweet cream and honey. Holly and I wend through the crowd, Holly and I are greeted by many of our local friends all dressed to the nines—the guys wearing freshly ironed shirts, gleaming cowboy boots, and oversized silver belt buckles with copper-embossed bucking broncos or alacranes at the centers. Giggling young girls roam about in packs—ripening tushes and fresh budding breasts barely restrained by the tightest of clothing—while the more matronly, aging women huddle amongst themselves, frowning in disapproval.

Past the main square, the pulsing heartbeat of the festival, an extensive outdoor market lines the main street leading out of town. From brightly lit stalls spills a profusion of goods—racks of spinning, flashing LED lighting; booths lined with hundreds of knock-off banda music CDs; several savory-smelling stands full of candies and nuts—succulent morsels of every imaginable shape and color; scores of clothing stalls displaying boots, hats, children's clothing, and buxom manikin torsos donning bright, stretchy, sexy clothing; and block after block of cheap, tinny, home goods —tortilla presses, buckets, tools, knives, and enough plastic goods from China to fill a fleet of semis. Overhead, the ubiquitous cohete bottle rockets, announcing the Virgin's coming, threaten to shatter the sky with their unnerving explosions.

"Where's the Virgin?" I ask a bystander.

"Oh, you missed her," the woman says, looking at me as if I should know better. "She came this afternoon." After a pause, she adds, "but there's no need to worry. You can stop by the church and see her anytime this week."

The Virgin, you see, has good reason to be a virgin and hang around the church all week. She's carved of wood and has nothing else pressing until she's carried on a litter by her passionate devotees to her next gig at another town down the coast.

Meandering back to the appointed meeting spot at the main square, Holly and I pass a large building that's a riot of activity. The cock fights. Outside, a handful of guys are milling about, passing a bottle, and inspecting a large gallo de pelea (fighting cock) that one of them is proudly displaying. We pass by on the far side of the street, knowing this to be the best place to go to if you're looking for trouble.

Arriving at the meet-up spot, several of our volunteers are drunk, and two are missing. We wait another half hour and then decide to leave without the stragglers. On the way down from the mountains toward home, we feel the crisp mountain air change back to the humid heaviness of the coast and hear the volunteers singing merrily in the back of the truck. Tomorrow will be a write-off as far as getting anything done, but it's been good to have a fun break after all of the ranch's recent stress.

✳ ✳ ✳ ✳ ✳ ✳ ✳

Within a few weeks we've settled back into a worn but happy vibe. By the time a month has passed, we've returned to the pizza parties, talent-night campfires, and group swing-dance lessons of the past. The volunteers even initiate the building of a playground out of recycled tires for the elementary school in town.

Despite this resurgence of good energy, Holly and I still feel bruised and raw. We swear that this is our final round of hosting volunteers or trying to partner with anyone. We also realize our own part in what's gone down and accept that some of the pain we're feeling is knowing that we could have handled the situation better as it was evolving. We vow to be more clearly communicate our truths with others and be from with our boundaries no matter how uncomfortable or inconvenient that may be.

As for Lillian, she stays camped at the beach for a time, never missing an opportunity to spread venomous words about Holly and me. We continue our policy of not responding or saying anything bad about her, but it's tough to hold our tongues with her nastiness continuing. In the end, we never receive a single peso for the retreat. However, we content ourselves that the projects she initiated are of some consolation.

Eventually, Holly and I overcome our aversion to the potential chaos that hosting volunteers can entail and begin, with timid steps, to bring a few back on at a time. Lesson learned by 'Shit Storm Lillian,' we're much more cautious these days and insist on knowing someone for at least a year before making long-term commitments to anyone.

22 - Animal Tails, Part 3
(Death Abounds, Shaky Deals, and Dying Trees)

A month later we were still recovering from 'Hurricane Lillian', but things were looking up. When Oprah lead off birthing season with a beautiful set of twins, we were happy to be bouncing into kidding season.

Unfortunately, the pleasant lull we were experiencing didn't last very long...

February 4, 2015

Having attended workshops on goat care at the Maine country fair while visiting each year, Holly and I have become fairly competent being our own country veterinarians. We also feel better prepared than ever for this year's crop of babies. We've even brought a microscope and have started examining the goats' and other animals' poo to assess and treat their parasite loading. The moms have been wormed, injected with vitamins and minerals along with their CDT booster (Clostridium perfringens + Tetanus), and extra rations prior to parturition, so that they're healthy and shining.

Today, we're giving selenium to the newborns, having learned that the majority of Earth's soils are selenium-deficient and the mineral is important for good muscle development in newborns. Their shrieks are unnerving.

February, 5, 2015

Seven a.m. Barely light out. I wake to screaming.

"No-o-o-o-o. NO-O-O-O-O-O-O!!!"

It's Holly. She's out in the corral. I throw on some shorts and go running out to find her.

"What? What is it?" I'm yelling as I run. I find her sobbing in the nursery where Gail and her new babies are being kept.

The babies, those perfect little packages of innocence, are alive but barely. Drooping like rag dolls, they twitch and try to lift their heads but are weak and formless, as if their bones have been crushed.

"She must have rolled on them," Holly says, nodding at Gail, who's over in the corner munching alfalfa, oblivious.

By noontime, both babies are dead.

The two of us go through the motions, doing our chores, making dinner, washing dishes, and reading a bit before bed. However, the mood is somber, and we're both deeply depressed.

"I don't know how much more I can take. Tomorrow needs to be a better day," Holly says dejectedly before switching off the light.

February 7, 2015

We are still feeling down, but we get a lift when we come back from the beach in the afternoon. One of our favorite goats, Mrs. Toggenberg, is in the corral with her two gorgeous babies, born while we were away.

"Ahhh, look, they've got toggles just like mom," Holly coos and fusses, referring to the two dangling appendages they each have on their necks.

After giving the newborns their selenium injections and making sure they're nursing fine, Hol and I finish our chores, have dinner, and get ready for bed. Putting on her headlamp, Holly heads out for one last check-in on Mrs. Toggenberg and company. Out there for over a half hour, I'm drifting toward dreamland by the time she comes back in.

"Are you awake?" she asks.

"No," I say. But it's no use. I can tell she's agitated, so I switch on the light.

"What's up?" I ask, propping on an elbow.

"It's the babies," she says. "Something doesn't seem right. They're too weak. Kind of floppity. They seem to be having trouble standing up."

"Well, they're only eight hours' old," I say to her. "You're bound to be paranoid after what happened to Gail's two."

"Yeah, you're right," she says. "It's OK. Go ahead and turn off the light."

February. 8, 2015

I wake in the predawn dark. Something's not right. Feeling over to Hol's side, I find the bed empty and cold. Putting on clothes and headlamp, I go out to the nursery where Holly is holding and rocking the new babies.

"They're not doing well," she tells me. "They should be stronger than this. More active."

It's the middle of the night," I try to reassure her. "They're sleeping. Come back to bed, sweetie. I'm sure they'll be fine as soon as the sun is up."

By mid-morning, it's clear there's a problem. The babies are stumbling around and have even started to exhibit some jerking motions.

Back inside, we scan desperately through our *Goat Medicine* guide, the two-hundred-and-fifty-dollar medical reference Bible for all things goat, and which, frankly, is way over our heads in terms of the technical level of information. In the book, we find several possible diseases that could account for the babies' condition. Feeling overwhelmed, we begin brainstorming our options. Can we get a vet in from Tuito or even Tomatlán, a solid hour and a half away? We try calling a couple of vets in the U.S. but our phone, a cellular hybrid with its feeble signal, isn't up for the task.

Meanwhile, two other moms have given birth. So now, on top of the worry about Mrs. Toggenberg's kids, we're busy as hell putting iodine on bloody umbilical stumps, laying out fresh hay, and giving the necessary selenium injections.

By nightfall, Mrs. Toggenberg's baby's are near death. Holly, believing the problem may be pneumonia due to the cold nights we've been having, has blown up an inflatable mattress in the kitchen and intends to spend the night there, cuddling the babies.

The truth is that we're both a mess and haven't a clue what to do. Tomorrow, we'll take the babies to find a veterinarian in Tomatlán. We consider going to our terrific domestic animal vet in Vallarta but decide that, in Tomatlan, we'll have a better bet of finding someone more tuned in to goats and any caprine diseases that may be making the rounds out here in 'El Campo.'

The night passes fitfully with neither us getting any real sleep.

February 9, 2015

"No need to take Mrs. Toggenberg's babies to the vet this morning," Holly informs me in the half-light in my half-conscious state. "They're both dead."

By mid-morning, another mother is birthing, and two of the four new babies born yesterday are beginning to show signs of the disease. Once we have the new mom settled, we decide again to head to Tomatlán. Scooping up all six babies, we settle them on towels and cushions in the back seat of the truck and start the bone jarring, washboard journey down the coast.

The vet we find seems competent enough and says the babies have a virus. He gives injections and loads us up with supplies for the twenty more we expect will be arriving soon.

Relieved to finally have some certainty about what's going on, we head back home followed by a long trail of dust.

February 10 - 11, 2015

Motherfucker! The meds don't seem to be doing anything. We are distraught and afraid. Speaking for myself, I feel as though I can't breathe—

like I'm being sucked down into quicksand or have been punched in the gut.

Our only ray of hope is that the Internet has come back on and we're able to Skype a couple of U.S. vets and do some better research online. Drowning in fear and sorrow, we grasp hold of this tenuous lifeline.

Holly soon finds several articles about selenium poisoning, and the symptoms seem to match the ones we've been seeing. Double and triple checking the dosage with the medicine guide and online sources, we seem to be correct with the amount we've been giving, but we find that the "Beef-Se" selenium formula we've purchased here in Mexico may be much stronger than the U.S. equivalent. After more research we become certain that the Mexican formula has the decimal point one place over from those recommended in our books. This means we've been overdosing by a factor of ten!

During the afternoon, the Internet is down for a couple more hours, but, in the interim, we decide to hold off on giving any more injections.

Next day, when the Internet returns, we read, horrified, numerous accounts of selenium overdosing. One article we find tells of an entire team of polo ponies wiped out by selenium overdosing by the team's vet.

February 13, 2015

This morning, after coffee, I take my trusty shovel and go out to the field below our house to bury the last of the babies that received the selenium injections. Finishing up, I survey the field that's now pockmarked with fresh graves of the eleven precious lives we've lost since this ordeal got started.

We're relieved, of course, to have finally found the source of the tragedy, and there are already five healthy frolicking babies in the corral, with more on their way. A pall of gloom still hangs in the air, however. We know, without saying, that it will be months, if not years, before we'll have put this horrible episode behind us.

✳ ✳ ✳ ✳ ✳ ✳ ✳

Not long after the baby goat tragedy, Holly and I have our own direct experience of life on the fringes of the narco world...

April 18, 2015

Today I'm nervous. Yamir has arranged a trade of thirteen of our goats for rastrojo (sacks of ground corn stalks used as an animal feed supplement), a very useful trade for the ranch. The goats are going to a nearby ranch owned by an ex-narco heavy now living as a legitimate businessman. I call him 'X'. We've sold goats to him before so I know he enjoys talking to me and is extremely interested in all things irelated to life in the U.S..

Today's the day X or his man will pick up the animals. The problem is we only have twelve goats for him because one died when the feed trough fell over on it yesterday. We're sad about the baby, and worried about shorting the deal.

Yamir is nervous, too, and he tries to talk sense into Holly and me. "Holly. Daniel. You can't short him on the deal. That's just not done, especially with X. Can't you just give him one of the other goats you'd planned to keep?"

Holly carefully selects goats to become a permanent part of her elite manada and isn't going to budge, but I have to give it to Yamir for trying.

"No way. Not happening. You're not taking any of the ones I've picked," she says to both of us.

After twenty-five years of marriage, I know the tone for 'non-negotiable' from Holly. Despite being a non-starter, I, too, give it a try. "Holly, I made the deal with X for thirteen. Now there's only twelve. You don't understand. This is Mexico. A man's word is everything here. He's expecting thirteen and will feel we've tricked him if we come up short. This is definitely not a guy we want to jerk around."

Yamir, doing his best to follow our English, concurs. "Holly, I know it's not my place, but Daniel is right. X is expecting thirteen goats. He's not a guy we want to chingar (fuck over)."

Holly's not having any of it. "The answer is no. You two are just going to have to adjust the deal."

'Man, talk about being stuck between a hard rock and a place,' I think to myself, and indicate this to Yamir with a pathetic, raised-eyebrows look.

An hour later, X's ranch truck rolls in with X himself onboard along with a couple of of gnarly looking ranch hands. Standing around the truck, Yamir does his best to explain the trough accident and the money we're offering to compensate for being short one goat.

"That's no problem," X replies. "I'll just take that one instead," he's says, pointing to the handsome little buck we're keeping as stud.

"Ummm, I'm sorry but that's my wife's favorite," I say, doing my best to balance meek with macho while knowing too much of either will come across as a lack of respect, or worse.

Silent, uncomfortable pause.

"Ha!" laughs X, finally. "Do you have any of that nice tequila you had last time I was here?"

"Sure, sure. Let me get some. Let's have a snort!"

Just then, Holly comes out of the house with a cutting board loaded with her latest batch of fresh chevre. Pulling out the tequila and some shot glasses, we toast the deal while the others load the goats into the back of the truck.

"Excellent cheese," X says to Holly. "How much does cheese like this cost in the U.S.?"

April 24, 2015

Today's worry is that the hundreds of trees we've planted over the years are all suffering without rain. Water from town has been inconsistent and, on many days, we barely have enough for the gardens and the animals. Even though we go through this same anxiety every year, this round seems particularly hard, probably due to the winter we've had and the stress we've been under. The reality is that, for up to nine months of the year, the sky here is a stingy old man unwilling to let go of a single drop. Then, for the rest of the year, it becomes a jilted lover, shamelessly crying for days on end. We'll get through it, we know, but the price to our psyches seems to get higher every year. We just need to get past this bad run we're having, Holly and I keep telling each other...

23 - Fear Factor, Part 3
(Day of Insurrection)

<u>From the U.S. Department of State Website, May 2015:</u>

"The Consulate has received initial reports of several fairly significant narco-related events around Guadalajara in the areas near Plaza Mexico, downtown, and at an unspecified location on the Periferico. Our recommendation to all American citizens is to stay put while we gather more information. Anyone on the road should continue directly to the nearest safe area and stay put. As we develop more information, we will share it with you."

<u>**May 4, 2015**</u>

This morning, we are up well before dawn, getting an early start for Vallarta. After making coffee, packing the cooler, and putting a few other things in the car, we bump on down the drive, headlights washing away patches of pre-day darkness. If all goes well, I'll catch the earliest five-hour bus to Guadalajara, see my periodontist at one o'clock, and then catch the afternoon bus back to Vallarta afterwards. Meanwhile, Holly will run errands in town and pick me up at the bus station in the late afternoon. Like a Mission Impossible field team, we have our assignment and are swinging into action.

The one advantage to coming in this early is getting the jump on Vallarta traffic. After a quick stop at Starbucks, Holly drops me at the bus station out near the airport.

"Good luck," she says, giving me a kiss.

"You, too." I kiss back. "Try to stay relaxed today," I add, knowing how stressed city driving can make her.

I buy my ticket and head to the VIP waiting lounge. The first-class, long-haul Mexican buses are a wondrous thing. VIP lounges, immaculately dressed bus attendants offering bag lunches and refreshments, and extra-comfortable, stretch-out seats with individual movie-on-demand flat screens all help make the trip more pleasant.

Today, in the station lounge, people are gathered around the large overhead TV monitors watching a story about a downed military helicopter on the other side of the state. Apparently, the chopper, carrying eighteen soldiers, was downed by a rocket-propelled grenade, and at least seven of the soldiers are known to be dead. It's assumed the attack is in response to an attempted capture of the new-generation cartel leader, Ruben Cervantes, a.k.a. El Mencho (The Blond Guy), the day before.

After tiring of the redundant news loop, I stroll around the station, anxious to get on with the day ahead.

Finally, the bus pulls in and we board. I settle in nicely, headphones pulsing a terrific Mexico-themed Ry Cooder album, Chávez Ravine, that I've recently downloaded. After snaking its way up the coast to Tepic, the bus takes the turnoff inland, heading east through the mountains. The morning is a beauty, with the mountains gleaming.

Then:

Ping!

Incoming text from Holly: U won't believe it. Fire at Banamex by Costco. Got there right at opening time. All sirens & fire trucks. Gonna try a different bank…

Me texting back: Which one?

Holly: Gonna try the BanComer by Plaza Caricol…

Back to my music which is synced in perfect rhythm to the scenery flowing by. Several times the bus slows to a stop in heavy traffic, and then, thankfully, starts rolling again. I'm mildly concerned already about encountering such heavy traffic this far out from Guadalajara but shrug it off. Having caught the seven o'clock bus should give me almost an extra hour, so I still feel comfortable I can make my appointment, especially if the traffic clears up once we're away from the coast.

I'm settling back into a state of mobile bliss when the bus shutters, slows, and comes to a stop in heavy traffic. Then it starts up again.

I try calling Holly, just to touch base, but after repeated messages of "all lines are busy," I give up and return to my music. Ry is singing in flawless Spanish:

> *"Un monton de soldados, jovenes y enganados*
> *Llevaron su bronca to Downtown LA*
> *Contra Los Pachucos, sin saber porque..."*
> *(A pile of soldiers, young and deceived*
> *Took their row to Downtown LA*
> *Against the Chicanos, without knowing why...)*

Then, once again;

Ping!

Holly: Something weird going on. When I pulled into Plaza Caricol, a dozen federal pickup trucks came flying in behind me, all sirens and lights. Big black hole where the bank windows used to be. Holy Crap!!!

Me: Wow. I saw on TV where a helicopter was shot down this morning. Better get somewhere safe till we know what's going on.

Holly: Starbucks?

Me: Hell no, not there. That could easily become a target. Try to check in early to the B&B you booked. BTW, did you know this is a holiday? I just found out. The banks wouldn't have been open anyway...

Holly. OK. Sounds good. Will keep you posted...

I switch on my back-of-seat flat screen, scanning for news, when the bus shutters, slows, and comes to a full stop. People are up out of their seats, talking in hushed tones and trying to see what's up ahead. Face pushed against the window, I can just make out a plume of smoke around the next corner and no cars coming the other way.

Oh crap, I think to myself, *first the things going on in Vallarta and now an accident here. What the hell is going on?*

Ping!

Holly: There's definitely something fucked-up going on! Passed two more banks blown up. Not a car on the streets. Pulled into Costco just as they were rolling up their big steel doors. Headed back to my Air B&B place now.

Me: Oh man! Definitely park yourself there for the day. Don't go out. Drive safe and keep your eyes open. I love you!

Holly: Will do. I'm scared. I love you too!

Mind racing, I start working through the possibilities. OK, worst-case scenario, I postulate. Clearly this is a well-orchestrated attack. New reports coming in on the TV are saying it extends to other states as well. If the narcos really do manage to cut off the highways and get control of some major cities, total anarchy is possible. Got to think of a plan to get Holly and me to the border. No, not possible. Something else. At least get back to Vallarta to be with her. Holly's B&B is outside of town. Fairly remote. Should be safe. At least for a while. Supplies. They'll need—we'll need—supplies so we don't have to go out. I'll text Holly and tell her to stop at an OXXO and get as much water, nuts, and anything solid that she can find. Aja. Got to text Aja and let her know some sort of plan.

In the thought-stream, another voice jumps in. "Dude, your blood pressure. Check out your pressure!" Responding to the voice, I refocus my attention. Sure enough, my scalp is tingling with pressure as all the morning's caffeine courses through my arteries. Whoa. Got to breathe. Calm down. Not a good time for a panic attack. Serves no purpose. Besides, this is the test you've been prepping for with all that meditation and mind training. GET A GRIP! You know the drill. Steady on, old boy. You can think your way through this. You've always done well when the going's gotten tough. Deep breath… Another… Good, that's it…'

After half an hour, the bus lurches back to life and begins crawling forward. Staring dumbfounded as we round the corner, I see several tractor-trailer trucks engulfed in flames. There are scores of police vehicles, and a huge bulldozer has pushed the trucks off to the side of the road. Police and military everywhere are working to get the traffic moving. So this is it. It's really happening!

Ping!

Holly: OK. I'm at my B&B. I'm watching the news. There's shit blowing up all over Jalisco. More than a dozen banks and a bunch of Pemex gas stations in Vallarta alone. Supposedly a response to a narco leader getting captured. I tried to call you but all the lines are busy. What a mess. I'm really scared!

Me: I know. Me too. They blocked the highway, but we're through it now. I'll head back to Vallarta as soon as it seems safe to. Trying to figure out some sort of plan now. Stay put at the B&B. It will be our meet-up point if they take over the cell towers and we lose connection. I'll get there, I promise. I love you!

Scre-e-e-e....h-i-s-s-s-s. Airbrakes pumping bus to sudden stop. More traffic snarl. More billowing black smoke up ahead.

In the meantime, I try texting the dentist at her personal number. Immediately I get a response back telling me that she's monitoring the situation and that there are no disruptions within the city. Most of the trouble's been on the highways or around Vallarta. She adds that it's a holiday, so traffic is light, and she's fine keeping the appointment or making it later if I'm able to make it.

Amazing! Call me crazy, but I doubt there are many U.S. dentists who'd risk going out during a narco insurrection to keep an appointment for a check-up—and on a holiday, no less! But we're often reminded that's how people are here.

And, sure enough, an hour later, we've cleared the second roadblock and are rolling freely into Guadalajara, where everything seems normal.

Chatting up the taxi driver about the situation on my ride from the bus station to the dentist, he shrugs it off.

"Yeah, those Nuevo Generation cartel guys are just throwing a tantrum because the feds almost got El Mencho," he says nonchalantly. "We've seen worse when they burned all the buses a few years back. The narco's did this on a holiday as a warning and didn't intend to hurt any civilians. They're saying that, so far, not a single person other than soldiers in the chopper they shot down have been hurt. It'll blow over. No need to worry, my friend."

Finally, I'm able to get a call through to Holly. The reports she's hearing also confirm the lull. Other than the string of bombings at banks and gas stations that weren't even open yet for the day, there's no other activity reported, and things are already returning to normal.

Being a holiday, there's no receptionist at the dentist's office. Ringing the bell at the front door and peering inside, I see her coming down the stairs, the cheerful picture of health and beauty, as always. All's well, and I'm given a good cleaning and favorable checkup.

Taking another cab back to the station, I'm just in time to make the 3:00 P.M. bus which, to my relief, is nearly empty. In my seat and headphones on, exhausted from the day's intensity, I lapse into dreams of machine guns and dentist drills.

Section V

Finding the Flow (Summer 2015 on...)

"What day is it?" asked Pooh.
"It's today," squeaked Piglet.
"My favorite day," said Pooh."
— A.A. Milne

24 - Toward Sustainability, Part 4
(Building the Good Life)

It's been a rough patch, to be sure. Still reeling from the Lillian episode and the selenium poisonings, Holly and I haven't been at our best as of late.

This is the point where many projects like ours falter and die. Far too many homesteads, farms, ranches, eco-villages, and permaculture initiatives do. Many of them fail to hit critical mass due to being underfunded, but many others die on the vine from the harsh reality of the amount of work and inevitable hardships involved.

Holly and I are in the fortunate position of moving toward an earth-based lifestyle with adequate funding. However, even with financial concerns only a minor background issue for us, being modern settlers has definitely taken its toll. As our time to head back to the States for 'summer vacation' approaches again, Holly and I should be happy, but, instead, we've been snipping at each other a lot, and the viability of what we're attempting here is increasingly coming into question. "This just isn't fun anymore," Holly has said to me on more than one occasion recently.

I try to console Holly by telling her I'm not attached to 'things,' that our well-being as a couple is more important than this project and that I'm perfectly willing to put the ranch up for sale and move on, if that's what's needed. Meanwhile, my internal ego-voice is saying: "Yeah, right, amigo. You? Quit this thing and just sell it and walk away? Who do you think you're kidding? Doing that would be like death for you."

Another complicating factor is that our daughter, Hillary, having hired a natural-building architect friend of ours to build her house here at the ranch this past year, is now a vested partner. Her wanting to be here also raises the hope that one or more of our other four adult children may one day want to follow her lead.

We've also invested a tidy sum to drill a well and are halfway through the process of subdividing a handful of lots in order to have others able to become vested participants. This further complicates the idea of giving up and abandoning the project.

In my funk, I think about how, aside from the cold, the main impetus for selling our businesses and transitioning here was that we were in constant responsibility-overload mode. Now it feels as though we've dragged that all down here with us.

Increasingly, I find myself crawling through a sludge of mild depression, barely able to keep my head above the muck. I sit for a meditation, regain perspective, and feel better for a while. But relief is fleeting...

<u>July 5. 2015</u>

"They worked like dogs for over thirty years to get ahead and then took all of their retirement savings and bought a huge money pit in an unstable, third-world country. They deserve to be punished. Your honor, I rest my case!" my deceased mother implores in a dream.

Except now she's not my mother. She's a British prosecutor, with formal waistcoat; ruffled blouse; curly, grey, powdered wig; huge, scaly, reptilian face; and weepy, yellow, alligator eyes. The court isn't really a court, either, but a renaissance theatre with carved oak banisters and candlelit footlights creating a dramatic uplighting on all our faces. Yes. That's it. We're on stage now. Out in the gallery, I recognize not only many of our friends but animals also. Our burra, Lupita; our deceased Cocker Spaniel, Amy; lots of familiar goat faces; and several large, leering lizards that I don't immediately recognize. Everyone is laughing and jeering. "Lock them up. Lock them up," a chant begins. It's an indecipherable cacophony of animal-speak and garbled human voices, but the intent is clear. From the stage, which is now turning in a circle like a giant merry-go-round with Holly and me in the center, I try to give an impassioned defense of our actions but find, to my horror, I have no tongue.

I wake with a start. *Whoa*, I think to myself. *What the hell did that one mean?*

Then, I understand exactly. If Holly and I had to defend our actions of the past twelve years at a sanity hearing, we'd be unable to mount much of a case.

On the other hand, lying here in the dark, I'm equally unable to think of anything I'd have done differently. Even now, I imagine someone offering us ten million dollars for the property, and, try as I might to think of where I'd rather be or what I'd rather being doing with my life, I come up blank.

Strange mix, this. On the one hand, I can totally understand anyone who thinks we're crazy for making our retirement one of toil and uncertainty, but, on the other hand, I also understand completely why visitors here often say things like, "Must be nice to be living the life!" or "So this is what paradise looks like."

The truth—as with most truths—is probably somewhere in the middle. Yes, it's true this little project of ours wouldn't be for everyone. Not by a long shot. But yes, it's also true I couldn't imagine a richer, fuller, more interesting life.

So where are we at with it at this point? I continue my thought train. *What have we accomplished? Where are we going?*

Lying here, still slightly disoriented by mental echoes of the dream, I'm feeling the need to make an assessment.

I get up and go to the kitchen, make tea, and head to the couch under the palapa where, wrapped in a blanket, I sink deeper into my darkness, wondering what the meaning of all of this is? I try to call up visions of the good times we've had here—laughing in the surf, watching spectacular sunsets with waves crashing over the rocks at Lover's Beach, playing with baby goats, walking the back of the property, going to soccer games, or attending the myriad fiestas—weddings, quinceañeras, birthdays, and other lively events with our local friends. But the images I'm able to access are only dull, tarnished facsimiles of former joy.

My head is spinning now and I feel a mild panic. *I can't give this up. I can't! But it's tearing Holly and me apart, and what's the point if the fun is gone and it's nothing but drudgery?*

OK, calm down, I council myself, taking a sip of tea and bundling the blanket tightly around my shoulders. *I need to break it down into bite-sized pieces. Do an analysis. Find some objectivity…*

And so I start my midnight assessment.

In the cons column:

The past five years—despite some bright spots—have been tough, with the chronic water problems, chronic people problems, chronic animal problems, chronic shit-breaking and equipment-failing problems. We've also taken on far too many projects and have spread ourselves too thin. On top of all this, life here is frequently made difficult by a dysfunctional bureaucracy that makes every new step—from surveys to permits—like wading in hip-deep, wet cement.

On a day-to-day basis, I'm constantly dealing with things breaking, the quality of the most basic materials and equipment here being crap. Even the sheetrock screws here are often crooked! And the problem is only getting worse with time. Basic PVC tubing, for instance, once good and rugged, is so thin these days that you can break it by hand. Fencing that used to last a decade now goes rusty and falls apart within a year or two. Even the pumps I bring down from the States to fill our cisterns last only a year or two despite their five-year warranties. Replacement would be a simple matter if we were in the States, but we're not. This means I have to buy and bring down extras of all critical components such as solar chargers, inverters, pumps, pump controllers, filters, and specialty tools.

Another con is that no matter how much one cleans, or hires help with cleaning, life in El Campo is a dirty, dusty proposition. I believe Holly has borne the brunt of this latter issue. Even though I know she loves it here deeply, if after finishing this assessment I were to say to her, "Let's pack our things and sell the place," I doubt she'd put up too much of a fight.

In the pros column:
In my gut, I feel this is the right thing to be doing. The world is in trouble. I feel strongly that every drop of oil I burn makes me a willing participant in its destruction, along with all the violence and suffering such destruction wreaks. Pursuing a life of true self-sufficiency and sustainability is the only way I know of to opt out of the corrupt, broken, violent, corporat-acrocy system, and there's no better place I know of to do so than here in Mexico with it's lax rules, ample sunlight, easy climate, and nearly nonexistent property taxes.

One big positive is that once our cob house is done, our big, five-year infrastructure project will be complete. So, in theory at least, the above 'con' of being spread too thin should soon start to dissipate. With the infrastructure-building slowing down, many of the stresses we've suffered over unreliable workers and continually breaking equipment and materials should also diminish. The filth factor also. Once we get the house done and some landscaping and better ground cover in place, much of the dirt and dust should also begin to dissipate. The social stresses around volunteer help should diminish as well. With the building done, we won't need so much help.

With these problems solved, the rest of the time we have on this planet can be spent going deep into a wealth of hobbies and interests—reading, writing, cooking, meditating, music, and exercise—all set against a background of learning about gardening, bees, aquaponics, brewing, fermenting, and virtually endless other fulfilling pursuits. In short, abundance is within reach, the ultimate goal of all this striving.

Going back inside to make more tea, I see the near impossibility of all of it. The tea is from a package, produced and shipped from who knows where. The gas for the stove is pure fossil fuels. The cup I drink it from is commercially produced. The water for the tea is pumped to the property using the town's fossil fuel-driven electric system. Of course, I could ultimately produce all of these things without being complicit in the killing system, but a life of that level of self-sufficiency seems impossibly far away.

And how did I—and, to a lesser extent, Holly—ever come so far from having this project be an intriguing novelty and entertaining diversion to being a damned annoying need to be pure, unwavering penitents of the Holy—if not self-righteous—Church of Sustainability?

I'm particularly sensitized by the book I'm reading, *The Sixth Extinction*, which details how a staggering half of the world's entire species of plants and animals are in rapid decline or are already extinct. I've also been affected by the television documentary, "The Years of Living Dangerously," which shows how climate change is displacing entire populations and leading to famine and civil strife the world over.

A passage from another book I read recently, Daniel Quinn's, *Providence*, comes to mind:

"Who can live with a light heart while participating in a global slaughter that makes the Nazi Holocaust look like a limbering-up exercise? We look back in horror at the millions of Germans who knew, more or less, exactly what was happening in the death camps and wonder what kind of monsters those people were. In fifty years our grandchildren (if they survive) will look back at the billions of us who knowingly and wantonly laid the entire world to waste and wonder what kind of monsters we were..."

Following this new thread, I feel both inspired and discouraged. Through this lens, I view what we're attempting here at the ranch as important. But I also consider the way Holly and I are going about it as somewhat of a farce. While we've talked a good line about living sustainably—and, yes, we've come a long way, having learned to build naturally, harness solar, grow food, and raise animals organically—we've also maintained a substantial carbon footprint. Summers, for instance, when things here heat up, we fly the coop and head for the cushy comfort of the United States. We've also continued traveling extensively overseas with a massive carbon footprint and do our fair share of keeping Amazon Prime in business. With every drop of oil we still continue to use through our travel and purchases, we're like those complacent Germans—not only looking the other way but actively participating in wanton destruction and suffering on a planetary scale. Can't we be doing better???

Reasoning further, I question, 'If we do fail at achieving critical, sustainable mass here, isn't that failure due—like the failure of the vast majority of relationships—to a simple lack of commitment on our part?'

Suddenly I feel a new resolution germinating and taking hold deep down in my core. Like a mariner at sea who has passed through storm, and who, with the storm's passing, is released to a still roiling but gradually calming sea and is seeing a swath of light sweeping the horizon from a distant cliff, guiding the way to safety, I understand clearly now the route I must take. I know I must double down on and commit more fully to this ambitious but do-able project of ours and see it through.

I step outside under the brilliant, jeweled, veil of stars—the same ones gazed upon by the ancients—and am filled with wonder. The cosmos, at least, is something that is completely sustainable and incorruptible—something we humans cannot fuck up. The night is calm and quiet save for the background thrum of insect life and the rhythmic pulsing of the ocean in the distance.

Tomorrow, I tell myself, I'll start anew and double down on my effort to find my way here. This property and all that surrounds it is the biggest gift, with the greatest potential, I've ever experienced. While perfect as is without any intrusion on my part, I also feel the land's joy at the prospect of being given purpose and to have all of its disparate, independent voices—plant, earth, animal, and even human—singing together, as one would conduct an orchestra, in order to have it become a place of learning and hope in this troubled world.

Realizing I can, and need, to be doing more to extricate myself from the systematic, systemic worldwide violence, and help raise awareness for others, a newfound sense of commitment washes over me. I feel tremendous relief. Now I'll be able to return to bed, sleep soundly, and rise tomorrow ready to take on whatever comes with renewed sense of purpose and enthusiasm.

July 6, 2015

Adrift on an undulating sea of dreams, I wake two hours later than normal. Holly brings coffee, asks if I'm all right.

"Sure, sure," I tell her. "I was up for a while last night. That's all."

Sitting up in bed, flipping open my computer, and checking emails, a vaguely familiar address pops up in the in-box. Andrew Jones. *That's the guy I wrote to about teaching a permaculture workshop here next winter,* I remember. Andrew, a well-known permaculture instructor operating on the world stage, has done projects with one of permaculture's superstars, Geoff Lawton, and is one of the founders of the eco-village Biosana in the Baja.

Excitedly, I open the message. Andrew says yes, he has some free time this coming winter. He's looked over our project and would be very interested in teaching a permaculture certification course at our ranch! This is thrilling news, and I can't help but imagine it's a harbinger of the rewards my renewed commitment will surely bring.

<u>October 7, 2015</u>

Today, I launch the blog—Sustainable Mexico. In it, I discuss all the ways I believe pursuing sustainability makes good sense here in Mexico. Using our experiences, I explore the many advantages—from virtually nonexistent property taxes ($250 per year for one hundred acres!), to minimal licensing and regulation for food or other cottage-industry products, to plentiful sun that can be tapped for making electricity, pumping water, and dehydrating food. Other advantages include inexpensive labor and lax or nonexistent building codes making natural building much more do-able. Finally on the list is a climate that eliminates heating costs and makes growing food possible all year round.   These things all add up to vastly reduced carrying costs making sustainability achievable with far less effort.

　　Thinking about these things, I realize I love my great, clean, predictable country of origin, but I love my adopted one even more, flawed as it is, and feel I can live better and more sustainably here.

<u>December 21, 2015</u>

The Winter Solstice. We'll strive to be lazy today; however, our solar panels and batteries will have to work extra hard to compensate for the abbreviated hours of sun. Other than that, Sunday comes easy to the ranch. Outside our wide-open screened windows, a deep aquamarine sky gives way to the day's first streaks of pink and gold. High on the ridge, a giant, stately organ pipe cactus stands in mute silhouette against the pinking horizon. In through the window, a gentle breeze breathes 'Good morning' while huge banana-palm fronds rustle 'Buen dia' in a sing-song call and response.

　　Other soft songs of morning begin as well. Listening close, one can hear a far-off rooster in the village doing his part to lift the sun. Then another joins in from our neighbor's hilltop. Finally, our own rogue band of feckless gallos begins their own obligatory chorus. Joining the tuning orchestra comes the hollow "clomp, clomp, clomp" of the timpani drums— baby goats using an overturned water tank as springboard for the day's activities. Meanwhile, Rambo, our new attack kitten, is already in full swing and beginning his training. Head popping out of a laundry basket, he scans the room. Whoops, there's the enemy—a mad pounce at the carpet fringe, brief pause, and then whoa, look out! Counter attack from a blowing curtain sends him flying to the bookshelves for cover. All good practice for the mice and lizards he'll have to contend with later.

Finally, the sound that starts my own rhythm section—Holly in the kitchen grinding the coffee!

✻ ✻ ✻ ✻ ✻ ✻ ✻

After a late start, it's a scramble, but throughout the fall we've managed to nail down plans for the PDC (Permaculture Design Certification) course with Andrew Jones. The registrations have come in at a dribble, and we almost abort, but, by Christmas, we have enough to make it a go. There's a lot of work to do to get the facilities up to snuff after our summer away, but Holly and I are thrilled and giving it our all.

January 17, 2016
Tomorrow the PDC course begins. Holly and I are anxious and excited. The instructors, Andrew and Shenaqua, arrived yesterday, and they're wonderful. Together, we all walk the property and make our final plans. Andrew seems impressed with the general layout and all the demonstration projects we already have in place.

January 28, 2016
Just like that, it's the last day of the PDC course. Tears and hugs all around. It's been a terrific week of learning and loving camaraderie. It's also been super inspiring to be surrounded by people, many of them young, who really get it, really get what we're doing to our biosphere, and yet, despite the seemingly insurmountable challenge of making it right, are committing themselves to being part of the solution.

Andrew is an inspired leader and teacher. Both wise and learned, he's brought a wonderful sense of mindfulness and fun to the multi-faceted jewel of permaculture. Through Andrew's eyes, Holly, Hillary, and I, along with a dozen other students, have learned about all the energy zones and natural resources affecting a property and how to coordinate the myriad elements of plant life, animal life, building materials, solar energy, and human energy into an integrated whole of sustainable, even regenerative, affirmation.

During the weeklong workshop, culminating in a massive, singing, rollicking, hug fest around a bonfire on the beach, we also had numerous skill swaps—everything from dancing and drawing instruction to a talk on creating a mobile, freelance livelihood. (See a video of the PDC at the Rancho Sol y Mar YouTube Channel).

Tomorrow, we'll return to our regular projects with the help of Billy, Lina, Ali, and Beto, stragglers who've opted to stay behind for a while.

With renewed vigor and sense of purpose, our project feels like it's finally finding its feet and walking a buen camino toward a more sustainable future.

February 7, 2016

Today was a good day. Ultimate Frisbee on the beach this afternoon followed by spear fishing. I spent forty-five minutes stalking a big bota fish, trying to get at his hidey-hole. Didn't quite have the cojones (balls) to go down into the crack, particularly with the issue I was having with the snorkel strap coming loose, plus the surge of current going in and out of the little cave he lives in. 'I'll dance with you another day' I say to him, but it comes out all bubbles. The reality is I almost never catch anything and enjoy this more for the challenge of the chase. Things like this are what keep life fun for me.

Now, glass of wine in hand, I'm sitting here on the roof, reflecting, the day's glow of experience melding and flowing with the red and purple hues of sunset. This is my bell ringing. My time to deconstruct the day, reflect on life, and get some perspective.

Still buzzing with head full of permaculture musings from the course, I realize that an aspect of sustainability that often gets overlooked is the importance of fun. If any human activity or project doesn't have an element of fun to it, it has far less chance of continuing long-term and being truly sustainable.

Buoyed by the PDC course, an idea starts taking hold: Why not go all the way in and shoot for a completely sustainable, carbon-free existence? I begin imagining the possibilities and considering the effort it would take.

The more I think about it, the more I realize what a massive undertaking it will be. Not an undertaking as in lifting or hauling, but an effort of the other kind—of the will involved in changing habits. Even in our relatively earth-based existence here, Holly and I are still thoroughly addicted to—i.e. dependent on—fossil fuels. Where would we be without our bimonthly trips to Home Depot, Costco, and all the other stores we shop at in Vallarta, not to mention the truckloads of supplies we drive down from the States every summer?

'Well,' I answer myself rhetorically, 'Maybe I should try to find out! After all, what better place or time to do so. I've got enough staples here to survive. I can grow the quick-producing tropical fruit—bananas, papayas, pineapples, passion fruit, and limes—with both hands zip-tied behind my back, and our fledgling food forest—filled with tens of varieties of longer-term trees such as soursop, star fruit, pomegranate, guava, jack fruit, chayote, fig, and many others—is well under way. I have milk, cheese, and yogurt from the goats; eggs from the chickens and ducks; and fish from the sea. Kitchen-garden annuals can be a challenge to grow in tropical climes due to pests and fungi but are doable. I have no heating or cooling energy needs aside from the refrigerator and fans in the summer, all of which, plus my other ancillary energy needs, are easily covered with the solar photovoltaics, solar water pumping, and solar water-heating systems already in place. Being retired, I don't have to worry about transportation to or from a job.

'OK,' thinking to myself and feeling the first buzz of excitement, 'maybe this carbon-free idea wouldn't be so massive after all. Maybe it would be easy? If I stop expending the time and energy now used for travel and buying stuff, I'll have more of both left over for the things I've been telling myself are important but I never make time for—meditating, music, reading, exercise, and relaxing!'

I see my sense of mobility as representing freedom on one hand, and unconscionably destructive behavior on the other. I consider my fossil fuels use, from the most basic, jumping into the car to go to the next village, Vallarta, or even back to the States, to the most intensive, hopping on and off planes to visit friends and family or to travel purely for pleasure. Can I give this up?

This will also be a tough sell for Holly. Being a major travel enthusiast who started a woman's travel club—and who still has an extensive bucket list of destinations for us to see—I know she'll be disappointed to hear this absurd new idea of mine. Perhaps making it a year-long experiment rather than a cold-turkey, forever commitment will make it more palatable for her —and not quite so overwhelming a prospect for me? Yes, that seems right. I'll try it for a year. That'll be a good challenge and a suitable compromise.

With that the die is cast. I'm not sure how and when I'll make the break with fossil fuels, but I know the biggest hurdle will be changing the lifetime of habits I've built up around consuming and travel. As a longtime student of the Buddhist monk Thich Nhat Hanh's teachings, I'm familiar with the mind training for dissipating habit energy. I know that just like smoking cigarettes, watching TV, eating meat, and other negative habits I've left behind in my life, I'll feel better without them, and, with time, won't even miss them.

For now, that's enough to consider. It's almost dark—time for me to climb down from the roof and help Holly put all the animals into their pajamas, read them a story, and tuck them in for the night.

25 - Animal Tails, Part 4
(Pajaretes, Bee Stings, and Spider Bites)

As Holly and I regain our emotional footing throughout the winter, and I consider a more committed move toward true sustainability, we experience a run of interesting animal events. One ridiculous reptilian episode involved Rogelio, a bilingual Mexican national who was volunteering with us for several months…

February 9, 2016
Egg production by our chorus line of attractive hens has fallen off recently. Investigating, our volunteer Rogelio has discovers that a curmudgeonly old Gila Monster (called a scorpión here in Mexico) has been helping himself to the eggy bounty. Now, I personally find scorpiónes—known for a nasty, infectious bite and for never letting go once they do latch on—to be intimidating. Never one to back down from a challenge, however, Rogelio, using the noose-on-a-pole I'd rigged up for catching snakes, has just captured the old boy and stowed him safely in an Igloo cooler.

Since we have a trip to El Tutio planned for later in the day anyway, Rogelio and I decide we'll take 'El Chapo' (the name of Mexico's most notorious drug lord, which Rogelio has now given to his reptilian captive) along for the ride and give him a new home somewhere along the way.

With hissing El Chapo loaded into the cooler in the back of the pickup, we hit the road.

A few miles out of town we're stopped for inspection at a military checkpoint. After searching the cab of the truck and clearing us to leave, the commander suddenly waves for us to stop again, comes over, and raps on my window.

Zzzzz-uddd. Window down.

"By the way, what's in the cooler?" the commander asks, nodding toward the back.

Oh, man, I'm thinking. *Do we tell him we've got El Chapo in there? Would he find it funny?*

Knowing my history of butchering cross-lingual jokes, I decide to forego any attempt at humor. However, a swirl of other thoughts now has their way with my feeble, paranoid mind. *Is transporting animals illegal? Could it be considered a dangerous weapon? Should I offer a bribe? Or would that make matters worse?* My mind races.

Seeing me in my paralyzed state, Rogelio—native Spanish speaker, former time-share salesman, and all-around natural bullshitter—takes over.

"It's a scorpión, señor," Rogelio replies, leaning over to address the commander through my window. "We caught him this morning and we're transporting him to a more suitable location."

Is he serious? I'm thinking. *A 'more suitable' location?.* Wouldn't the commander wonder why we didn't simply kill the damn thing? And what are a Mexican and a gringo doing cruising the back roads in this big, narco-looking beast of a pickup truck, anyway? I'm sure he's sure there's something fishy going on.

"Can we open it?" asks the commander.

"Yeah, fine, but be careful" Rogelio warns.

"Be careful?" the officer repeats, stiffening into a more alert posture.

"Because there's a scorpión inside," Rogelio reminds him.

After talking to one of his men, the commander scrutinizes us but says nothing. In the rear-view mirror, I can see two soldiers climb into back. They heft the weight of the cooler and one of them peeks under the lid. The moment is tense.

Finally, the soldiers jump down and the first one pulls the commander aside. They talk in a hushed huddle.

The commander returns to the truck.

"Ees a scorpión you hab een ze box," the commander says to me, speaking English now.

"Yes, yes," I affirm. "We caught it this morning."

"How much?" the officer asks, deadpan.

"How much?" I parrot, confused.

"How much wee'll jou sell 'eem for?"

Oh man, he can't be serious, I'm thinking. Is this some sort of a trap? He can't be serious right? Is he fucking with me, trying to get me to blunder into a snare like the one Rogelio caught El Chapo in? Or is it possible he really wants to buy the wretched thing?

Apparently I've frozen up. Rogelio is speaking up on my behalf.

"No, sir, I don't think that would be legal for us to do," he offers. "We're transporting him to a more suitable location," he says again.

Still poker-faced and impossible to read, the commander takes half a step back. Is he pissed? Have we passed or failed some sort of test, or simply pissed him off to the point of arrest this time?

"OK, amigos, have a good day," the commander finally says, motioning us onward as if nothing has happened.

✳ ✳ ✳ ✳ ✳ ✳ ✳

Despite the period of relative calm we've been experiencing this winter, we do have one more tragic animal experience that sets us back.

February 10, 2016

Driving to Villa Del Mar today, I see a spectacular wild cat cross the road in front of me, right by the crucero near the back gate to our property. Orange with spots like a leopard, the graceful, powerful feline, about the size of a German Shepherd, is a beautiful sight.

On returning to the ranch, I pull out a guidebook and identify the animal as Pantera Onca, a wonderful reminder of the wildness of this place.

February 11, 2016

This evening, I'm up on the roof, my favorite sunset hangout. I'm not normally a big pot smoker, but this evening, seeking to enhance the bliss at the end of a good day, I've broken out my stash and am puffing away. Over the ocean, the colors have peaked and are now settling into the deep, soulful purples and blues of coming night.

Suddenly Holly, who's gone out to the goat pen to tuck the ladies in for the night, let's out a scream. "Oh no-o-o. NO-O-O-O-O-O!" She hollars, hysterical.

Vaulting down the ladder off the roof and running for the corral, the flying kite of my rooftop reverie comes crashing to earth. In the middle of the pen, Holly holds one of our favorite goats, Luna, in her arms. There's blood everywhere.

"It's her neck," Holly croaks out. "She's been attacked!"

With all the self-taught veterinary experience kicking in, and feeling myself transition wrenchingly from useless stoner to triage EMT, I rip through the Tupperware box of supplies, pulling out alcohol, cotton swabs, syringes, penicillin, analgesics, and anti-inflammation meds.

"Here, let me have a look," I say, prying Holly's arms from Luna's ravaged neck. Luna, pure white, has the sweetest, calmest temperament of any goat we've ever had, but now she's a writhing, fearful mess. Buzz gone, Holly and I clean up the wounds. Though horrified to see long deep gashes on either side, we' relieved to find that the jugular is intact and the wounds, though gnarly, appear superficial. After dressing the injuries we give her injections, then fix up a pen for her—doing our best to make her comfortable for the night.

"No way those are coyote bites," I say to Holly. "It's the damn panther I saw. I'm sure that's what did it."

The following day, Luna's condition is stable but she's huddled in the corner of her pen, fearful of her own shadow. We decide we'll leave the rest of the herd in the corral for a while until we can redo some fencing that will keep them in an interior paddock.

$$* * * * * * *$$

By Spring, after no further sign of the cat, we begin letting the goats back out to the back pasture. Luna bears the scars of the attack as well as psychological ones. Always timid and fearful now, she never mixes with the herd, and is always hanging back, afraid and alone. One day, months later, she doesn't come back at all. Searching the back forty, I find her remains under a huisache tree, probably the victim of coyotes or the pack of stray, feral dogs that have been sighted several times on the Villa road recently.

Yet another, one-off, wild-animal encounter happened a few weeks after Luna's Panther attack.

February 13, 2016

This morning I'm taking some guests for a hike to Tehua. Emerging from the far side of Lover's Beach, we head up the trail that traverses the cliffs around the headlands. The morning is cool and breezy—a perfect day to show these folks some of the best that Mayto has to offer.

A few hundred yards along the trail, we see a large termite nest that hangs low, about shoulder height, on a tree. Stopping to show the group the nest, I explain that when we have baby chicks to feed, we cut the nests down and bring them back to the chicken pen, the millions of termites inside serving as wonderful, high-protein food for the growing chicks. Swinging my machete, I demonstrate how we feed the chicks each day by chopping a chunk out of the rock-hard nest, causing thousands of squirming termites to spill out. As I take several good whacks at the nest, the group of three ladies and one guy stands behind me watching. I'm confused and then suddenly horrified to see not termites tumbling out but...a swarm of angry bees!

"RUN FOR IT!" I yell to the others, pointing the way up the trail.

With that, the group is in motion—running, swatting, screaming, and crying. I'm using my hat to try to swoosh the buzzing madness away from my head and shoulders while also swatting at the back of the woman in front of me. One of the gals, a big Norwegian woman with blond hair, is screaming louder than the rest, "We're going to die. WE'RE GO-I-N-G TO D-I-E-I-E-I-E-E!!!"

A hundred yards up the trail, the squadron of fighter bees peels off in formation and returns to their base. We, the vanquished, retreating army of giants, lie about the thicket, panting and moaning. Despite having been in the rear, I'm not too bad off and have suffered only a handful of stings. The Norwegian woman is whimpering softly and appears to be in partial shock.

I monitor the situation and am relieved to see the Norwegian woman quickly recovering her equilibrium. She has only a dozen or so stings, so I decide to stay with the group and get them all to Tehua as quickly as possible rather than doubling back for help.

Forty-five minutes later, we're sitting around a table at Liz Adriana's restaurant, drinking cold beer, laughing and retelling the story of the attack, over and over.

February 14, 2016

To make up for yesterday's ordeal, I've offered to take the group of bee-war veterans over to Villa Del Mar for pajaretes (a beverage containing cane alcohol mixed with straight-out-of-the-tap cow's milk and chocolate), the Mexican national breakfast drink of champions. As normal, the usual gang of Sunday suspects, a group of men from town are gathered at Jorge Espindola's corral, chatting and enjoying the morning. They're all happy to see me pull in. The four, hearty-looking women and my one guy friend pile out to join them in the corral.

Jorge's brother, Lupe (pronounced 'Lew-Pay'), hands each woman a big styrofoam cup with powdered 'ChocoMil' and instructs them to go over to Jorge who's seated on a stool beside a cow, smiling and beckoning. Taking the cups, Jorge's big cowboy hands squeeze and squirt warm, frothing milk into each one. Looking unsure, the women take their cups to Lupe, who pours a healthy slug of cane alcohol into the frothy mix. Timidly, the women take a sip. Smiling wide, chocolatey, 'Got Milk' smiles, they drink the beverage down, several helping themselves to seconds and even thirds. Meanwhile, cup in hand, I circulate around the corral, shooting the breeze with the local guys.

"Daniel, why don't you come on the Cabalgata to Talpa with us this year?" one of the cousins pipes up.

"Yes, join us," the others all nod and grin enthusiastically.

The Cabalgata, which I've heard about before, is a week-long horseback pilgrimage to the sacred city of Talpa, far up on the spine of the Sierra Madre coastal range.

"Porque no? (Why not?)" I respond, hearing the buzz of the pajarete talking.

Driving back to the ranch, my guests are all singing and laughing. The morning's breakfast drink sloshing about in our bellies is both nutritious and fun, and yesterday's drama is a distant memory.

* * * * * * *

Yet one more bizarre animal episode rides into town on a dream a few days later...

February 16, 2016

I'm dreaming that our cat, Rambo, is trying to wake me up. He's clawing me in the buttocks; however, in my dream, Rambo only has a single claw.

Now I'm in a nether world, half awake, swatting at Rambo, telling him to leave me alone.

"Ow!" Holly says. "You just hit me."

"Oh, sorry. I must have been dreaming," I say, getting up to go to the bathroom and realizing that Rambo is nowhere around.

In the bathroom, I notice there's something wrong. My eyes are stinging. They feel like they've got sand in them.

Rubbing them on my way back to bed, I also notice feeling odd and light-headed. "This is strange," I say to Holly, who's on her way past me to take her turn in el baño. "My eyes are all scratchy, and I feel kind of dizzy."

Returning to the bathroom, I stand under the shower for a minute, rinsing my eyes. That doesn't do it, so I get out the eye wash and try that. Tipping my head back to use the rinse, I nearly pass out.

"Whoa," I call to Holly. "Something really strange is going on."

Concerned now, she's in the bathroom helping me. After using the wash, I'm heading back to bed when, oh boy, I feel dizzy and again nearly lose consciousness.

"Holly," I say, "I'm going to the car. I need to go to the hospital. Bring my clothes."

We're in the car, me pulling clothes on and Holly driving through the pitch-black night toward Vallarta. Driving through the mountains, I nearly pass out several times. At one point, a horse appears at the side that sets off a hallucination—a fragmented trail of horse-like images flowing along beside the car. Later, I notice I've been scratching an itch on my butt cheek for some time, and I suddenly remember the dream.

"I think maybe I've been bitten by a spider," I tell Holly, who's ashen with worry and driving like Mario Andretti.

After an hour and a half, we're nearing Vallarta, and I'm beginning to feel a little better. The stinging, itching eyes and the dizziness are subsiding.

Pulling over on the outskirts of town to see if the symptoms will keep diminishing, we both are on our iPhones researching spider bites. We don't find anything conclusive but do find mention of the symptoms I've been having in a couple of places. Neither are the most common effects of a spider bite, but it seems to be a possible cause.

Another half hour and the symptoms are nearly gone. Turning the car around, we head back to the ranch.

Exhausted, and with the sky just getting light, we arrive home. After stripping and remaking the bed, we crawl back in and dive into sleep.

✳ ✳ ✳ ✳ ✳ ✳ ✳

Finally, finishing up Season Ten or Twelve or whatever it is now, we have one more bizarre little animal episode...

February 18, 2016

"Dan, Dan, wake up! I think there's something attacking the chickens!"

Donning my headlamp and pulling on shorts, I snatch up my twenty-two-caliber rifle and am out the door in a flash, followed by Holly, who's wearing nothing but a bright red hoody. On the way out the gate, Holly grabs a machete, and the two of us rush across the yard, unlikely super-heroes heading after some unknown villain. Out in the chicken coop, there's definitely a ruckus going on.

At the coop, we immediately see the problem—a good-sized possum is scaling the wall. The chickens on the perches are cackling in terror, still sounding the alarm. As much as I hate killing anything, I know possums will tear through a chicken coop, killing simply for the sake of killing, so I'm resolute about what needs to be done. Frozen in my headlamp beam like a convict caught by a searchlight, the loathsome animal turns and hisses at me with a hideous toothy grin.. Leveling my gun, I pull the trigger, and, with a loud crack, the possum falls lifeless to the ground.

Now Holly is taking up the action, swinging her machete with surprising zeal. Chop, chop, chop, like Lizzy Borden's unstoppable ax, the machete blade falls on the expired animal.

"You motherfucker. You stay away from my chickens!" she yells, her shouting syncopated with the blows she's delivering.

Standing back a safe distance, I watch the gruesome spectacle by the light of my headlamp. Truly, I've never seen Holly like this before. Wearing nothing but the red hoody, delivering blow after blow to the bloody mound of possum pulp, she's still yelling profanities and showing no signs of letting up.

"Hon, hon, it's OK. He's dead," I say to her.

"He's a possum, dammit," she replies, panting and swinging. "They act like they're dead, but, but…" Coming to her senses, she starts slowing up.

Note to self, I think while watching the spectacle, *never even joke about eating one of Holly's chickens.*

The chickens' terror has now turned to laughter, and yes, Holly's's starting to laugh too. We're all laughing in comic relief—me, Holly, and the ridiculous chickens. But not the possum. He's quite dead. I'm sure of it.

✳ ✳ ✳ ✳ ✳ ✳ ✳

We were still laughing about the image of Holly in nothing but her red hoody, swinging her machete, when, a few days later, a more ominous animal episode invades the fun roll we'd been on…

26 - The Rise and Fall of Poor Old Colorín Part 1

Together with Fernando we had purchased Colorín (pronounced Color-een) about five years ago. The running joke was that Holly and I had gotten the 'bad end of the deal'—which meant Fernando had purchased the front end so was responsible for the feeding, while Holly and I had purchased the back, so we were responsible for clean-up. Fernando loved Colorín, and with cold Corona in leather Harley Davidson beer holder attached to the saddle, Fernando could make Colorín dance like a Lipizzaner.

 The other two horses we had were much more aloof. Not Colorín who'd often stop by the house looking for snacks or whinnying 'hi.' He'd also make the rounds down at The Lower Hamlet, checking in with guests and making small talk—the chattiest horse since Mr. Ed.

 Owning Colorín over the years was a wonderful experience. The biggest problem we had with him is vampire bats. I'm not kidding. Vampire bats. Probably because of his blood type, the bats, which are common here, made Colorín their number-one target. Once the sun set, the bats would find a succulent spot, usually on the side of his neck behind his ears or even the soft tissue around the anus, and lick the fur away with an anticoagulant, analgesic saliva that makes their work so discrete that a large animal like Colorín doesn't even notice it is happening.

 Once, when we arrived home in the car after dark, Colorín, ass pointing toward us, was blocking the drive. Standing in the headlights, Colorín turned and revealed a vampire bat splayed out on the side of his neck. Poor Colorín freaked when I jumped from the car, yelling and brandishing a machete.

 We ordered Colorín a full cover-up for protection including a spiffy head mask that Holly brought back from the States. The outfit, which we put him in most nights and started calling his pajamas, looked like a super-hero costume. Either it worked to scare the bats away, or else it made them laugh so hard they couldn't suck straight. Either way, he was less of a bloody mess in the mornings than he'd been without it.

February 19 - 23, 2016:

For half a year now, our three geldings, Colorín, Canelo, and Chepipwe (Chepe), have had their run of the back of the property. Today, I've decided it's time to bring them forward and re-socialize them with humans. Planning to go on the annual cabalgata with some of the local caballeros this year, I have to start training whichever horse I decide I'm going to take. I'd prefer to take Colorín, but he's getting older and isn't strong as Canelo. It'll be a toss-up.

 I start the move to the front pasture with Colorín, since he's already at the gate, looking for grain and a bit of loving. The other two horses ostracize Colorín, and he's usually alone looking sad and forlorn. He's looking particularly crappy at present from the many months he's been out back without proper care. I notice he's thinner than normal despite there being plenty of rich, green pasture available, so he's overdue for his worming treatment. I dose him with the standard anti-parasite medicine and suffer a pang of guilt over having left him out back unattended for so long. Once watered, bathed, and fed, I let him loose to explore the overgrown front pasture, which is chock-a-block with fresh, tasty forage to munch on.

Watching Colorín over the next several days, Holly and I both begin to worry. Head drooping and coat looking terrible, we decide to fetch Victor, a teacher at the high school in Villa Del Mar who has moved to the area recently and who is, supposedly, a university-trained veterinarian. Arriving at the ranch, Victor confirms what we suspect. The worming medicine I gave Colorín didn't sit well with him, probably the result of a heavy load of parasites attached to his intestinal walls all dying off at the same time and creating some internal bleeding and possible intestinal blockage. Victor doesn't seem overly concerned, however, and gives Colorín a shot of antibiotics.

"Keep him tied so you can control his eating. Alfalfa's best, not too much grain, and give him his meds once a day for three days. Don't worry, he'll be fine," Victor tells us before we drive him back to start the day's classes.

Over the next several days, Colorín improves enough that we put him back in the main pasture with the other two horses.

A week later, and still thin as a stick, he's starting to droop again. I let him out to graze along the road, deciding to bring him back up to the house in the morning to better feed and keep an eye on him. The fact that we're about to leave for a week for our daughter Aja's wedding in Austin will be a challenge, however.

In the morning, Hillary is walking fast up the drive toward the house. "Have you seen Colorín?" she asks, half out of breath.

My first alarm bells sounds.

"He's lying in the road and won't get up!"

Crap, crap, crap! sounds my internal mantra. "Where is he?" I ask, full-on terrified now.

"He's down by the turnoff to my house," Hillary replies. "He's been there since last night."

"Since last night?"

Now, switching over into damage-control mode, I'm thinking hard, weighing possibilities, running through the decision trees of possible outcomes and worst-case scenarios while the body part of me is in solid motion, grabbing the bucket containing feed and a lead rope, and running down the road.

At the bottom of the drive, I find Colorín stretched out with his face in the dirt. Head rising as I approach, his eyes are drained of life. Brain still whirling, I'm arranging the burial in my mind, or, if he doesn't die, planning the contingencies, since we'll be gone for a week. Sickening thought, but Nacho, our trusty backhoe guy, will have to be called right away. We'll need to get on his schedule to come pre-dig a grave in case of the worst.

In the meantime, I manage to coax Colorín, staggering, to his feet and lead him back toward the shelter of our yard. *This place really never wants us to leave*, I'm thinking to myself, mind jumping ahead and imagining calls back and forth from Texas, probably in the middle of the wedding ceremony, getting updates on Colorín's condition and making difficult decisions.

But, for now, thankfully, he's walking well, or andando boracho (staggering like a drunk) more like. Almost to the house now, I'm calling out to Holly, "I think he's OK," when, kerplunk, he's down again, grunting and snorting. "Crap," I mutter to myself, the brief candleflame of hope snuffed out again.

Jumping into the car, I head over to Villa for Victor.

Finding Victor should be easy, since he lives with the rest of the teachers in dormitory housing—a cement bunker of a building at the far end of the abandoned, littered athletic field. Victor's is the last of four cell blocks in the building. His door is always open, metal-frame bed bare except for a lumpy pillow and threadbare sheet bunched at one end. Clothes strewn over the single chair or on the floor, Victor is usually there, lying in bed reading or sitting at the flimsy card table grading papers. Seeing the empty room now, I feel sad that Victor—well into his thirties, noble in bearing and bald as a cue ball, and who, we've learned, teaches veterinary medicine weekends at the University in Tepic, six hours away—should have to live so shabbily. I make a mental note to tip him well when this is over.

Back in the schoolyard, the janitor woman, child in tow, is sweeping leaves out of the dirt courtyard. "Victor? Yeah, he left early for a run on the beach. He should be back any time," she informs me.

Finally, Victor arrives, jogging clothes noticeably damp with sweat from the morning's run on the beach.

On filling Victor in, he's convinced that Colorín still suffers bloat from the parasite die-off and recommends a different medicine that I'm certain I don't have on hand. Agreeing to go with me to El Tuito, an hour away, to make sure I get the right stuff, Victor hops into the car, not even bothering to change.

This is how it's done here in el campo (the country). With almost nonexistent phone service, and marginal Internet, 'sneaker net' still prevails as the go-to means for tracking someone down, getting help, or making an appointment. It's definitely a big part of what keeps life here so spontaneous and unpredictable. Coupled with this spontaneity, everything, and I mean EVERYTHING, is taken in stride, with little thought given to veering hard off the day's path to help someone out. It's a beautiful dysfunction and a constant lesson for us.

Back from Tuito with the medicine, Victor doses Colorín and demonstrates to us how to give the follow-up injections ourselves. He also takes a blood sample, which I load into a cooler with ice and immediately head to Vallarta.

The following morning, we receive the results of the blood tests and learn that Colorín has Anaplasma, a life-threatening parasite. This new knowledge precipitates another consult with Victor and another run to El Tuito for different meds, but, by day's end, Colorín's been dosed up and seems to be doing a little better.

The following morning, Colorín is back on his feet and, though weak, he's eating well. Relieved, it looks like we'll catch a break this time.

February 24, 2016:

Tomorrow, we leave for Aja's wedding in Austin. Today is packing day, plus the usual fifty thousand things that pop up at the last minute before leaving what we fondly refer to as 'The Bubble'. Even though we'll only be gone five days, the pre-flight checklist is long. I start out just after sunrise, making the rounds, trying to bring everything up to snuff, as we'll be leaving before Yamir and the two building interns show up for work. Both water storage cisterns full and food forest watered: check. Solar batteries topped off and fully charged: check. New sack of grain unloaded and mixed with corn for the chickens and ducks: check. Anything vulnerable to rain stowed in case there's one of the rare winter storms that only seem to hit when we're away from the ranch: check.

All through the drill, I've had the still-sick Colorín in the back of my mind.

March 1, 2016

Our trip to Austin is a fabulous celebration of our daughter Aja and her wife Jamie's wedding, surrounded by family, long-time family friends, and scores of Aja's and Jamie's extended, roller-derby family. It's been a wonderful time, but, all through it, I've been worried sick about Colorín.

Now a week later, we're back at the ranch and find Colorín doing pretty well. He's definitely lost muscle mass and is looking lackluster, with ribs well defined in the afternoon sun, but hey, he's got a decent appetite and is walking around fine, so I'm confident that he's on the mend. I won't be taking him on the ride to Talpa as hoped. But he's alive and functioning, and I call that enough.

27 - The Ride to Talpa, Part I
(La Subida - The Going Up)

For years some of my local caballero (cowboy) friends have invited me to go along on the ride to Talpa. The week-long, three-hundred-kilometer horseback journey to the pilgrimage city of Talpa De Allende, high up in the mountains of Jalisco. In the past I've declined because Holly's birthday falls the same week. This year, knowing of the recently renewed invite, Holly has graciously encouraged me to go, and I've made the commitment to be a part of the expedition. Despite feeling trepidation, I vow to be on the ride, come hell or high water (hopefully not both).

The route on the Cabalgata is a series of trails and dirt-track roads that lead straight up from the coast onto a main spine of the Sierra Madre Occidental Mountains. I'm imagining my leathery, unkempt compadres disagreeing every couple of hours about which fork to take, and my gentile, vegetarian sensibilities challenged by the offerings of dried beef, days-old tortillas, breakfast tequila shots, and whatever form of rodent gets hunted along the way. Having recently killed two rattlesnakes here at the ranch, I also can't help but wonder, 'How does one keep snakes from snuggling into one's warm, inviting bedroll there by the coals of the dying fire?'

Though only ten of us will be going on this pilgrimage, we'll be in good company, as tens of thousands make the journey annually from all over Jalisco and Nayarit, usually on foot, but, in the more extreme cases, crawling on knees or even prostrate for stretches.

While religion is the driver, our group's motivation is also very much about male bonding and camaraderie. If nothing else, for me, it will be the ultimate immersion into country-speak Spanish, the slang-ridden local dialect I've struggled with for many years now. I'm seeing it as the best opportunity imaginable to take my integration here to a deeper level.

Layered onto this is the chance to play out one of my most powerful childhood archetypes—that of the rugged cowboy traversing mountains of adventure, bedroll and tin coffee pot strapped to the saddle. As I approach sixty years old, the opportunity for this kind of therapeutic role-playing is rapidly diminishing.

Early March, 2016 (two months prior to the ride)
The Ride to Talpa begins with getting the horses in shape. But also, one's butt!

With Colorín still recovering, I decide my mount for the journey will be Canelo. At about fifteen years old, Canelo is a bit old for such a trip, but he's stocky and strong, and I'm confident he'll make it OK.

The die now cast, I sip my coffee and think about what I've gotten myself into.

Yamir arrives for the day's work, bright and bristling, and, as is often the case, he's practically clairvoyant, already a half step ahead of me.

"Daniel," he starts in. "Escuché un rumor que intentes montar a Talpa con los muchachos de Villa! (Daniel, I heard a rumor that you intend to do the ride to Talpa with the boys from Villa Del Mar!)"

"Sí, es la verdad," I reply, marveling at the speed, and accuracy, of the rumor mill here. "Christ, amigo," I say to him, "you can't fart here without everyone in Cabo Corrientes knowing what variety of beans you've been eating."

He laughs and, without skipping a beat, proceeds to deliver a machine gun, country-Spanish-speak sermon about how my training needs to start immediately!

"Which horse are you taking? Canelo? I think you should take Canelo. He's the only one strong enough to make it all the way there. You're going to need to start training. You need to ride at least a kilometer up the beach, twice a day. This isn't just for the horse, you know, but for your nalga (ass) too. If you don't do the training, Canelo might keel over halfway there, and you could die of saddle sores. Eight full days of riding, you know. You're going to have too much fun! The Espindolas are going again this year. They like to party and ride like Pancho Villa. Maybe their cousins Juanito and Jorge too. We're going to need to get you in shape, prontisimo, amigo! And Canelo will need shoes!"

It's always like this with Yamir. Nothing is ever short or simple. With an exuberant brightness, he's constantly probing and prodding.

So yes, Yamir. Today we can begin working Canelo and start to make this thing real. Like so much in life, my initial impulse is fear, but right behind it comes the shove to push through. Part of the fear is ego—not wanting to appear foolish. I'll need to build up my endurance and get better at the riding itself. Though competent, I'm not without fear of these big, potentially unruly beasts, and a trip through the mountains will put my novice horsemanship skills to the test.

Another part of the worry has to do with Canelo, the chestnut-brown Mexican quarter horse I'll be relying on. A number of years ago, I rode Canelo in a roundup, moving a neighbor's cows to our back fields. Never before or since have I experienced such bonding with an animal. We were pushing the herd of unruly bovines right down the main street of town, people laughing and flapping their arms around, trying to help keep the wild-eyed beasts from veering off into yards, gardens, side streets, or into their stores.

Suddenly a huge bus rolled through, scattering the herd in every direction. Throughout that afternoon, Canelo repeatedly read my signals, cutting this way and that, often at a full gallop, heading off stragglers and driving them back to the herd. An amazing experience that I'll never forget.

But, aside from that day, Canelo has always been a total brat—even more so lately because he's been left out back for months. He bites, he kicks, he's mean as hell to the other horses, and he nearly killed our dog Chanchito last year with a nasty kick to the head. Still, Canelo is a comfortable ride and, of the three old timers, he's the only one with the remotest chance of being able to get me all the way to Talpa and back.

April 24, 2016 (three weeks prior to the ride)

I start my training regimen today. Everyone says that a month of riding will get both butt and horse in shape. Now, with less than three weeks to go, Canelo is still fat as a sausage, and my butt is about as muscular as mantequilla (butter).

"Your ass is gonna be hamburger," Yamir teases me, holding the reins as I toss the saddle over Canelo's ample back, preparing to ride him for the first time in months.

Yamir, over the past couple of weeks or so, has been increasingly anxious that I start training 'right away!' Knowing Yamir as well as I do, I can't help wondering what his angle might be.

"OK, Yamir, I get it. You've made a bet with your friends, haven't you?"

"Huh? Que? What are you talking about, Daniel?"

I've got him now. This is my favorite part—that sweet second or two when I can catch him off-guard and have him thinking I know something he's up to, or that I might have gotten the jump on him in some other way.

"No, really, Yamir, I appreciate that you've at least bet for me rather than against me."

Now he's definitely taking the bait.

"What the hell are you talking about?" he asks, anxious to get back to his comfort zone—controlling the spin on the conversation.

"You've bet that I'll survive the ride. I appreciate that," I deliver deadpan. "Your friends are betting Canelo will die, or I'll come crawling back crying. That's why you've been so anxious for me to start training. How much do you get if you win and I make it back OK? You need to split it with me, you know."

"Ah, pinche Daniel…", he shakes his head with a half grin, finally getting the joke.

Heading out through the back of the property, the sun is peeking over the hills to the east, streaks of light highlighting golden tufts of guinea grass; proud, Spanish moss-draped guayabillo trees with their glistening, smooth green bark; and colorful, flitting Orange-breasted buntings with their iridescent indigo backs and shocking, orange undersides.

What took me so long to get to this? I wonder. And why are so many things like this—simple life pleasures right here at hand that dumb inertia keeps me from taking advantage of?

What a waste it is to always be consumed by workaholism—that self-important self-image of working all day and being productive—rather than the subscribing to the importance of not missing out on the things I love most. Simple things. Usually things of little or no cost, and so easy and accessible here. Getting down to the beach for a swim every day, for instance. And remembering to take my fishing rod or snorkel for that extra bump. Giving myself the nod and knowing it's OK to pick up the guitar or a go for a walk on the property with Holly, read a book, or simply swing in the hammock. What's the blockage that constantly keeps me from indulging in these things?

Well, I'm doing it now. Riding a horse out through the back gate in this spectacular morning light. And I've got a great excuse to do so every day for the next several weeks. Yeah!

May 11, 2016 (four days prior to the ride)
Late afternoon and I'm ready to kick back and relax with a glass of wine when our dogs, Chanchito and Pirate, sound the alarm:

"Arrfff, arrfff, arrfff, Someone's coming! Someone's coming, arrfff, arrfff!"

In a cloud of dust, half the guys who'll be going on the cabalgata pull up to the house in a variety of vehicles—a muffler-less motorcycle, a ridiculously decrepit pickup truck without any doors, and a homemade Mad Max cross between go-cart and dune buggy, low to the ground and painted florescent orange and green. They're here, as promised, and only a couple of days late, with the farrier brought in special from Tomatlán to shoe all our horses for the trip.

With TEN-TIMES-TOO-LOUD, distorted banda music blasting out of speakers mounted to the frame of the dune buggy, beers are passed around and the farrier, a gruff, no-nonsense hombre, pulls his gear from the back of the pickup and sets to work.

"Is he going?" I ask Cesar while motioning to Piri, one of the group. Cesar, the youngest, handsomest, most well-groomed of the lot, is the only one of the group who speaks any English.

"Sure he is," Cesar responds. "He's always gone. He's small, but he's tough."

At five-foot-two and weighing in at around ninety-five pounds soaking wet, Piri is the 'special' Espindola brother. Often mumbling something unintelligible but apparently happy enough to be a part of the tribe, he seems to be an often ignored but essential component of the group.

For months my caballero friends have been telling me my horse is much too old and fat for the journey. But I know better. My golden-brown gelding Canelo is a stocky, handsome fellow, and his age is debatable. Several of the guys going on the trip claim to have known Canelo back when they were boys of eight or ten, putting Canelo's age at more than twenty. Seizing the perfect opportunity now, they once again make sure to remind me of his advancing years.

"Daniel," one of the guys pipes up "who's older, you or your horse?"

"I'm pretty sure he's the first horse I ever saw," another chimes in.

"Pfshaw, that's bullshit." I posture as if I have some clue of what I'm talking about. "Our vet from Vallarta floated his teeth last fall. Says he's eighteen, tops."

"I'm pretty sure my grandfather owned him before Jorge's dad," pipes in Juanito. "That would put him at, hmmm, let's see, about fifty."

Laughter and more beers passed around. Blaring banda music punctuated by the farrier's tap, tap, tap, clip, snap, and rasping sounds.

Turning their attention now to Canelo's ample girth, the group begins to make jokes about his portly figure. Beyond humiliation, Canelo's eyes are bugged out in sheer terror and he looks at me pleadingly as his hooves get filed, sawed, nailed, and hacked into shape.

"Daniel, are you sure he's not a cow?" Jorge asks, sending the group into beer-spewing laughter.

"Daniel, you could sell him for chorizo and buy two regular-sized horses!" Lupe advises thoughtfully.

Despite the laughter and bravado, I have to admit, if only to myself, I'm concerned. For nearly a month now, I've been working Canelo steady, trying to get him in shape. I've hired Efren's son, Freddy, to ride him mornings for an hour or two, and I've been on him myself, almost daily, over to Ipala, an hour away and back, and working him up to decent running form on the beach. Despite limiting his feed and singing him the theme from "Rocky" every morning, I haven't managed to cajole the roundness out of his ample belly.

With the ride to Talpa less than a week away what's left of my cocksureness about Canelo's ability to make the journey is fading. A thought comes to mind: Do they make diet pills for horses?

May 10, 2016 (Cabalgata, Day 1)

As planned, we converge on Don Juan's house, ready to leave well before sunrise so as to make El Tigre up in the foothills before the sledgehammer sun begins its work in earnest. The inky darkness is lit by a single, bare, fluorescent bulb beside the house and the random, jerky, flashlight beams of the other guys arriving. Not much talking now as gear gets organized in the back of the white pickup truck, 'La Gringa' that will provide our logistical support, and saddles are given their final adjustments. I feel jittery and awkward—out of my element.

After dropping off my gear, I sling myself up into the saddle and ride over to wait with two others, Jorge and Lupe, under the eerie glow of the town's one yellow streetlight. Canelo is restless and paws at the dirt, picking up on my nervousness, no doubt. One by one the riders assemble—cowboy ghosts in the pool of light—big, good-natured Jorge on his giant roan; Don Juan and son Juanito on their undersized mules; Brian, the only other gringo (although practically Mexican, having lived here half his life); young, handsome, well-groomed Cesar on his equally beautiful white mare, Chula; wild, crazy, bald-headed Lupe; and, last but not least, Piri, the scrawny, toothless, special brother.

The mood is hushed but excited as the group nods greetings to the new arrivals and we all check our gear. Like brethren of a biker gang north of the border, we're all wearing matching 'chaleco' vests adorned with a large embroidered patch on the back—a horseshoe emblem with the words 'Cabalgata 2016' and 'Villa Del Mar' around the outside. This year's vests are something of a disappointment, being that they're cheap Naughyde rather than real leather as were the cabalgata vests of the past, but no one says anything about it.

"New hat?" Juanito asks Cesar, admiring the perfect, white cowboy vestment.

"Every year," Cesar answers, grinning and tipping his fine new sombrero to Juanito.

Finally, the group is gathered and ready to leave.

"Single file," announces Don Juan. "Daniel, you follow me."

With that, we fall into formation and go cloppity-clopping up the hill to the small village church.

In the pre-dawn darkness, the group of men is subdued, with only the clomping sounds of the horses and soft jangle of tack breaking the night's silence. All family—brothers, cousins, uncles, or, at the very least, related by marriage to each other—it's a ragtag group, to be sure. Despite his modest size and disheveled appearance, Don Juan, whom the group all calls "Chido," is clearly the alpha cowboy of the lot.

Next in leadership is the other gringo, Brian, who manages all of the construction at Hakuna Matada, the most significant gringo property holding in the area. Brian impressively manages to be both a good friend of these guys and also patrón and boss to many of them (throughout the days ahead, I'll often marvel at how thoroughly Brian has assimilated Mexican campesino culture while deftly blending the roles of both patrón and friend).

Jorge, Chido's next youngest brother, is a handsome, robust fellow. Mustachioed and classically Mexican looking, he owns the largest herd in the area and is host of the Sunday morning pajarete gatherings—the one I took the bee attack veterans to.

Next in the lineup is Lupe, a rugged, virile, bald-headed, Yul Brenner lookalike who scares me a little. Nice enough guy, often smiling and joking, but I get a mild volley of warning flares when around him.

Following Lupe is Juanito my longest-running friend here, Chido's son, and the youngest of the group.

Bringing up the rear is Piri.

Completing the team are our support members—noble, quiet Gilberto and his even quieter son, Pancho, who will be driving La Gringa and meeting us at our overnight stops along the way.

At the church, Chido jumps down from his mule, goes up the steps of the open structure, and switches on the light—a single bare bulb hanging from the ceiling midway to the altar. Following suit, the rest of us dismount, tethering our horses to whatever bush or tree is handy. Mimicking the others, I take off my hat and follow up the steps.

Now begins an odd ritual of cowboy prayer, the ten of us holding hands in a circle by the altar, heads bent, assembled around the ring of hats that we've placed at our feet. Chido leads us in a rambling benediction: "Padre Dios, benedictanos en esta viaje sagrado (bless this sacred journey we are about to undertake). Keep us safe from the perils of the trail and help us avoid temptations of the flesh that may lay in wait for us. Please,

Father of all Fathers, bless and protect our noble horses, our families who await us, and our truck, La Gringa, that will make the journey with us."

It's reassuring to know that our truck will be protected.

Following the blessings, Chido switches off the light, and we mount back up, the starry shimmering black curtain overhead a true firmament.

Going down the hill, we pass once again under the streetlamp and then turn left onto the main dirt road heading south out of town along the coast. As we leave the outskirts, the stars overhead are joined by an ethereal flashing of fireflies across the fields, signaling our departure. Added to the light show, occasional sparks are kicked up by the hooves of our newly shod horses striking rocks in the road, and handsome Cesar's face and perfect white hat are stage-lit by the iPhone he's checking one last time for Facebook messages is icing on the visual cake.

Ten minutes later, we pass through Ipala, the next town south. As the thinnest hint of daylight starts showing off to the left, somewhere in the village the strains of banda music, announcing the day, have already begun.

Hanging back a bit, I watch the group of silhouettes—riders and horses—pass through puddles of light cast by the town's handful of streetlights. It's a dreamlike, ethereal scene.

By midmorning, we leave the main coastal track and begin following a trail inland toward the mountains. Mist hangs in the lowlands, and the air is fresh. Passing over a small rise, the three or four riders ahead are silhouetted against the orange blaze of sunrise.

We begin passing through majestic stands of old-growth hardwoods— giant Caoba (mahogany) trees; bright-yellow, blossoming Prima Veras; grand, sweeping Parrotas; and gnarly barked Avios—all punctuated by massive, twisting agave plants, some of them head-high, even on our horseback perches. Taking this all in, I can't remember a land so stunning.

Even my hardened compatriots, who make this trip every year, seem caught up in the glory.

"Daniel, Daniel. Look, up ahead. An orchid tree!" Chido says, reaching over, grabbing my arm, and pointing as we ride by an amazing specimen—a sprawling hundred-foot-tall tree completely covered in orchids.

Passing through another grove, Juanito pulls up alongside and is grabbing at me as well. "Look, Daniel, these are all Capomos!" he says grinning and gesturing toward the stately giants that produce an abundant fruit similar to coffee and which the indigenous peoples long used as a sacred beverage.

The excitement of the trip—and the appreciation of Nature we're experiencing—is palpable, and it's wonderful to see this softer side of these otherwise tough, crude, Mexican cowboys.

Then, along with the rising sun comes the obligatory cowboy's breakfast drink: tequila.

"Piquete de verga? (prick of the pecker?)" offers Chido, grinning, handing me the traditional gourd canteen that hangs by leather straps from his saddle. The gourd gets passed around the group as we ride and, even though the harsh bite of tequila burns, it feels like the appropriate way to meet the long, tough day ahead.

With the tequila burn, I begin wondering about breakfast. "Hey Lupe," I ask, pulling up alongside him, our horses settling into a perfect cloppitty-clop rhythm with each other, "Umm, are we going to be stopping sometime for breakfast?"

Lupe looks at me sideways and laughs but says nothing. I imagine him putting his own spin on the classic line from the movie, 'Treasure of the Sierra Madre:' "Breakfast? We don't need no stinkin' breakfast!" My stomach grumbles a feeble, acidic protest. We ride on.

At some point early on, Juanito coins a joke that becomes a running theme for the trip. He's fallen behind, probably having stopped to adjust the ridiculous, full-sized pillow he's brought to sit on to compensate for not having gotten his butt in shape for the trip. The group stops in the shade to wait. Trotting up the road from behind us, Juanito calls out, "No me dejes sonso," (Don't leave me ravaged—"sonso" being a currently popular slang word for leaving one's partner sexually ravaged). In an effected, nasal, feminine voice, he stretches out the last syllable "No me deje s-o-n-so-o-o-o-o..." in way that cracks everyone up and, almost immediately, others are repeating it, each trying, in turn, to perfect the annoying accent.

And so, in the manner of all good guy trips (and girl trips too, I imagine), we have the official journey joke, usually a simple word or short phrase like this one, that will get repeated, ad nauseum, throughout the duration.

Near noontime we come to Highway 200, the main, two-lane road that runs south along the coast. The rush of cars and trucks is jarring, a violation of the spectacular nature we've been riding through. Crossing the highway, five or six of us huddle in the shade of a billboard, waiting for the others to catch up. There's a moment of tension as each rider times his crossing to the cars and trucks going by with their violent swoosh of noise and wind. After just one morning riding through wilderness, our world has already become more primitive and peaceful. It's clear that our horses feel it too—threatened. Horses are like that. Not smart in the way of dogs—or even goats, burros, or pet parrots—but smart in their pure, raw sensitivity.

Then, right on cue, as the last of our motley crew has crossed over the asphalt no-man's land, La Gringa pulls up for our final rendezvous check-in before we head off into the remote interior. There, in the splayed rectangle of billboard shade, a few snacks are passed around, gear adjustments made, and plans are confirmed with the driver for this evening's rendezvous spot. Then we're off again, leaving our accommodating billboard standing alone.

'Wait. I hate being stuck here. I want to have an adventure too. I want to come with you!' I hear the billboard, wearing a faded announcement for last year's political candidate, crying out.

The highway is the last of any significant civilization we'll be seeing for several days, and the riding now takes on a more serious rhythm. Passing through several nameless villages, we slowly begin our ascent into the mountains. Parts of this stretch are truly sublime. On one memorable tract we ride along a straight dirt path between fence lines surrounded on either side by a vast plantation of palmas reales, the type of palm used for thatching the roofs of palapas in this region. Doctor Seuss-ish in their appearance, the palmas reales are beautiful and odd, their gangly trunks topped by surprising shocks of spikey, punked-out 'hair.'

As the heat comes on the day, the easy banter of the morning yields to a silent, serious, determined plodding of hooves on hard-packed earth.

Another hour in and the landscape has changed to a more barren scrub as we ride ever upward to meet the blazing sun. With the lush tropical woodlands behind us, we ride through another, long, trench-like path carved into the earth between the fencerows, a meter below the level of parched, hardscrabble fields of corn and sorghum.

Driven by the heat, the wind whips up to a near gale, carrying a curtain of dust as thick as a blanket. One by one, each of the riders reaches back and digs through his saddlebag to find and don whatever bandana, sunglasses, or other protection he has available. Head down and squinting, I glance up and wonder at the spectacle—a stoic, sepia line of trudging caballeros making their way toward an unachievable horizon, wind whipping dust motes off the hooves of their mounts in what could be a scene straight out of a classic Sam Peckinpaw western.

Finally, we're riding through a more forgiving, wooded glade.

Entering yet another shabby, forgotten town, ragged dogs run alongside, barking. Pulling up to the town's only indication of commerce—the ubiquitous aborrotes tienda (variety store)—with one large sign announcing 'Chido's Paraiso (Chido's Paradise)', we stop for lunch. Our own Chido, Don Juan, greets the owner with grand slaps on the back. Several others of our group, veterans of past cabalgatas, follow suit and greet this doppleganger Chido. It's clear to me that this apodo (nickname), Chido, is reserved for leaders, and that the two Chidos present enjoy the same leadership status.

As the newbie, gringo, quick-study, I'm careful to watch how the others remove the horses' bridles ('frenos' or 'brakes' as they're called here) and loosen the belly strap so the horses, too, can have a bit of a respite. Sitting at plastic tables or straddling the low cement wall in front, the men wearily pass around big, two-liter bottles of Coke as the owner's wife brings out steaming plates of beans, rice, and fresh tortillas.

Lunch soon over, we're back on the trail.

By mid-afternoon we're beginning a more serious climb. Passing out of the barren, lowland terrain, the hillside we're moving up grows increasingly dense with old-growth forest closing in. Following several hours of this, we pass yet another biological demarcation where the spectacular hardwoods give way to an arid landscape of agave, long-needle pine, and jagged outcroppings.

This is some of the most glorious scenery I've ever seen, and though tired, I also feel exhilarated—almost high.

As the day begins to cool, some of the earlier jocular teasing and joking returns.

"Oye, gringo," Juanito calls to me from up ahead, pointing to the massive, meters-high, phallic profusion of a century plant, "that one looks like my chili, only smaller!"

Though a lame attempt at humor, after ten hours in the saddle, we all crack up like children.

Riding into yet another shabby village, with the usual pack of mangy dogs yappity-yapping to announce our arrival, we make our way to the parched brown, soccer field—our home for the night—where La Gringa is waiting. As the fire is stoked and tents and other gear are unloaded, I help Chido bring grain to the horses tethered near a stream running alongside the field.

After a fine dinner of fried fish, I string my hammock between a set of goal posts and am fast asleep.

May 11, 2016 (Cabalgata, Day Two)

Today has been a blur. Rising steady into the mountains, we've passed through a variety of landscapes—dry, open fields; gorgeous, old-growth stands of pine and hardwood; and steep, jagged vistas hinting at even greater mountain grandeur ahead.

As dusk approaches (or perhaps it's us approaching it?), we pick our way along a forbidding canyon trail until, just before dark, we pop out onto a wide dirt road. Another kilometer on and we arrive at a roadside posada—a rustic guest house carved out of the hillside—equipped with an ample corral. We dismount, pull off the saddles and tack, and turn our horses and mulas out for the night.

Canelo has been struggling and sweating excessively for the past couple of hours. As everyone settles in for the night—hanging hammocks or laying out bedrolls on the long, open veranda while waiting for a dinner of sizzling strips of carne asada grilled by the innkeeper's wife—I return several times to check on him, jealously securing him extra rations of alfalfa and a bit of extra grain. Talking softly, I do my best to convince him he's doing a great job of it, but inside I'm worried about tomorrow's crossing of the mighty spine of the Sierras we've caught glimpses of throughout the day today.

"Don't worry, old boy, I know you'll do fine. You always do," I tell him unconvincingly.

Next, it's time to find the right spot to bed down. I settle for a spot on a shed-like porch where my buddies Juanito and Pancho have already hung their hammocks and are settling in for the night. Beside us, just outside the porch, a giant pig, snorting and snuffling, seems none too pleased with our intrusion.

Just as I'm drifting off, Juanito comes flying out of his hammock, cursing and flailing. Silently, an army of ants has risen up out of the underworld and is overwhelming our quarters, the advance forces having swarmed up the post, down the hammock line, and into Juanito's sleeping bag!

"Pinche hormigas! (fucking ants!)" he yells while stomping about in his underwear and swatting uselessly with his pillow at the surging mass of vicious, biting arthropods.

Pancho and I are up now too, laughing and shining our flashlights about while trying to avoid getting bitten. Others who've been milling about in the kitchen arrive to investigate the commotion. The ants, which seem to have multiplied by some dark magic, have taken over the entire ramada. Juanito, Pancho and I, having abandoned our roost, are with the rest of the guys who are doubled over laughing at the sorry state of our bivouac spot. Even the grumpy old pig is having a good laugh.

The ants, meanwhile, amassing for a final, decisive invasion, are fanning out, flooding the entire patio, scurrying up the posts of the ramada and marching forward to doom or victory. Just when all seems lost, the innkeeper's wife arrives to our rescue. Armed with a bucket of soapy water, she begins sloshing bowlful after bowlful of the pungent liquid over the undulating hordes. Drawing into itself, the ant army begins retreating, the momentum of the battle having turned in our heroine's favor.

With good, hearty, tequila laughs, the lot of us pass the bottle one last time before turning in again. The pig, attempting to downplay his embarrassing show of good humor, returns to his more respectable, curmudgeonly posture, grumbling his steady disapproval of our presence throughout the long, cold night.

May 12, 2016 (Cabalgata, Day 3):

After the pig-snorting, tequila-drenched, hammock-strung, ant-invasion-dream night, the arrival of sunlight is an unwelcome jolt. Chido, our tireless leader, is already up, rummaging about, calling out jokingly, "Danyell, get over here and help me get this lazy-ass, good-for-nothing horse of yours fed and ready!"

"Yeah, yeah, coming," I call over, tumbling out of my hammock and pulling on my jeans. A mere forty-eight hours in, and I'm already starting to hallucinate.

After a nothing breakfast of too-sweet coffee, watery scrambled eggs, and leathery tortillas, we're back in the saddle, continuing upward, the pass we're heading toward a seemingly impossible quest. By the time the sun is cresting the peaks, Canelo is already faltering. With each rise and switchback, I fall farther behind. Juanito, on his undersized, lumpy-gated mule, hangs back repeatedly to wait for me.

"Daniel, maybe you shouldn't have been feeding your caballo so much flan before the trip," he jokes.

Rising up ahead of us, the mountain pass, still more than a mile away, looks ominous.

Now the entire group has stopped to wait for me at a sharp bend in the road. Always in control, Chido takes charge.

"Daniel, you change with Piri. It's the only way that old nag of yours is going to make it."

As much as I'm embarrassed for my boy Canelo—that buffed, ornery, stud of a horse whom I'd hoped would be one of the most macho of the bunch—I realize Chido is right. Without the switch, Canelo may not make it over the mountain passes that lie ahead. Reluctantly, I switch mounts with Piri. Even after adjusting the straps, Piri's feet barely reach the stirrups and flop loosely to the sides. Meanwhile, now straddled across Piri's pint-sized mule, Piroline, my feet are practically dragging in the dirt. With the adjustment made however, Canelo, carrying sixty pounds less weight, is much better able to keep up, so I'm relieved.

Midday, and we're getting nearer the first pass. Crossing to the east-northeast, we traverse several open glades of tall grasses and rambling, griselda-berry thickets. The views over the valleys to either side are staggering. As we continue along an abandoned logging road, Chido abruptly shouts, "Atajo!" and veers off to the side.

Thinking he's said "a taco," I'm confused. Then I realize he means 'a shortcut,' as our leisurely morning jaunt turns into a fast-paced thrill ride. All of us catch the buzz and begin splitting off, finding our own routes through the undergrowth, dodging and weaving our way steeply up and up and up toward the ridge. Pulling my camera out of my bouncing saddle bag, one hand on the reins like the movie-star cowboys of my youth, I record, in video mode, the headlong rush of reckless energy. Up ahead, the thinning pines and scrub give way to ever more spectacular vistas as Jorge, atop his massive yegua (mare), Lila, a full head taller than the rest of our group's mounts, is in his glory, laughing and throwing himself forward in perfect rhythm with the horse's graceful, lumbering strides.

Finally, topping the ridge, horses snorting and still excited, we dismount. From where we stand on the single-track dirt road, a narrow walking trail leads even further up to the left toward the peak. Tethering our horses, we walk the final hundred meters and come upon an ornate shrine set into the rocks with mountains dropping away on all sides. Hats off and heads bent, the group gathers around, crossing themselves. After prayers, we all gather for a photo op, taking turns passing our cameras and smart phones around.

Soon after, beginning our descent, we come to a fine, shaded viewpoint where La Gringa is waiting, fire already blazing and breakfast ready: instant coffee and packs of multi-colored, sugary cookies as the morning's fortification.

Following 'breakfast', we cross two more passes before beginning our final decent, all but hurling ourselves into the valley below. The horses, glad they're no longer fighting relentless gravity, follow the pull and gain momentum. The switchback dirt road we're on reveals vista after vista out toward the grand highland valley we're headed toward, a vast, manmade grid of farmland.

Finally, the track empties out onto a long, straight, cobblestone road. Riding past low stone farm houses, we cloppity-clop along together, grouping up into threes and fours, making small talk and allowing the horses—which feel the excitement of our destination nearing—to break into an occasional gallop before settling back into a more reasonable amble.

After noon, we arrive at the outskirts of Talpa. Crossing a bridge and joining a larger artery, Chido starts barking orders. "OK, muchachos, chalecos on (put on your vests!) and form up, two by two. Daniel, you're up front with me!"

As we ride past the big park down a long boulevard and on to the central plaza, onlookers turn, smile, and occasionally clap for our modest procession, though we're far from being novel in this city that plays host to thousands upon thousands of pilgrims each year.

We reach our destination—the Cathedral Nuestra Señora del Rosario. A dozen or so of the group's family and friends wait for us outside the Cathedral, dressed in their finest clothes. Horses tethered and hats off, we enter the church just as Mass is beginning. We're only a small part of a throng of hundreds of worshipers including several large pilgrimage groups, each identifiable by the coordinated t-shirt or workout-suit uniforms and colored logos, which, like the patches on our vests, identify the group's town of origin, Talpa, the date, plus a flame, cross, or other pilgrimage symbology. The church is crowded and we have to settle for standing in the central isle, everyone but me crossing and uncrossing themselves.

Hanging back to take in the spectacle, I try to open myself to the fervor, but, as is usually the case in situations like this, I feel conflicted and disconnected. While I marvel at all the passionate devotion and belief, I'm unable to let go and become part of it, tainted by the certain knowledge of how destructive the Catholic Church—with its potent political structure and endless hunger for power and control—has been in this world. Standing here, watching like an alien, I accept that I won't experience the catharsis I was secretly hoping for on this sacred pilgrimage. Worn thin by the trail and feeling a bit lost, I find myself mourning the numb, rational part of myself that will never be able to be swept away on the waves of total surrender like all the others here.

28 - The Ride to Talpa, Part 2
(Talpa)

After Mass, we move to benches in the park in front of the church. Wives, cousins, and close friends who have come by car to meet up with us are all in a giddy, festive mood. There are several mariachi and banda bands circulating the grounds and, after a group decision, Lupe goes over and hires a fine-looking group to play for us. Juanito goes for six packs of Corona Light and bags of chips, and there, in God's front yard, the party has begun!

The beers flow and the music blares for hours. Not surprisingly, these country cowboys can really dance, especially Lupe, who, still wearing his spurs, is busting crazy dance steps with his beautiful, robust niece, Elena. Watching Lupe dance, I realize that my initial feeling of being frightened of him has melted away completely. The smiles and joking I thought insincere have turned out to be genuine, and he's proving to be one of the happiest people I know.

Chido and his wife, Estella, dance sexy and close as if their wedding day—thirty years past—was only yesterday. Numerous bystanders join in and it's a full-on fiesta in the happy churchyard.

Even Piri, who's managed to score a bottle of rumpopo, the sickly sweet, rum-and-eggnog-like beverage that's a specialty of the region, is shuffling about in an attempt at dancing. When not taking slugs of the beverage, Piri has it stashed securely in the bulging back pocket of his oversized, gathered-tight-at-the-waist-with-twine jeans.

Coming on nightfall the crowd thins. The band is paid, empty beer cans collected, and our group heads off, well lubricated and swaying, to turn our horses out to pasture in a large vacant lot not far away. Reuniting with friends and family downtown, we tuck in for dinner at some relative's restaurant where we're toasted for our accomplishment and given the royal treatment by everyone present. Finally, exhausted—or at least I am—we make our way to the hotel that's been booked for our stay.

The owner, an old friend of Chido's, shows us to our one, large, dorm-style room. But something's not right. There are ten of us overripe, trail-weary cowboys, but only five beds. Hmmm. Am I understanding this correctly? In my head, I do the math several times, each time coming up with the same unwanted answer—ten divided by five equals two. There's going to be two of us to a bed!

Without further ado, all the guys start pairing off and deciding who's going to be sleeping with who. Chido, of course, wants me, his pet gringo, by his side. I acquiesce, which turns out well because, before long, he heads out to a party with his wife and friends, leaving me the bed to myself, possibly for the entire night.

Meanwhile, the rest of us settle in for some well-deserved shut-eye. At least that's the way I'm hoping and expecting it to be. It's close to midnight now, and we've been riding, praying, and partying since before sunup. What's left to do but sleep, right? Ha. Silly me. As I'm stretching out, completely zonked, a spirited discussion starts up—a sudden breeze on embers of a fire that I thought for sure was going out.

Juanito: "What do you guys want to do tomorrow?" (Tomorrow is one of our two days free before heading back.)

Lupita: "We have to take Daniel (Dan-yéll) up to the mahplay forest!"

Pancho: "Hell no, you stupid cocksucker. The waterfall. We have to take him to the waterfall!"

Most of the rest of the group join in: "Yeah, definitely, the waterfall!"

Brian: "OK, then, amigos, what should we bring to eat?"

Jorge: "How about those excellent tamales that Chido's cousin makes?"

Lupe: "No way, man. I'm sick of all the pussy food we've been having. I'm ready for some carne asada."

The group: "Yeah, me too. We've got to have carne asada!"

Goofy Piri, who hardly ever says anything except in mumbles to himself but who has been sucking on that bottle of Rompopo all afternoon and is definitely feeling the spirit move him, says; "And chiles. Grilled chiles. I want grilled chiles! I'm gonna have grilled chiles!"

The group chants hysterically, "Chiles, chiles, Piri wants chiles! He's got to have chiles!"

The raucous joking goes on like this for nearly an hour, as I lie here feeling shellshocked.

Finally, finally, the commotion settles down.

Timidly, I ask if anyone minds if I turn out the light—a great glaring fluorescent bulb hanging from the middle of the ceiling.

"Sure, no problem," several of the others reply.

I get up and switch out the light. It's nearly one in the morning. I can't remember being so exhausted.

Then, like an errant spark on that stupid fire that refuses go out, Cesar crosses the room, using the line of beds like a pontoon bridge. He reaches for the TV mounted high on the wall, and turns it on. He surfs through the channels until, fresh breeze igniting those damnable coals again, several of the guys simultaneously shout, "The soccer game is on!" and are instantly up out of bed, hooting and hollering.

"That's it," I roll over and tell the wall. "I'm done. Spent. Cooked. Destroyed."

But also, somewhere in the reptilian recesses of my mind, despite my own flame having gone out hours ago, there's still an ember glowing. Here it is, I realize suddenly. Here's the cathartic pilgrimage revelation I've been hoping for—or at least some twisted version of it. Here's the joyful, enduring, effervescent heart of the Mexican experience, found unexpectedly in the form of a smelly, half-drunk, exhausted, beautiful, bro-mantic, two-to-a-bed, one-in-the-morning, pilgrimage-infused television soccer game in Talpa de Allende.

Rising from the ashes, I sit up in bed, take the bottle that's handed me, and rejoin the fray.

May 13, 2016 (Cabalgata, Days 4)

After breakfast we stop for provisions, and have a quick check on the horses who are happily munching alfalfa in their corral at the edge of town. Piling back into La Gringa, we head out to the waterfall. Spirits are high, and the air has a crisp, bracing chill to it even though much of the valley we pass through is covered by a gloomy carpet of smoke from the post-harvest, slashed-and-burned fields. Heading back in the direction we'd come the day before, we turn off the main road and follow a winding route up a side valley.

Pulling off at a bridge with a good-size creek running underneath, we unload our bounty—iron cooking grill, coolers filled with meat and beer, towels, and several aluminum lawn chairs and pick our way upstream. At the point where my arms are ready to come unhinged from helping carry one of the coolers, we reach our destination. It's a dramatic, hundred-foot-high waterfall and picture-perfect swimming hole. Perfect except for the trash. Apparently, we're far from being the only ones that know about this spot, and an impressive collection of partiers' garbage has accumulated here over the years.

This, sadly, is one of those reminders that, as much as one might love this beautiful country, it's far from an idyllic paradise.

Today, however, I'm in for a pleasant surprise. Digging into one of the bags of supplies, Chido pulls out several large trash bags and passes them around. Then, by unspoken signal, we fan out and begin a serious cleanup. Impressed and encouraged, I feel another surge of respect for this ragtag group of traveling companions.

After stripping down to underwear for an initial swim (poor Piri's underwear sagging precariously from his skinny frame like a surrender flag), the crew sets about gathering leña (firewood) and preparing the meal. Jorge, our resident salsa chef, grills tomatoes, tomatillos, and chiles and ritually crushes them into the stone molcajete he's brought for the purpose. Onions and garlic are chopped, meat sliced thin, beers popped open with the butt-ends of cigarette lighters, and a fine Mexican comida is underway.

Siesta follows, with leathery cowboy bodies stretched out on whatever rock, tree trunk, or smooth patch can be found.

The rest of the day is spent whooping, hollering, splashing, and diving from the rock cliffs facing the pool.

May 14, 2016 (Cabalgata, Days 5)

Today, our second 'day at leisure,' the guys are excited to take me to see a special reserve called Los Mahplace, or something like that. They're all jabbering over breakfast, telling me about the amazing forest there. It's not until one of them explains that the trees have leaves like the one on the Canadian flag that the lightbulb goes off and I realize the name of the place is actually 'The Maples'. But how can this be? Maple trees in Mexico? I have my doubts.

An hour later, we're winding our way up a switchback road on a beautiful, old-growth-forested mountainside. Turning off at a parking area and trailhead, a sign for the reserve does indeed say, "Silvestre de Los Maples" (Forest of the Maples). Following a hiking trail down a steep ravine, I feel as though I've been transported to the White Mountains of New Hampshire. Rather than the arid, subtropical landscape I've grown so accustomed to, the forest here is a unique micro climate—a museum replica of a northern forest with luscious, green, deciduous trees everywhere. Then, there they are, maple trees! The guys all want to be the first one to show me the leaves.

"Yes, yes, these are definitely maple trees. The exact same ones we have back where I came from in New England. And yes, yes, they're one of the main trees in Canada too. And yes, really strange to see them here," I tell the group.

The next couple of hours of hiking is like being on an elementary-school field trip. Playful and excited by everything, the guys scamper up fallen tree trunks, leap over bubbling streams, and lock arms around some of the larger maples to demonstrate the great tree's girths to me. Every new mushroom or caterpillar is handed around to everyone in the group— rough-and-tumble cowboys oohing and ahhing over the simplest of things.

And there's still one more place they're excited to show me. Another twenty kilometers up a steep grade the road dead-ends at a parking area. Through the thinning stand of pine trees, I can see the great, jagged spine of the Sierra Occidental range dropping away on all sides. We hike a short trail to where the last of the trees gives way to a bold outcropping of rock. Scampering and climbing to the peak, the guys all pass phones around and take photos of each other from every possible vantage point. The view from here is stunning—a 360-degree mountain panorama that rivals any I've seen before. This is it. After three grueling days on horseback, two hours by truck, and a last climb by foot, we've reached the top, the apex, of a most memorable journey!

By the second night in Talpa, the buzz and inspiration of being in this sacred city has begun to fade, and we find ourselves holed up in large, modern sports bar directly across the street from the looming cathedral. Under the shimmering, fluorescent glow of big-screen TVs, I marvel at the efficient symmetry of the locale—drink and carouse here and then cross the street to pray for forgiveness. Repeat.

Dinner is a savory, nutritious mix of Mexican bar food: popcorn, a cardboard-based pizza simulation, and cold Vienna sausage links.

The Ride To Talpa:

This page from upper left: Brian Mitchel Wallace, Canyon Edge, Pine Forest, Cesar & Juanito, Jorge, Morning Prayer
Next page from upper left: Las Minas Trail, Pajarte Breakfast Stop, Fine Cesar, At The Homestead

Photo Page 4 (The Ride To Talpa)

29 - The Ride to Talpa, Part III
(El Regreso - The Return)

May 15, 2016 (Cabalgata, Day 6)

We have many kilometers of riding ahead of us today. We leave the sleeping city of Talpa de Allende in darkness. The streets are still save for hooves striking cobbles and the occasional madrugador (early-rising) vendors we pass carrying bundles of merchandise or opening up their tin food stalls for the day. Aside from cups of coffee or sweet corn atole purchased from the one open food stall we find, we begin our day, as usual, with grumbling, empty stomachs—at least mine is.

Leaving behind the last, glowing pools cast by the city's streetlights, we cloppity-clop out into the countryside, a sliver of growing moon and a vast, shimmering curtain of stars overhead. The air is frigid and other than the plodding hooves, we ride in silence. Beside me, Cesar is making one last check of his iPhone, face and hat lit eerily like the first morning, some past lifetime ago.

By mid-morning we're starting to climb, but still no breakfast. Man, these guys are tough. "Don't worry," they tell me when my questions about food take on a desperate tone, "we've got a special breakfast planned for you today!"

Passing through a tiny, alpine-looking village, we turn off the main track and pull up to a large, well-kept corral that's terraced into the rocky hillside. Coming out to greet us, accompanied by a raucous gaggle of barking dogs, is a dapper gentleman and his heavy, country wife. Tying up the horses, we scramble up fences and stone walls of the picturesque corral for more photo ops, and to watch as the husband and wife prepare our breakfast.

I should have guessed it. Parajetes! The guys all laugh at the fine secret they've managed to keep from me all morning!

May 16, 2016 (Cabalgata, Day 7 + Holly's Birthday)

The return trip takes us on a different route, more north through the quintessential old mining town of Cuale and up past the newer strip mines—giant scars carved into the breasts of mother earth. Following the narrow mining roads, we come upon vistas more dramatic than anything so far. Rivaling views of the Colorado Rockies, though rendered even more spectacular from the back of a horse, great bulwarks of stone fall away many thousands of feet toward the coastal plain below.

Our only encounter all afternoon is with two campesinos hauling fen-ceposts in a old, rusty, green pickup truck that crawls along the tortuous path like a prehistoric reptile.

At the final ascent over the massive hurdle of rock, the road peters out to a little more than a walking trail and then practically to nothing. For an hour more, we inch our way upward in single file until we're forced to dismount, tugging and cajoling our fearful horses and mules over a rough, jagged obstacle course of car-sized boulders. Just inches to our left, the ground drops away into the dizzying void.

After this last challenge of nerve and rock, we continue down and down and down until, once again, the landscape begins opening her arms, welcoming us back to the foothills.

At lunchtime, we stop at a series of pools in a beautiful river that feeds one of Jalisco's main reservoirs, Cajón del Peña. Saddles and clothes off, we lead our horses into the pools, washing them down, splashing each oth-er, all laughing and playful.

Stretched out in the shade after lunch, saddle bags for pillows, I find new insight into that wonderful word 'siesta'—a nap so good that it's a celebration

Following the river farther down and crossing over at a broad, shallow stretch, we stop, mid-current, for a perfect photo op—a gnarly group of bandana-ed desperadoes atop horses snorting and pawing at the flowing water.

Farther on, along the gravel banks, we ride through a grove of huge, full, guamúchil trees laden with ripe, red, twisted seed pods. Moving from tree to tree on horseback, the lot of us pick great handfuls of the bursting pods, laughing out loud as we fill our mouths and stuff our saddlebags with the delicious, cottony, candy-like fruit. With the treacherous part of the journey behind us, a wide, rambling river alongside, bountiful gua-múchil trees overhead, and the comfort of home less than a day's ride ahead, a sense of joyous celebration takes hold of the group, and we all begin laughing—at nothing at all.

I realize in this moment that I love Mexicans! I truly do. Experiencing these beautiful men who've all had to struggle and toil so hard to get by, I'm blown away by their seemingly endless joy and enthusiasm.

But it's more than that. Here's the thing. If I were ever to be in a life-threatening, survival situation, any of these guys would be my first choice to have at my side.

Hmmm. What's this new diamond revelation I'm feeling? Cabalgata enlightenment? Spiritual epiphany? Exhaustion?

I came on this ride with a vague hope for something profound. Maybe I'll have a real breakthrough with learning the country speak, I'd thought to myself. Or perhaps I'll be struck dumb by some understanding of real faith that's always alluded me. Doubtful, but maybe... Now, however, I see in crystalline flashes of light shimmering off the river beside us, that revelation can be much more subtle and simple. Like Dorothy waking up after her crazy dream, I feel as though I've found my way home.

Well, almost home...

"Aiye-e-e-e!" Fine Cesar is yodeling up ahead, thrashing his mount into a full run along the river. The rest of us, mouths still full of guamuchile and stuffing last handfuls of it into saddle bags, pick up the jubilant call to action and go chasing after him.

Late in the day, we cross over one, last, jagged ridge, and with it, one final stretch of atojos—the steep, winding short-cut paths that cut the corners of the switchback roads we've been traveling on. We're all weary and happy now, definitely ready to be back in our own beds.

Finally, the gravel track empties us out at Highway 200, the familiar coastal highway. We have to wait because the intersection we've arrived at is a mile-long snarl of traffic and heavy paving equipment. Waving and clapping, the highway crew defer to us, ushering us past a long line of stalled traffic. Soon we're nearing our last significant milestone—the town of El Tuito, the municipal seat and our bivouac stop this final night.

"Challecos on!" cries Chido. "Single file!" And here we go now, cheesy naugahyde vests on, proud, triumphant, clomp, clomp, clomp, riding alongside the highway into El Tuito.

Unfortunately, our homecoming in Tuito is sown with a bit of confusion. We arrive at a vacant lot prearranged for us to corral the horses for the night, but, beyond that, there's disarray about what we're doing for dinner and where we'll be staying. The lot of us slink around, completely spent, awaiting direction. Finally, La Gringa arrives and, after some debate, it's agreed that we're to bivouac here in the corral with our horses for the night.

We pitch our tents or string our hammocks to whatever we can find (I string one end of mine to the tailgate of La Gringa and the other end to an old truck trailer parked at the property, while several of the other guys lay out their bedrolls on the rock-hard truck bed rather than bothering with the tents), then saunter, stiff and bowlegged, into town. After more indecisive rambling, we decide on a new restaurant owned by a friend of Juanito's—an ambitious combination of blaring banda music, big-screen soccer action, and the usual lame bar food.

After rounds of cervezas and yelling at mute TV screens, we stagger back to our undignified campsite at the edge of town. Two of the guys, poor pathetic Piri and jovial, good-natured Jorge, never bothered to set up their bedrolls. Exhausted, they opt for the front seat of La Gringa and curl in together.

Rocking in my hammock, I marvel at the mass of stars streaking back and forth overhead, and then pass out.

May 17, 2016 (Calbalgata, Day 8)

Well, this is it, the final day.

As usual, we strike camp in darkness and are saddled and on our way as the first sounds of banda music and church bells begin wafting across the town.

We're clomping down the very familiar stretch of pavement that runs from Tuito in the foothills to the coast. Behind us, a crimson sunrise bathes the fields of maize and sorghum in a luminescent glow.

An hour in, we take the left-hand turn I've always wondered about—the one with two signs: "Bioto" and "Reserva de Jaguar." Despite all the incredible vistas of the past week, the stretch here is still, by any measure, magnificent. Once again, as they did the first day, members of the group delight in pointing out precious finds to me, the newbie, as well as to each other. Here a giant strangler-fig vine has woven and wrapped its way up a massive caoba tree, while there a pair of spectacular, multi-colored Guacamaya parrots break cover and fly off through the forest.

Stopping at a tienda comunitaria (community store) in the tiny village of Bioto for soft drinks and snacks, I ask the owner about the jaguar reserve.

"Yes, that's Don Jose's place," the store owner responds. "He gets a generous ayuda (support) from the government for the project. I think he had a jaguar there once."

Riding on, we're almost out of the mountains by late morning. The group is nearing home turf now, the pace picks up a notch, and there's a palpable sense of excitement taking hold.

A bit farther on we're slowed.

Passing through a narrow connecting path between parcelas, we come to a desolate, depressing scene—a broad, open swath of felled woodland half a league wide and twice as long. The low, sprawling foothills ahead reveal a shamefully naked landscape being cleared to make pasture.

"Must be old José Louis is getting ready to grow his herd again," comments Jorge.

Trunks and limbs of old-growth trees lie broken and defeated for as far as the eye can see. Amidst the carnage, smoke rising from smoldering piles of burned brush lends to the gloomy, apocalyptic atmosphere.

We ride on silently, picking our way through the sprawling wreckage.

Soon, our route comes to a steep ravine we'll have to cross, but the trail is blocked by an impenetrable mass of fresh-cut timber. The group falls silent except for an occasional swear word under the breath. "Did they have to take every last tree?" Jorge complains to no one in particular.

"Pinche motherfuckers," Juanito adds.

Ahead is a group of paisanos squatting by a small stream, machetes at their sides, taking their morning comida.

"What the fuck are you guys thinking?" Cesar starts in, angered by the carnage, but he's immediately cut off by Chido. "They're working, guey. Earning a living like everybody else," Chido says to Cesar reproachfully.

As we ride on, I refrain from asking any questions that would probe the disconnect between these cowboys' wondrous love of Nature and the fact that every one of them, either currently or sometime in the past, has raised cattle on land cleared the same way. Nor do I mention anything about the connection this scene shares with the heavy consumption of the beef they so love. As in every other corner of the globe, Nature's sacredness is second in priority to the appetites of humanity. Perhaps I'll share that awareness some other, less emotional, time, but for now, I'll hold my tongue and ride on in silence.

At the edge of the next cleared field, we come to a hill we have to traverse. At this point, the trail we're following is blocked by piles of noble, fallen tree carcasses.

"So how do we get through?" Lupe asks to no one particular.

We all dismount and begin trying to pick our way through the tangle, leading our horses on foot.

"Here, you all wait," Chido commands, handing me the reins of his mula. "I'll go ahead and scout a way through," he says, words already dying behind him as he disappears into the tangle ahead.

After five or ten minutes, the group grows antsy and discipline breaks down.

"I'm going to go see if he's OK," Brian announces.

"I'll go too," says Juanito.

"Hell, let's all go," pipes in Lupe.

With that, we're all scrambling up and over logs and branches, making our way up the treacherous hillside. By the time we crest the first ridge, we're all completely scattered and calling out to each other:

"I think I've got a good route here," someone shouts.

"Me, too. I'm already at the top," another chimes in.

"Where's Piri? Has anyone seen Piri?" yet another voice calls.

"I've got him. He's here with me," Jorge's voice booms from somewhere off to the side.

"Awie-e-e-e, awie-e-e-e!" comes a shout from the next ridge top. It's Chido, who seems to have forgotten to come to get us once he found the way.

"Stick to the left, back toward the bottom of that other hill," he calls out. "It's clear going after that."

"What about your damn mule? I've still got it," I call out to Chido. Having a second mount in tow has made my scramble all the harder.

"Good, bring it," he shouts back.

Arghhhh, I'm thinking. A week on the trail will reveal the rough spots in any saddle.

Emptying out onto a large flat valley, we pass one last stretch of downed arboreal soldiers and smoldering charcoal fires before leaving the great, sad wasteland behind.

Following a broad, flat arroyo, enthusiasm returns and we all break into a joyous race toward the waiting coast. The horses, knowing they are on home turf, need little prompting. We're all in full gallop along the sandy riverbed, whooping, hollering, and splashing through occasional pools of water and dodging and weaving our way past various obstacles— looming boulders, fallen trees, and large piles of sun-bleached flotsam halted halfway on its journey to the ocean the previous rainy season, and stranded here since.

Slowing to a trot, we pass out of the riverbed and follow a dirt road that runs alongside.

"That's my house up ahead," says Lupe, pointing to a dwelling and cluster of trees atop a small rise. "This is my parcela," he adds, waving an arm to indicate a fine, broad acreage, hundreds of meters wide.

The country here is beautiful and lush with magnificent trees resembling willow and cottonwood lining the sides of the arroyo we've been following. Windrows of stunning Prima Vera trees are adorned in masses of brilliant yellow blossoms that appear to have been put on especially for our arrival. Overhead, billowing white clouds of imagination drift across the crystalline blue sky.

After a brief organizational stop at Lupe's house, we set out on the final stretch, soon reaching the main gravel road linking the villages of our region along the coast.

"Chaleco's on!" calls Don Juan Espindola one last time.

At the crossroads, where the road we've been following meets the main road, a small red pickup truck is waiting. In the back of the truck is a three-piece mariachi ensemble. On cue, they strike up a lively chorus, and the truck pulls out ahead of us, leading the returning heroes into town.

Turning at the same intersection where we'd first gathered under the solitary streetlight a lifetime ago, we follow the mariachi truck toward the church on the hill. Riding two by two, Chido insists that I ride up front with him at the head of the procession. A good-sized crowd has gathered to welcome us home, and we arrive at the church to enthusiastic clapping and congratulations.

In the church, a short, final prayer of thanks is given. Much of the village is on hand to join in thanking El Señor de los Señores (the Father of Fathers) for having given us safe passage.

After that, the crowd moves together en masse to the open air "Salon de Eventos"—a palm grove with picnic tables—a few blocks away. Barking dogs, ragged children, teens on bicycles and motor scooters, heavy-set mothers carrying babies, and scuffling old timers all join the procession. At the grove, the mariachi band climbs out of the truck while hardly missing a beat. Bowlfuls of birria (goat stew) are scooped from large steaming vats, plated with rice and tortillas, and passed down the tables along with endless rounds of ice-cold cervezas.

Overhead, clouds drift across the majestic blue. Looking down, they smile great puffy smiles and wonder what all the fuss is about. The palms below wave back their friendly saludos.

30 -The Rise and Fall of Poor Old Colorín Part 2

June 17, 2016

Well, this should be an interesting day.

Dawn rolls in on schedule, and I'm up to meet it, already worrying about the morning ahead. My current distress is what's to become of Colorín. The new round of blood work came back clear of Anaplasma, but he's still a pretty sad-looking bag of bones. On top of being frail, fresh grass from the season's first rains has given him an epic case of diarrhea—new insight as to why they call it 'the trots'. With Holly off at language school with her sister, I'll have to handle the situation alone.

A quick look out the back window to where I have him tied to keep him from eating more grass and… WTF? He's gone! Having been a commercial fisherman in my younger days, I'm confident of my knots. But nope, a second look and, definitely, he's gone, rope and all!

My dominant thought is I hope he hasn't gone down to the pond, which is one of his favorite places to hang out and graze. In his staggering, weakened state, the mud there would be tough for him to extricate himself from and, if he falls, a rare horse drowning could result. But hey, I'm staying in the moment and not jumping ahead to all the possible worst-case scenarios, right?

I know I need to go look for him, but I've also got other things pressing. A big item on the docket for the day is keeping everything moving forward with the backhoe that's cutting a new, less steep road up to our kids' building lots. That, and having to find out from the workers why so little was done yesterday while I was away in Vallarta (the "Big Shitty"). The backhoe brought in for the roadwork has a new 'chofer' (chauffeur as locals here call heavy-equipment operators), one I haven't used before, and, so far, I'm unimpressed. Aside from getting the machine stuck precariously on the side of the hill within the first half hour on the job, he and his helper have already called me twice this morning on the walkies to get me to fetch them things they forgot to bring with them such as drinking water (!), brake fluid, a machete, and a chainsaw.

Having a sick horse and backhoe here at the same time gives rise to another issue bubbling up in the scummy pond of my brain—the potential burial. Handling funeral arrangements for animals gets more complicated the larger they are. I'm acutely aware that once a piece of heavy equipment leaves the property, there's no telling when it will ever come back. Even in taking care of Colorín, this backhoe question has influenced my decisions. The easiest way to care for him, for instance, would have been to put him in the goat corral. The problem is, if he died there, the backhoe wouldn't be able to get to him out. Instead, I've been keeping him tied out back under the big guayabillo tree. While fearful of jinxing Colorín's fragile recovery, I keep coming back to the idea of at least digging a grave while I have the equipment here. I'd like to believe I'm not superstitious like that, but I think everyone is, on some level.

After a quick coffee, I go to look for him and am relieved to find he's only about thirty yards away. I lead him back to his tree, but he's stumbling and nearly falls several times on the way down the small hill. Somehow, there's nothing quite so helpless as a large animal that's sick. Smaller animals seem to have more of a sense that there's something wrong and go into an instinctual, self-protective mode, curling up in a ball and tucking away someplace safe. Big ones, on the other hand, seem completely clueless that there's a problem and act as if they should still be able to go wandering about and behaving like normal. They act bewildered as to why their body is betraying them so.

Once Colorín is settled back into his spot under the guayabillo, I finish scarfing down a bowl of yogurt just as a dump-truck load of gravel for the kitchen floor shows up. Halfway through the dumping, I realize that I've ordered way too much. Even though, at 3,500 pesos (about $200 dollars), it's not a huge deal, I deplore waste and am frustrated with myself.

Yes, this day intends to be a fine one indeed.

Things have settled down by mid-afternoon, and the specialty horse vet, Claudia, whom I've been waiting for days to have come out from Vallarta, has finally arrived. She seems competent and begins probing and prodding her way toward a diagnosis. Deciding that he's got a secondary infection resulting from the one-two punch of having diarrhea on top of a compromised immune system, she writes out a prescription. She tries to be optimistic, but Colorín's wobbledy-ness has her worried.

"I'm comfortable we've got the diagnosis and treatment right. Let's just hope we caught it in time," she tells me.

I ask her about the possibility of leaving me a lethal injection of something in case he should deteriorate over the weekend. She tells me she'd be willing to use her license to purchase such an injection, but she isn't even certain it's available in Vallarta and, in any case, she definitely doesn't have anything like that with her.

"People here don't euthanize horses that way," she tells me. "They shoot them. Can you get a gun?"

I tell her I have one, but it's only a twenty-two-caliber, good for shooting possums but definitely not a horse. I tell her I can ask around about something more suitable, if it comes to that.

After two hours with Claudia, I've learned more than I want to know about horse triage. Assuring me that the situation is under control and that I'll do fine giving Colorín his new injections and the saline drip, Claudia packs away her things and leaves.

After tidying up the aftermath of medicine bottles, syringes, IV tubing, bottles of saline, alcohol, cotton swabs, and latex gloves, I hop on the moto and go to check out the progress on the road. I'm excited to see how it's going, but my hopes are dashed when I come to find all the great machinery noise I've been hearing all day is nothing more than another neighbor's tractor still trying to pull the original backhoe free from the precarious perch where it's stuck.

The original two guys, the operator and his helper, have multiplied into a small group of locals. They're all stopped now, waiting for yet another neighbor's larger tractor to come. Despite the lateness of the day, and the occasional crack of lightning from a threatening sky, they're all sitting around as if time had no meaning, drinking beer, laughing, making a party of it. This is classic Mexico, and, like so many relationships gone sour, I realize that if I'm not careful I'll end up hating the things about this place that I first fell in love with.

Breathing deeply, I recalibrate my gringo attitude, have a seat, and accept the beer that's offered.

Hanging out there with them I'm starting to relax when the storm that's been brewing finally starts to unleash. *Crap!* Realizing that Colorín is going to get soaked—something that would likely be the final kiss for him—I fly down to the house on the moto, barely able to see for the pelting rain. Untying Colorín, I lead him staggering to our front porch where he'll be dry for the night.

Pulling out a couple of big beach towels, I dry him off and then remember we still have what we jokingly call his pajamas—the strap-on horse suit we got to try to keep the vampire bats off. (The fact that Colorín is more loved by the bats than the other horses could be the cause of his illness, as vampire bats are carriers of innumerable diseases.) *Perfect,* I think, fetching the suit, putting it on him, and tucking him in for the night there on the front porch.

With rain pouring all around and a couple of massive C-R-A-C-K C-R-A-C-K, suck-the-breath-out-of-you lightning strikes, I manage to get his tether adjusted so he won't stagger and fall off the porch. It's only a few inches' drop, but, in his state, a fall on a short lead could be disastrous.

By the time this is all done, it's time for his IV saline drip. Ugh. The porch light is dim, so I don a headlamp and go at it. Despite all the practice I've had this week, I struggle with the procedure tonight, growing a little more tense each time the big, sixteen-gauge needle punctures his neck, but misses its mark. By the time I do hit pay dirt, needle sliding deep into vein, there's blood all over the place including inside the sleeves of my latex gloves. That's a worry. Even though yesterday's lab work showed Colorín to be free of blood parasites, it's not 100% conclusive, and there are other possible zoonotic diseases that can be transferred to humans.

That'll be a good story, I tell myself. I can hear it now: "How'd he die? " someone at a cocktail party will ask. "I heard he got AIDS from a horse, " someone else will reply. "Wow, a horse? " A third person will chime in, "That's sick—but impressive!"

Colrín's treatments completed, he seems to be resting comfortably. I, on the other hand, am a total wreck.

It's 9:45 at night and I'm at my desk writing. The rain has slowed to a drizzle. In the distance, there's still annoying shouting, laughing, and large machinery noises coming from the hill where the guys are undoubtedly soaking wet, and good and drunk. One thing I know for sure; there's nothing in this world more tenacious than partying Mexicans trying to get a piece of heavy machinery unstuck.

Added to the irritating sounds, there's a constant scratching coming from behind the bookcase. I know it's a crab that's managed to find his way into the house There are billions of these curmudgeonly critters clawing their way into every conceivable cranny now that the rains have started. The crab is as stuck as the backhoe. In my foul mood, I wonder if maybe I'm just as stuck in this absurd ranch life I've chosen? The scratching keeps up and is annoying but is not worth bothering to move the bookcase to remedy.

Next on the irritating noise list comes the sound of a loud gush of liquid out on the front porch. I figure it's a horse-sized squirt of diarrhea but, going out, I'm relieved to find that he's only peed.

Beyond exhausted at this point, I decide to reorganize the bikes, Tupperware containers of dog and cat food, and anything else Colorín might stagger into and stumble over during the night. Despite my efforts, he takes up a third of the porch, so I can't possibly move everything out of harm's way. I realize that keeping him out of trouble in his drunken state is likely to be a marathon I'll be running for most of the night.

The next three days pass in a suspended state.

August 5 - 7, 2016

The Internet, which has been a disaster as of late, comes on for a while on Friday afternoon to inform me that the weather we've been experiencing has strengthened into a tropical depression and now has a name: Javier.

Ha! Tropical depression! I think to myself. *I guess that sums up the way I'm feeling pretty accurately.*

It's been hard—really hard—having Holly away through all of this. With construction, sick animals and all the rest to be done here I'm spread too thin and my reserves are spent. I feel drained and defeated. Fuck Javier. I'm christening this storm Danielito, *my* tropical depression.

Somehow, Colorín and I muddle through the weekend together. During breaks in the rain I take him on brief walks. Each outing is a nerve-wracking experience, him wobbling and stumbling so. But Claudia said it would be good for his intestines to keep him as active, so I continue. At least the weather is cool, and there are signs he's improving. I'm on the phone with Claudia several times a day now, relating any new developments, reviewing his treatment plan.

"He still has diarrhea, but there were a few small balls mixed in this morning," I tell her.

"Balls?" she asks. "That's good. Very good! A horse has thirty meters of intestine, you know. It will take some time for the diarrhea to work itself out. Be patient, my friend. We're on the right track."

I'm also catching a break from the noisy road work. After all the drama of the machine having been stuck, it returned to work Saturday morning and promptly blew one of its massive tires. Now it's in town at the mechanic getting fixed. With the ranch returned to a more normal rhythm, Colorín seems stable (no pun unintended) and, by Sunday morning, the storm is passing.

Sunday afternoon, I'm feeling upbeat enough to load my kayak into the back of the truck. I spool new line on my reel and make ready to go fishing—something I've been promising myself for weeks now.

Not so fast, though. Before getting all the way to the beach, a gusty wind kicks up from the south, so I call off the trip and head back up the hill just as a fresh round of rain is starting. With one more small defeat piled on, I'm beginning to take this personally.

Back at the house, I try to divert myself by digging through our stale mix of DVDs, pulling out the fourth season of The Sopranos series. What a decadent thing to be doing, watching a video midday! The dialog and acting, which once seemed so fresh and innovative, now appear overdone and stilted. This combined, with Colorín's constant shuffling and scuffling out on the porch, has me diving deeper into the muddy waters of depression. Shutting the video off mid-episode, I'm feeling ever more alone and sorry for myself. I know I'll be fine. I can take any amount more than this, but sometimes it feels good to indulge in self-pity.

Outside, Colorín is having his own mood swing. He seems to be agitated and growing weaker. The practical side of my brain kicks in, imagining the effort involved in getting him off the porch should he collapse there for the last time. Without the backhoe as an option—no way to get it to the porch—and no good direct lead for a vehicle to pull him out, it would be a matter of getting six or eight guys to try to carry him by hand, or by using a hand winch to drag him inch by inch across the yard. Ugh.

The wind is still gusty, but the storm seems to have finally passed, so it's time for Colorín's porch stay to end. Gently coaxing him along, we make our way out to the driveway where he collapses. This is it, then. He must be down for good this time. Covering him with numerous beach towels and blankets, I make myself a comfortable spot, put his head into my lap, and sit with him for an hour or more in the gathering darkness. Gusting winds aloft bring forth a mob of threatening clouds that blot out the feeble light of the new moon.

"Motherfucking shit," I swear under my breath as a light drizzle begins again. Soaked and cold, I head back inside. It's killing me to leave him out there to die in the rain like this, but it's as it has to be. I'm out of options. It is what it is.

The night continues gusty with periods of rain. Fitfully, I dream of angry gods and flailing monsters, waking often throughout the night.

Monday Morning, August 8, 2016

Finally, at dawn, I drag myself upright. The day already has a distinct, heavy feel to it. Looking out the window to where I'd left Colorín to die during the night, I do a double take. Shit, he's not there! He's gone again!

Outside I see he hasn't moved far—just a couple of meters off to the side—but, low and behold, he's sitting upright and still alive! I'm shocked and flooded with a mix of relief and dread. "Really, amigo," I say, rubbing his cheek, "it's OK to let go. You've fought so hard, been such a beautiful, noble spirit being. It's OK to move on to other pastures. You'll be surrounded by fillies and nothing but the most delicious grasses to graze."

So many thoughts swirling through my head. *Should I take charge of the dying now? A simple plastic bag over mouth and nose, and he'd be gone in a minute.* Of course, there'd be a struggle—i.e., suffering—which is, above all, what I want to avoid. Maybe I should reconsider using my twenty-two. A shot directly to the temple would probably do the job. I've done the deed once before with our beloved Mrs. Toggenberg, who had to be put down, so it's not that I'm unwilling or unable. I just don't want to make a mess or cause undo suffering of any sort. And who knows whether dying naturally—even if it entails some suffering—isn't ultimately better than the violence of a bullet ripping through flesh and bone?

I know that my dilemma is strictly a gringo one. The reality is that such minimal deference is given to large animals here that Claudia, despite being an excellent, even world-class, horse vet is barely scraping by with only a couple of clients willing to pay for her services. For the trip out Thursday, she charged 3000 pesos plus the meds, about $250 total, an amount that would seem trivial in the States, especially considering the five-hour, round-trip drive, but an expense that my neighbors would consider exorbitant—the cost of buying a good horse being only about double that.

It's still early, but I call Claudia one more time to update her and ask if she'll check into the injection, which Holly could bring back from Vallarta if necessary. Claudia tells me the supply house doesn't open until ten, but she'll check into it.

Meanwhile, I continue to weigh the options. From a pragmatic standpoint, it's best not to do anything until I can be sure of getting the backhoe here to dig a hole and transport the body.

At 8:00am Yamir the two guys working on the house drift in to work. Yamir reports that, over the weekend, he went by the mechanic's. The backhoe is still parked, and the tire is too damaged to fix. A new one is on order, but it may take a day or two.

"And Nacho?" I ask him, referring to our usual, go-to backhoe operator who was too busy to do this job. "Do you think we can get him to come and help us out?"

"I talked to him already, and he says he's tied up on the job in Tehua for several more days. He suggests trying to get the other chofer, Mike, to bring his rig down from El Tuito," Yamir replies.

"Well, let's call him and beg," I answer back. With that, we're boots off, in the house, making calls. The Tuito guy isn't available, but, with a bit of Yamir's unyielding lobbying, Nacho relents and lets us know he can send another operator over by mid-day.

Another couple of calls, and Yamir has lined up the loan of a high-powered rifle, a sixteen-gauge 'escopeta' that will dispatch dear Colorín without any chance of undue suffering.

It's done then. A plan is in place. As usual, the Mexican solution, though crude, is the right one for the toughest jobs that need getting done.

Waiting for the backhoe to arrive, Yamir and I sit talking. The subject rambles from my efforts this past week to save Colorín to the fuck-ups with the road work and, particularly, to my anger over a large tree that got plowed down by mistake.

Yamir: "You know, Daniel, six years ago when I started working here, I would have thought all these things you care so much about were silly. Most of the people here still would. Most people's minds wouldn't 'digest' your way of thinking. The tree is just a tree. Who cares? And the horse, just a horse. A great animal, yes, but not worth a quarter of the time, effort, and pesos you've put into keeping him alive. But I've been starting to see things differently lately. I'm not saying that I totally agree with your way, but at least now I understand why you do these things. My mind has been changing and is more open, I think."

Even though I try hard not to proselytize, to not be the arrogant gringo telling locals how they should live, the moment seems ripe, and I can't help but lob a slow inside pitch.

Me: "Thanks, Yamir. It feels good to hear that. So, the way I see it, and the way I care about these things, boils down to a single issue: Look at all the big problems our world is facing right now. Think of all the things that will make life for our children and their children so much harder than we have it. Think of all the fish gone missing from Tehua. Think of fields of chiles, tomatoes, papayas, and bananas that only a few years ago used to grow naturally but now require a massive use of pesticides and chemical fertilizers. Think of all the cancers so common to everyone around here. Think of all the news you hear about climate change and the problems ahead. So think about these things and see if you can tell me the one common element that's the cause of all of them."

Yamir loves BIG questions—big challenges like this one. Never without an answer for more than a second, he has to think this one over. "Greed?" he finally blurts out.

"Well, yes, that's a good answer, but it's not the one I'm thinking of."

Yamir frowns, thinking a bit more. He's hooked and squirming but finally gives up. "What?" he asks.

"The answer I'm thinking of is this: We humans believe we're somehow outside of and above Nature. We think it's our right and even our job to control it, manipulate it, dominate it. That's the bogus thinking that's gotten us into this mess! The only solution to all of these problems is to understand that we're part of everything, and that everything is a part of us. When a beautiful, life-giving, life-protecting tree is cut down, it's us we're damaging as much as the tree. When an animal we're in relationship with dies, a part of us dies, as well. Even though the connections don't always happen in a way that can be measured, collectively it's the thinking that we're above Nature and should dominate it that's the core cause of all the problems we have now."

Yamir sits listening, appearing to absorb this like a sponge. He's not faking it either, I'm certain. In fact, he who usually has all the answers isn't so much stumped as he is pensive and thoughtful. More pensive, in fact, than I've ever seen him.

This seems to be a particularly ripe time to spread the gospel, so I push the lecture a bit farther.

"Now, I'm not saying I'm right. I don't know that at all. It's possible that none of my efforts will amount to "verga" ("cock" or "dick" in the current Mexican vernacular) in the end. It's possible that nothing will ever change, and we're all doomed to a world of decline. But what I am sure of is that at the end of the day when I'm lying on my death bed, I'll be able to have peace from knowing I did what I could to leave the world a healthier place for my children and grandchildren. Yours, too!"

Despite the heavy-handed preaching, Yamir still seems intrigued and sits for a while without responding. Then, after a few moments, he answers, "Sí, Daniel, I think I understand."

Getting up, I go out front to check on Colorín again. He's resting peacefully, possibly having slipped into a coma at this point. As long as he's like this—definitely not suffering—I'll let his own end come naturally rather than usurping the process with a violent explosion. I realize it's a silly rationalization, a way of feeling better about the whole thing, but if Colorín's passing has been a means for Yamir's mind to have opened more, something worthwhile has been served by the dying.

And oh, the dying. I don't know that I've ever been so affected by a dying before, human or animal. I realize this big hard lump of emotion is wrapped up in the package of my deeper history—a combination of guilt over not having done more to get help earlier on (i.e., the core guilt instilled by my parent-gods over having not been more responsible as a child) and my powerlessness in keeping bad things from happening (osmosed pulsations from the plutonium core of my father's nuclear worry reactor). Whatever the reason, I'm taking it hard. Holly had her worst animal episode with Lupita's passing last year. Now Colorín's dying is my pain-body to deal with.

Poor, noble Colorín. Of the three horses, Colorín is definitely the special one with his geniality and talkativeness. Where the other horses will roam around on the fringes, doing whatever horse things they do in their corrals or out in their pastures, Colorín always comes right up and mingles with whatever group of people is around, whinnying politely for a little treat. In the evenings, he often sidles up the road, calling out a cordial greeting and checking in to see if there might, by any chance, be any spare grain on hand. One never has to worry about walking close behind Colorín. The thought of him biting or kicking is unimaginable. And, best of all, swimming Colorín down at Lover's Beach is as good a horse experience as there is.

It's evening now, and the horror of this death watch won't end. When Colorín was conscious, off and on throughout the day, I continued telling him it was fine to let go, that there's a perfect pasture waiting for him, but the closer he gets to the edge, the more determined he seems to stand and fight. To stand is his objective, and where, twenty-four hours ago, he was only trying to do so every hour or so, now he's kicking constantly, trying to gain purchase in the dirt and make a final stand.

Is this suffering? I ask myself over and over. Would a bullet to the head be a more dignified ending than this? Despite my efforts to line up a gun today, no one came through. I didn't try all that hard because he seemed peaceful, for the most part. But now, at 11:00 at night, the thumping of his pawing at the ground is a dreadful sound. I'm glad I've at least made arrangements for Victor to bring his nine-millimeter pistol in the morning, the one he bought after the kidnapping attempt. Also, the backhoe has returned and is parked at the ranch. I had them dig an adequate "fosa" earlier today, so everything's as ready as it can be for the dying.

Headlamp on, I prepare a syringe with the last of the analgesic and head back out to Colorín's makeshift hospital bed in the front drive (earlier today, Yamir and Felipe set up a scaffolding rig covered with shade fabric to keep the sun off him). Even in his dying throws, Colorín's power is awesome. Despite his state, now unable to so much as lift his head, I need to be careful of his occasional kick. Using a yogurt container, I scoop some water out of a bucket and poor it over his parched lips which are beginning to part in a horrible grimace. I have to be careful to avoid spilling any in his wide-open nostrils. He licks thirstily at the liquid for a few moments and then loses interest (or maybe it's a purely mechanical reaction?). After giving him the shot, I tuck in close, get his big sorrowful head up into my lap, and stroke his cheek and neck for a while. Within minutes, he's calmer, his breathing eases somewhat, and he seems to be back in a place of relative peace.

Pausing to take it all in, I look around. Straggler clouds of the departing storm system march across a gaining half moon. The thrum of crickets, frogs, and other night creatures merges and reverberates with my own inner vibration to the point that I can no longer clearly differentiate between self and other. The field below where I sit, Colorín's head in my lap, is an orgasm of lightning bug flashes—more than I've ever seen before. In sync with Colorín's labored breath, I sob and give thanks for having known this awesome being.

Back inside, I brush, floss, and tuck myself in. Tomorrow I'll end it, one way or another.

Nodding off to sleep, I hear the chorus of insects and then one last thud of hoof striking dirt.

August 9, 2016

Waking late this morning at almost 8 o'clock, the sun is already up over the back hill. I lie still for a moment, listening for any sign of Colorín still being alive outside, but I hear nothing. Slow to dress, I find myself dragging every step, not wanting to go out there. Looking out the door, a twitch of ear and slight moment of a leg tells me all I need to know. I have to hope the message sent to Victor to bring his gun today gets delivered. I go to Colorín, pour a bit of water over his cracked, shrunken lips. Greet the day.

Ten minutes later, Victor arrives.

"La pistola? No, Daniel, No la trajé. Creí que Joán estaba bromeando (The pistol? No, Daniel, I didn't bring it. I thought that Joán was joking when he told me you wanted it). But don't worry, Daniel. Felipe can go and get it." He gives the order to one of his workers who leaves on his motorcycle. Twenty minutes later, the worker is back. He hands a plastic bag to Victor. Victor pulls gun and bullets out of the bag.

"Wow, Smith and Wesson," I comment, doing the obligatory guy thing and admiring the well-worn agent of death. The pistol looks to be a good twenty years old and has probably been involved in God knows how many heinous discharges in the past. Victor tells me the chrome plating was in much better shape when he got it but was damaged through his own stupidity.

"Last year, when the soldiers were coming often and checking all of our houses, I took it out to my father's parcel and buried it. Later, when I went back, my father had planted corn and I couldn't remember where it was, exactly. I dug and dug for more than a week, ruining plenty of corn, then finally gave up. Months later, I was telling Juan Carlos about it, and he reminded me that Luzano had a metal detector. I found the pistola in less than an hour, but, as you can see, the chrome finish was ruined from being in the ground so long."

We share a laugh, but, as I hold that mortal piece of heaviness in my hands, my gut is constricting. Now it's a matter of waiting for the backhoe operator to show up so he can carry the remains to their resting place. Then I'll have no more excuses.

Returning to Colorín I see that he has finally passed over. I'm at once relieved, particularly at not having to perform the execution, but also I'm flooded with yet another wave of guilt and remorse. This probably could have been prevented if I had been paying better attention in the beginning.

And so it goes. With so much going on here—building crews, stuck backhoes, volunteers stumbling around, a gazillion animals to care for, and our own endless needs, bodily and otherwise—it's impossible not to fuck up, impossible not to have our pain bodies of guilt become self-fulfilling prophecy from time to time. Having both been diagnosed recently with skin carcinomas, Holly and I have been going through our own self-berating for not having done a better, more intelligent job of protecting ourselves over the years. So, the death of a horse is but a dollop of icing heaped on an already bitter cake.

For a couple more hours, I futz about, waiting for the stupid backhoe operator to arrive. Out front, I take down the shade fabric covering the scaffolding and drape it over Colorín to keep the flies and rising sun off him while he waits for his ride to arrive. I even cruise into town on the moto to look for the operator, but he's nowhere to be found. Finally, he shows and, within minutes, he has Colorín scooped into the bucket of his rig. I make weird mental note that a full-sized horse is a perfect fit for a backhoe bucket. From a distance, the stiff, rigor-mortis legs of a dead horse sticking out of the backhoe bucket look artificial—a child's toy horse being carried by a Tonka Truck.

In the loneliest funeral possession imaginable, I follow the back hoe to the grave dug yesterday toward the back of the property. Beside the site, Yamir has left a couple of bags of lime under a sheet of plastic. Tearing at one bag, I line the bottom of the pit. Next, the operator lowers the body into the grave and then pulls back out of the way. Opening the remaining bag of lime, I do my best to toss it outward in order to cover the body completely. A cloud of the powder wafts up, burning my eyes and lungs and, slipping in the loose dirt, I nearly fall into the hole on top of Colorín. Recovering my footing, I imagine the backhoe operator watching from the cab of his machine behind me—laughing probably. Down in the hole, covered in a thin, coating of lime, the death camp image of Colorín's powdery white grimace is beyond the macabre. I say a short prayer of sendoff, then signal the operator to begin filling the hole. It'll take more than a backhoe to fill the hole in my chest, however.

✳ ✳ ✳ ✳ ✳ ✳ ✳

So, what's the moral of this episode? What's the takeaway? I guess it's pretty much whatever I want it to be. For now, it's sadness and guilt. Later, I'll work on rationalizing it, giving it some other, more positive meaning.

That afternoon, I buy a couple of sixes and let the guys off work early. I explain that we're having a wake. They look confused, but when I mention Ireland they know what I'm talking about and nod their heads—an Irish wake shares a similar appreciation for death that the Mexicans have. Sitting around the worksite, drinking beer, we reflect on the day. A joke is made about how seeing the gun scared poor Colorín to death. Yamir is yakking away as usual, examining the gun, admiring its heft. Without a care on Yamir's part, the barrel of the gun casually points in my direction.

"Yamir, please," I implore him, nodding at the gun.

"Don't worry, Daniel, it's not loaded. You silly gringos worry too much," he chides me jokingly.

The others laugh.

For them it's been just another day.

31 - Central Casting, Part 2
(Castaways)

Approaching our thirteenth year, our adoptive country continues to provide us with a seemingly endless parade of dynamic, entertaining characters. This abundance of unique specimens here is a common experience we've heard shared by other ex-pats.

I believe there are three reasons for this phenomenon. One is that Mexico, simply by its roughhewn nature, attracts dynamic people. The bland or timid are much less likely to fly, drive or cycle to the land of tequila and narcos, much less find their way out to places like Mayto.

The second reason is that much of people's normal clothing—the usual costumes that tend to segregate people into tribes—from hipster gear to business suits—is replaced by standard-issue travel and beach clothing. The garb de rigueur here is a t-shirt and shorts or a swimsuit. This tribeless, unidress code makes it hard to tell bikers from bankers.

Lastly, there's what we call the 'glomming on' factor. It's a fact that travelers and ex-pats congregate with much less demographic stratification than they do back where they came from.

All these things combine mean that be it at, El Rinconcito, bonfires on the beach, or at our own 'Lower Hamlet' campground, we're likely to meet and hang out with poets, pensioners, potters, or presidents of corporations in equal and random measure.

At times, these encounters stretch our boundaries and cause us to reflect on or even question our lives. A common theme for this reflecting has been Freedom. Having grown up in "The Land of Freedom," we thought we knew what the concept meant. Now we see that notion was badly skewed, and many of the most basic freedoms there are systematically under attack. Living on this side of that absurd wall, our view of freedom has taken on a wider perspective. I often joke with my Mexican friends that you can't fart in the U.S. without a permit. Here in Mexico, on the other hand, you can do just about whatever you want as long as you're not hurting anyone. I believe it's this broader sense of freedom that attracts the dynamic, fringe element types.

Adding to this questioning of the meaning of freedom, we frequently have visitors who've opted out of conventional lifestyles altogether, instead living lives of constant travel and fluidity—many working seasonal jobs like tree planting or trimming marijuana to finance their journeys.

A perfect representative of this is a guy we met while returning to the ranch via the Baja this year.

October 10, 2016

Launching our kayaks to investigate a pod of lounging whale sharks at a remote stretch of beach in Bahia de Los Angeles, Holly and I are approached by a scrawny, wiry, dreadlocked apparition of a man. I mean, seriously, half of this guy's body weight is contained on his head in one of those colorful, Jiffy Pop, rasta dread-bonnets. With braided, beaded beard stretching down past protruding ribs to a boyish waste, this Rastafarian ghost of hippies past, wearing nothing but beads and thin, loose, multicolored cotton pants greets us enthusiastically.

"Top of the mornin' to you, fellow spirit beings!" he calls out, grinning from ear to ear.

"Hey," I answer back, circumspect, "how's it going?"

"Awesome, amigos, awesome! I was diving up there by the point earlier this morning and got into a whole school of skipjack tuna! If you all wanna stick around, we're gonna have a tuna party on the beach tonight! Nice kayaks you got there. You goin' out to play with the whale sharks? Completely rad experience, man. Have you tripped out with them before?"

Holly and I are speechless.

Then, "Is this place fucking far out, or what?" he asks with a satisfied guffaw.

"Yeah, yeah, it's pretty special," I reply. "Do you live here?"

"What, me? Yeah, man, sure. This is the definitely the locale where I've made my domicile. We've got a whole community here," he continues, pointing back to a small cluster of ramshackle houses up the beach.

"How long?" Holly asks.

"Oh, shit, man, I dunno. Ten years or so. Some of us have been here a lot longer than that. As long as there's water and fish, we'll be here forever. Maybe even longer!" he says, laughing. Pausing then, he seems lost in thought for a moment. "Or else we'll move on," he says with yet another outburst of laughter. "You all are welcome to join us, if you want. It's Mexico, amigos, and we're all brothers here. The more the merrier! Besides," he adds, "there's plenty of fish!"

★ ★ ★ ★ ★ ★ ★

A few days later we meet Cheri and Sam, newlywed refugees recently transplanted from the hype of SoCal. Cheri, mid-twenties, Sam, a bit older, maybe forty, are an interesting pair.

October 16, 2016

Handsome and vibrant, Sam and Cheri are referred to us by a mutual friend for their biodynamic soil amendment products and their marijuana-based CBD healing tinctures—both things that we are interested in. Over lunch at a hip pizza joint in Todos Santos Cheri and Sam explain their company and products with religious zeal.

"It's been amazing launching here," Sam tells us. "No licensing or controls of any kind! Definitely makes starting business a heck of a lot more doable!"

Over the course of lunch, it's unclear whether Cheri and Sam are trying to sell us product, looking for investors, or just plain, old-fashioned enthusiastic. After lunch, we pile into their beat-up '80s Jeep Cherokee, and they drive us out to their rented house on a desolate stretch of beach outside of town.

"Two hundred bucks a month," Sam says, showing us around the beautiful, newly constructed beach house. "I surf right out the door every morning. Can you imagine what a crib like this would cost back in the States?"

For the next several hours, we get our own private, whirlwind TED talk. Sam is on fire now, making us try his special Boron mix dispensed from a wine bottle, darting this way and that, pulling out samples of various products he's been working on—MDB oils, CDT tinctures, and cannabis edibles made from special strains of sativa and captiva that he cultivates himself.

"See this?" he says, making us sniff a vial of noxious liquid. "Totally illegal in all fifty states. But here? No way, man. I can sell this in the market, and no one gives a rat's ass! I can give ozone treatments, do stem-cell research, whatever I want here! I've actually been experimenting with some amazing biohacking ideas, like replacing my own gut flora. It was totally fucked-up before I exchanged it for a super-healthy friend of mine's shit. Literally, man, his shit! It sounds totally gross, I know, but I killed my problematic bacteria off with a massive dosing of doxy—doxycilin—then capped up some of my friend's fecal matter and popped it down! Easy!" he says, patting his new, improved tummy.

"Whoa, that's intense," I respond, practically speechless.

Toward evening Sam and Cheri drive us back to the place we're staying. Cheri, Sam and I toking from their fancy vape pen along the way. During the bumpy ride, Sam tells that before meeting Cheri a year ago, he'd been a medical supplies salesman in Chicago. When his eight-year-old son developed leukemia and died, he lost all faith in the medical products he was selling and headed to California.

"Since then," Sam tells us, "I've been doing my own research and am finding out that everything they ever taught us up there in 'Trumpzikistan' is a lie. A bold-faced lie!"

"Ummm, like what, exactly?" I ask him, curiosity heightened by my high-tech high.

"Like everything. Everything you've ever learned. Give me an example of something you've been taught and you think you know for sure," he says.

"Well, OK," I say, taking the bait. "How about gravity?"

"Ha. Gravity! Knew it! You probably even think the world is round, don't you?" he asks, neatly skipping past the actual question and evoking a memory trace of the rabbit hole, flat-earth conversation I'd had with my fisherman friend Alfredo at El Rinconcito many years ago. "My son and I were investigating that lie just before he died. We did experiments on the beach with a transit site. If Earth had the accepted mythological radius of four thousand miles," Sam says, reignited now, "then, according to our old pal Pythagorus, its curvature would equal approximately eight inches of elevation drop for every linear mile of surface. So we took measurements at one, two, and three miles, and guess what. Nothing. Nada. There wasn't any drop at all! If that round-earth bullshit was true, we wouldn't have even been able to see each other's knees at three miles, but with transit site revealing the truth, there we were, knees, feet, and all!"

"What about ships and the sun disappearing behind the horizon?" I protest meekly.

"They don't disappear *behind* anything," Sam says. "They just get smaller and, finally, you can't see them anymore."

We're stopped now, parked in the dark out front of the hotel where Holly and I are staying.

Sam continues his astounding roll. "Look, it's like this," he says, grabbing a Frisbee off the dashboard and producing a gold ball out of who knows where. He leans over the seat to demonstrate the earth as a flat dish with the sun moving around its perimeter.

Holly and I are pretty much speechless at this point, but we're enjoying the show.

Somehow, Sam manages to switch the theme to what's clearly another important subject for him—the Holocaust. Like a mountaineer nearing the summit, Sam is digging in for the final push now, determined to help us see how flawed and pathetic all our default, conventional belief systems are.

"So much of what you've been taught is bunk, my friend. Most of it even. Take the Holocaust, for instance. Five million Jews annihilated? Never happened!" Sam says outright.

"Whoa, whoa, whoa. Wait a second," I protest, though the vape pen is having its way with me, and I'm not even sure I'm not imagining this whole thing.

Seizing the pause, Sam continues, "If you took the total population of Europe in the nineteen thirties and calculated the Jewish population based on accepted demographics, there would only have been just over two million Jews, tops. Five million killed by the Nazis? Never happened, I tell you!"

"Even if the numbers were way off, that in no way proves it didn't happen," I say, rallying. "Whether it was five-hundred thousand or even five thousand instead of five million, it's still a fact. An evil fact. We've been to the Holocaust Museum and seen film footage of the liberation, testimony by the survivors, photos, all of it."

"Ha!" Sam enjoins. "All that was faked. Easily done. I suppose you even believe in the lunar landing."

With that, Holly and I offer a cordial goodnight and exit the vehicle.

Thinking it over afterwards, I begin to see this wild-eyed Sam person for what he really is. I see how a son was lost, only to be followed by further life traumas, the way malaria and dysentery follow tsunamis and earthquakes. I see a fiercely intelligent man who, in response to having his worldview shattered by the death of his son, created from the ashes a totally new, alternative reality—a reality based on the negation of every commonly accepted belief he'd ever been taught or indoctrinated with. I feel sorry for Sam, even though his brand of crazy is a scary one.

32 - Ready, Shoot, Aim
(How Things Work in Mexico)

Let me preface this chapter by saying, "I love Mexico." If, in the writing, I speak of her at all disparagingly, it's in the way one might speak of a spouse: "I love her madly, but she makes me crazy when she's getting dressed for a party."

Sitting here on the hill under our airy palapa, another prefect ten of a day is waking up and stretching its legs. It's mid-March, halfway through the dry season. Despite the parched, dormant landscape—what we lovingly call our 'nuclear winter'—there's dew each morning that causes what bits of color there are to pop and glisten. A mellow surf is massaging the grand arc of beach below, producing a soothing sound that wafts up to where I sit. A single, small, fishing panga bobs gently on the ocean's shoulders.

Being Sunday morning, I'm sipping my coffee and soaking up the bliss of having nothing pressing to do. Sometimes I can do this—just be—but far too infrequently. As my mind drifts with the rhythm of the waves, I begin reflecting on the bizarre web of how things work here in Mexico, and think back to an episode this past week:

November 9, 2016

This morning's Vallarta errands include going to the mechanic's shop to pick up a chainsaw I left off for repair a month ago. As I arrive at the shop, the owner, Pablo, is heading out the door to run an errand.

"Hang on, I'll be right back," Pablo tells me, not in a hurry nor expecting me to be in one.

Inside the one-room workshop is a greasy tangle of machines. Piled waist high are lawn mowers, chainsaws, weed whackers, generators, and pressure washers, all in various stages of disembowelment. The workbench, half hidden under the wreckage, is a brooding collection of machinery innards—piled close to the ceiling in places. An anarchist's mechanical fantasy.

Waiting, I look around for my chainsaw. I check the workbench area first, hoping to see it set aside from the rest, ready to be discharged, its repair tag, like a hospital wristband, ready to be clipped and removed. But nope, it's not on the workbench.

My search expands to under the bench and farther to the sides.

Still nothing.

Feeling a mild panic setting in, I start poking around the piles, timidly tilting a lawn mower here or moving a pressure washer there. Now I'm feeling the morning's coffee kicking in and my blood pressure rising. Somewhere in the tangle of synapses and circuitry that comprises the workshop of my logical, organized mind, a little voice pipes up, talking me down from the ledge, telling me not to worry. The voice is telling me that Pablo has undoubtedly stuck the chainsaw away somewhere special for me. I'm his special gringo customer, after all!

It's at about this point that Pablo returns, drying his hands on his shirt.

"Ummm, hey, amigo, I can't seem to find my chainsaw anywhere," I say to him in the most casual voice I can muster.

Pablo gives me a blank look followed by a moment of hesitation. Then, with a cheerful grin returning to his face he says "It must be here. I worked on it last week."

Together, Pablo and I begin the search anew, with Pablo making more bold advances and reaching deep into the morass to uncover any possible hiding places. We're a team now, Pablo and me, sifting through the rubble of a collapsed building, looking for a lost friend we believe to be trapped inside.

Finally, at a loss, both literally and figuratively, Pablo turns to me and shrugs.

Now comes the part where I realize there's a choice to be made. I can feel my default control mode kicking in, wanting to get all gringo on the guy, making a stink, exerting pressure. MAKING HIM FIND IT! Or, it occurs to me, there's another option. It seems unlikely, but, borne out by my experiences during the years of living here, I decide to give it a try: "We-e-lll. Ummm, do you happen to have another saw you can give me instead?"

For a moment, Pablo's face is blank, and then, with a slight head bob to one side, he shrugs. "Sure," he says. Looking down to his right, he picks up the first chainsaw he sees, a pretty decent McCulloch, much beefier and newer-looking than the crappy Homelite I dropped off. "How about this one?" he asks, handing me the saw.

One pull of the cord and it screams awake, then settles into a smooth, throaty hum. It's perfect.

Now, my other default mind, the guilt one, kicks in. This is too good a deal. He must be joking. I don't deserve it. "Uh, fine," I say. "This will be fine, but what do I owe you?"

"Naw," he says, grinning, "we're good".

November 10, 2016

It's the day after the chain-saw episode and Holly is in one of the fancy department stores in Vallarta buying a new refrigerator. Handing the sales clerk her credit card, the clerk asks her for some identification. Berating herself for having left her ID in the car, she switches gears and attempts a gambit. Turning to a couple of friends who are visiting from the States, she asks if either of them have any identification on them.

"Sure," our friend says, reaching for his wallet and looking a little confused. "But he needs *your* ID, doesn't he?"

Holly shrugs, takes his ID, and hands it to the sales clerk. Without hesitation, the clerk copies down the necessary information and completes the sale.

＊＊＊＊＊＊＊

They're all around, these stories. Hundreds of them, large and small. They're amusing and fun and, en masse, they help shine a light of understanding for us on the Mexican way. Like tortilla soup for the gringo soul, they help us become more "Mexican" about this much-too-serious life of ours.

But what is it that's really going on here? Why are Mexicans so relaxed about it all? What lies behind these cultural vestments of super-chill attitude? I often wonder.

Whenever I contemplate this, I come to the same conclusion: Time. It's all about time. Mexicans and gringos process time differently. I see that our perceptions of, and relationship to, time is the root of most of our cultural differences. For myself and most of the americanos I know, the bulk of our energy is spent planning and working toward some distant future. But, for the Mexicans I'm acquainted with, the future doesn't receive anywhere near as much attention.

The reality Mexicans embody seems more firmly planted in the here and now. I virtually never hear Mexicans lamenting the past with could-haves and should-haves that I'm so used to hearing from people stateside. It's not that they don't emphasize the past and future. It's more like these time-based abstractions barely even exist for them.

For most Mexicans I know, especially those born and raised here in el campo, the future is a vague, far-off notion. I believe it's this lack of attachment to all things future that explains many of the vagaries of Latin culture. It's a hell of lot easier, for instance, to hang out in the hammock all afternoon or shoot the breeze with friends in front of the local store for hours on end if today is all there is and tomorrow, like the local bus, may not even show up. If time is simply the present and nothing more, there's no sense of it being limited or wasted. No hurry, no stress, and no consequences.

One of the most obvious effects of this cultural time warp is the general lack of planning one finds here. The fact is, whenever momentary flashes of insight do lead to plans being made, they're quickly baked to cinders by the Mexican sun and then washed away by beer.

For Holly and me, casual followers of contemporary spiritual teachers like Eckhart Tolle and Thich Nhat Hanh, this Mexican way of living in the moment is something we aspire to. The flip side of the coin is that it chafes hard at our linear mentality and makes us bat-shit crazy at times is the profound lack of planning.

A cliché that exemplifies this concept is the word 'mañana.' It took me a long time to truly understand this word. Like most others, I always thought mañana was meant as a joking, fun way to legitimize procrastination. Living here, however, I've come to realize that with a tomorrow that's only vague at best, saying mañana actually means something more akin to 'not now,' or even, 'not ever.'

While Holly and I know, deep in our psyches, that this present-centric perspective is the very best medicine for our overburdened, overproductive, workaholic gringo lives, it still, twelve years in, hasn't finished sanding down all of our intractable edges.

One reason is that this mañana-tude tends to wreak havoc on one of the most basic forms of planning, organization, and discipline we still embrace: building something. Rarely, if ever, are architectural plans used for building, at least not out here in el campo, and building crews rarely show up for work with the necessary tools or materials. Having managed a half-dozen construction projects here in Mexico, I don't think I've ever heard a worker say he was running out of anything until it was completely gone. Even though I've drilled my help on giving me advanced notice about necessary supplies, I still get blind-sided by this culture gap.

Worker: "Daniél, we need more nails!"

Me: "OK, thanks for letting me know. I'll be going to El Tuito Thursday and will pick up a couple of kilos of nails then."

Worker, a puzzled look on his face "But we need them now. We just ran out."

-or-

Crew Boss: "Daniél, we need more drain tubing for the retaining wall we're working on."

Me: "How much do you need?"

Crew Boss, looking at me quizzically and pointing to the obvious hole in the wall where his guys are working: "Three feet, enough to go through the wall." (like, duh.)

Me: "Ummm, what about tomorrow and the day after? Won't you need more then for the other drain holes you'll be making? Shouldn't I buy it all in one trip?"

Crew Boss: "OK, sure, if that's what you want. I didn't know if you'd want to spend all the money this trip."

✶ ✶ ✶ ✶ ✶ ✶ ✶

It's not only supplies that being so in-the-moment affects either. The standard construction project goes like this: A trench gets dug; a foundation poured; and brick, cement, and block become walls and floors according to rough dimensions agreed to beforehand. Finally, there's the big day when extra help is rounded up to 'colar' (pour) the roof, followed by the obligatory drinking of cases of cervezas. Room layouts and other minor details are fudged throughout the process.

Once the shell is complete and all the cement forms have been pulled away, the abañil (construction boss) and the owner of the building take a stroll around the inside, making decisions as to where wiring and plumbing will be run. Then, as tradition dictates, out come the grinders and the noisy, dusty, cutting-in of channels for plumbing and wiring begins. Ready. Shoot. Aim. The guys in my crews think it's strange that I run all the wiring conduit and plumbing as the floors are made and walls are going up rather than waiting until later (including testing it before closing it in—the paranoid weirdo!).

As further testament to the non-future, respiratory masks, safety glasses, and hearing protection are never worn, unless, each time, I insist on it. Why worry about such abstract things as getting hurt or losing one's hearing—things that haven't happened yet, or may not ever?

Yet another stereotypical aspect to building here are the ubiquitous half-built structures one sees all over Mexico. The assumption I used to have, and which I've heard other gringos express, is a sad lament that so many projects get abandoned. This isn't it all! The reality is multilayered and goes back, once again, to the concept of time and Mexicans' relationship to it.

Mexico, until the past decade or so, was never a culture of debt. Without loans, people build when they have money available and stop when it runs out. This doesn't mean the project is dead. No, not at all. It's common to see a dramatic rise in building activity after the Christmas holidays, because every employee gets a Christmas bonus of approximately one month's wages as mandated by law. Bonuses in hand, everybody then runs out to buy piles of brick and sand and bags of mortar in order to re-awaken their dormant building projects. Watching over time, I've seen that virtually every building project eventually ambles its way across the finish line. Meanwhile, an equal number of partially built structures have replaced the finished ones, thus giving the false impression to passers-by that the whole place is a graveyard of failed, half-built construction hopes and dreams. Not true!

Another aspect of building in Mexico that I'd be remiss to leave out is the ubiquitous Coke break. Every day at around 10:30 in the morning, work crews all over Mexico send a representative to the nearest tienda to buy at least one giant, two-liter bottle of Coca Cola for their mid-morning break. This happens at every job site everywhere, probably hundreds of thousands of them, without exception. The national addiction to Coca Cola is that strong.

There are a couple of sad statistics about Mexico that get tossed around frequently, and these reinforce this perception. One is that Mexico is ranked number one in the world for diabetes. The other is that it's the number-one, per-capita consumer of Coca Cola.

For about a year, Coke, in collaboration with the national highway system, ran an interesting promotional campaign. Covered in a shrink-wrap logo, every highway tollbooth we passed through that year looked like a bottle of Coke. At the toll, drivers had a choice. For an extra six pesos, the toll taker would reach behind him or her and pull an icy cold Coke from a full-sized Coke refrigerator and hand it to the lucky driver. My guess is that this marketing campaign eventually got nixed due to the obvious costs involved, rather than any lack in popularity.

Yamir and I have discussions about these sorts of cultural differences, including nutrition, all the time.

Yamir: "Daniél, your tomatoes look like crap, and the ones that have survived so far are getting devoured by plaga. You need to fertilize them and spray them for pests."

Now, I know that he knows that I know that he's teasing and testing me, and he that knows full well what my answer will be, but I take the bait. "Yamir, you know we don't use chemicals here. That stuff kills all the good-guy bugs in the soil and causes cancer."

Yamir, ready, "But how can you get cancer tomorrow if you starve to death today?"

OK, Yamir. Very funny. You got me.

It's just part of our repartee, but there, crouched down low behind the bushes, listening in and snickering at the little joke, is the intractable cultural truth of the matter.

✳ ✳ ✳ ✳ ✳ ✳ ✳

Another fun cultural mash-up here is that, like pets, gringos nearly always end up belonging to a Mexican. Yes, you read that right. Gringos nearly always end up belonging to a Mexican.

When Holly and I first read about this phenomenon years ago in Carl Franz's terrific guidebook, The People's Guide to Mexico, *we laughed at the goofy flip-flop in perspective. In the book, Franz describes overhearing two Mexican women talking:*

First Woman: "You wouldn't believe it. My gringo doesn't want me to use any bleach in the wash anymore."

Second Woman: "That's nothing. My gringo doesn't eat any sugar!"

It was a fun way to view the fact that many Americans down here have their dedicated Mexican facilitator. One often sees these couplings around Vallarta—a Mexican and his gringo, shopping in Home Depot or Costco, the Mexican translating questions to store staff or helping carry giant boxes of gringo merchandise out to the car.

Then, one day, it happens. I overhear Yamir refer to me as 'his gringo' to his friends, and a lightbulb goes off. Despite my always having thought of the relationship as being completely top down, I suddenly see that I truly am "his" gringo, his possession, every bit as much as he's mine. I reflect on all the times I was frustrated with him—or, in the early days, suspicious that he might be stealing—but couldn't bring myself to cut him loose because of the dependence on him. Fortunately, with time, I've learned to trust his integrity, and from his frequent help in navigating the delicate minefields of local politics to organizing special deals on building materi-

als and ranch supplies to the buying and selling of animals to keeping us filled in on the local chisme, Yamir's indispensability has us locked in— possibly for life!

* * * * * * *

Entering into the culture of mordidas (bribes or, more literally, 'bites') is yet another perspective shift, another doorway to better understanding and assimilating to life in Mexico. Personally, I believe it's far too easy and oversimplified to paint Mexico with the corruption brush and buy into the accepted notion that corruption here is worse than anywhere else in the world. If anything, the corruption here is more straightforward and less institutionalized than in the U.S. Holly and I, for instance, have always felt that paying taxes in order support the manufacture and deployment of bombs that drop on innocent people overseas—all to protect the interests of Big Oil or to make huge profits for the rest of the military-industrial machine—is the very worst form of corruption there is.

On the other hand, bribes here are often no more than supplemental income for underpaid government workers. Yes, upper-level bribery enables the drug trade to continue unchecked, and undermines Mexico's democracy. Though wrong, this pales in comparison in the planetary-scale destruction financed by the U.S. taxpayer.

Personally, I'd rather have it the way it here in Mexico. than to be paying to support Big Business's war machine (which, as U.S. citizens, we're still required to do, even though we're full-time residents of Mexico and use virtually none of the stateside governmental services).

If I had only two words to describe the difference in morality on either side of the border, I'd use 'malleable" for Mexico and 'rigid' for points north. One of my favorite authors, B. Traven, writing about Mexico nearly a hundred years ago, put it this way:

"As every official had his finger in the pie in some way or another, no inspection was made. What would be the point? Life is much more cheerful when things are not looked into too closely..."

In a way, it all gets back again to relationships. The first time I paid a mordida (a bite), Holly and I felt used and indignant. Now, after living here more than a decade, we both view the occasional 'propina' (tip) as being more like a random tax or facilitation fee. The big difference for us, having this perspective, is, that by paying this kind of tax, we're participating in a form of symbiotic relationship that's much more benign than buying bombs and making rich those who build and drop them, as we do when paying our taxes in the United States.

An amusing example of this new, improved perspective happened when we recently got shaken down for a minor traffic violation while in Vallarta running errands:

November 20, 2016

Oops. Just made a bad left-hand turn…

A traffic cop working the intersection does his thing, blows his whistle, and pulls us over. It's a tight, busy thoroughfare, so he comes up to the passenger window—Holly's side.

Me: "What's up, officer? Is there a problem?"

Cop: "Didn't you see the sign? There's no left turn at this intersection."

Me: "Oh, gee, I'm so sorry. I won't ever let it happen again."

Cop: "License, please."

Me: "Yes, sir, of course (handing him my license)."

Cop (looking it over as if considering whether this is going to require jail time or not): "I'm going to have to fine you. I'll need to take your license until it's paid. You can pick it up at city hall in the morning (hauls out his ticket pad)."

Me: "Oh, no, that's not possible. We're only in Vallarta for the day. Isn't there some way that we can pay it now?"

Cop (looking around): "Well, I suppose we could work something out, this time."

Me: "Great. Thank you so much. How much will it be?"

Cop: "Five hundred pesos."

Me, acting respectful but incredulous: "Five hundred pesos? That's far too much. The ticket would only be about fifty pesos…"

Cop: "Well, I'm sorry then. You'll have to deal with City Hall to get your license back."

I'm about to make the counter offer. I figure we'll settle at two-hundred-fifty pesos, about fifteen dollars. That's definitely on the high side but will be well worth not having to stay overnight and spend hours at City Hall in the morning. (I did this once—toughed it out on principle and paid the ticket. I waited half an hour in one line to get the ticket processed before being sent downstairs to a second line to pay and get a receipt and then sent back upstairs to a third line at another office to show my receipt and collect my license. All together it took over two hours!)

Holly pipes in: "How about some cheese?"

The cop and I both look at her, confused, until, for my part, I realize we have a cooler full of fresh goat cheese we'd brought to town to sell to the one organic food store in the city or to give away as gifts.

"Cheese?" The cop perks up. "What do you mean, cheese?"

At this point, I imagine he's thinking it's some slang expression he hasn't heard before or maybe just really bad Spanish.

"I make goat cheese," Holly replies, "Queso de cabra."

"Really?" replies the cop as Holly reaches over into the back seat and starts opening the cooler.

I can't believe he's actually interested.

Pulling out a roll of chèvre, Holly hands it to the cop.

"Will it last out of the cooler until lunch time?" asks the cop.

"Sure," replies Holly. "It would even be fine to save it and take it home this evening."

The exchange made, we're on our way and, a few minutes later, as we drive by the other way, the cop, back in his position on the corner, gives us a big, friendly grin, blows his whistle, and waves us on through the intersection despite the red light.

"Well, that certainly puts an interesting spin on the word 'mordida,'" I say to Holly.

"Yeah, literally a 'bite' of cheese," she replies laughing.

✳ ✳ ✳ ✳ ✳ ✳ ✳

Other bribe situations we've gotten tangled up in haven't all been quite so smooth as the cheese incident. It's taken years, but we've gotten adept at understanding the permit process here. It goes like this:

Permits for throwing up buildings are easy to get. Even so, most people here in el campo don't bother, preferring instead to bet on the notion that tomorrow may never happen. Other permits, such as drilling a well or subdividing a parcela, can take years or are cost-prohibitive. All the locals I know skip past these technicalities too.

Whether one goes the legal route or skips it, if the municipal or federal inspector—underpaid and overburdened with paperwork—happens to show up and discover the infringement, the results are often the same. The conversation goes something like this:

Property Owner: "Oh, I'm sorry. I didn't know a permit was needed."

Inspector: "Hmmm, well, I'm going to have to write you up. The multa (fine) could cost you thousands of pesos. Maybe even a hundred thousand!"

Property Owner: "Is there some other way? Say, how about if we go have lunch and talk about it?"

Inspector: "Well, OK. I am a bit hungry. But I doubt there's anything I can do to help. I'll think it over while we eat..."

Or, in the case of obtaining a permit:

Government Official: "No, I'm sorry, that's not possible. There have been changes in the environmental laws, and we're not allowed to issue that kind of permit anymore. It's a shame. If you'd applied, and the permit was dated six months ago, you'd be all set (hint hint)."

Applicant: "Oh, crap. I really need to get this done. Say, I'm heading over to lunch. Would you care to join me?"

Of course, these examples are oversimplified, and certain permit applications or offenses can take months or even years to extricate oneself from. That's why, for us, even though it's been a hassle, we've gone overboard to keep all of our legal affairs, other than traffic violations, scrubbed and clean. As gringos and assumed to be wealthy, getting caught in a serious bribe event can amount to the financial equivalent of having a date with a vampire.

Stories abound of gringos who've ignorantly or arrogantly ignored the process and, in a couple of the more extreme cases we've heard about, they find they've eaten a really bad burrito that's nearly ruined their financial health. One local friend described government officials as being like sport fishermen. "The hook goes in," our friend says, sticking a finger into his mouth and pulling his cheek out of shape, "and then they play you for as long as possible," he finishes, pantomiming a fisherman reeling in the big one.

One of the most extreme examples of Mexican fluidity came about recently when a friend of ours died. First hospitalized in Vallarta, in the state of Jalisco, his condition was deemed fatal and he was transferred to a more economical clinic in one of Vallarta's satellite cities over the border in Nayarit state. Within days of his death, his widow was informed that certain inheritance issues were going to be vastly more complicated since her husband had died in a state different than his residence. With the help of a facilitator friend of the family, the doctor readily agreed to redo the death certificate, certifying the man had died in the state of Jalisco instead. Easy.

A similar, but happier, example occurred this past winter. Our daughter, Aja, and her wife, Jamie, were here on vacation along with Jamie's brother and ex-wife. The brother and his ex have two kids together and had split up several years previous, but, after time apart, had fallen back in love. Instigated by Holly, and catching a wave of Mexican spontaneity, they decided that, if possible, they'd like to get remarried at Lover's Beach before leaving. Having already been through the drill once, they wanted to keep things low-key—just a local Justice of the Peace to preside over the service, with our family as witnesses.

With only two days of vacation left, it was a bit of a scramble.

February 14, 2017 (Valentine's Day)

We go to the Delegation office in Mayto to see if it's even be possible to organize the ceremony and license on such short notice.

"Sure," says the Delegado, while his wife, the town Clerk, quickly produces the necessary form. After I translate the form and the couple fills in the blanks, the clerk/wife reviewes it and starts checking off the list of municipal requirements: Passport? Check. Drivers licenses? Check. Blood test? What? You haven't had your blood tests yet?

"Oh, crap. They leave on Thursday and today is Tuesday. How are they going to get a blood test in time?" I ask.

"Tuito?" the wife asks her husband.

"Doubtful," he responds. "It'll have to go to Vallarta for processing. At least twenty-four hours. They're better going to Vallarta themselves. Probably get it done in a couple of hours."

Translating this to the engaged, they decide that, with just one day of vacation left, a trip to Vallarta for a last-minute blood-letting will be too be much hassle. Clearly disappointed, they decide to bag the idea.

"That's OK. Thanks for trying. It almost worked," they say to me.

I inform the Delegado of the change of plans.

At this point, the Delegado and his wife begin having their own side negotiation. Finally, the Delegado speaks up: "It's OK," he tells the group, "we don't need the blood test. It's not really all that important."

"Ahhh." Sighs of gratitude all around.

Then the Delegado remembers something. "You're going to need rings, though. We can't do it without rings."

With that, we're off to El Tuito, a town not quite large enough to boast a jewelry store. I stop by Juanito's tienda first to see if he knows where we might score some rings.

"Anything will do," I tell him. "The nuptial couple isn't all that picky at this point."

Juanito says he thinks his wife sells rings in her store across town. He'll take us there.

Rummaging under the counter, his wife produces a plastic box with a selection of about twenty dime-store-quality rings. The bride sees hers right away, a gleaming faux diamond appointment. The groom doesn't have any choice. Only one fits. Forking out the ninety pesos—about four dollars—we head back to Mayto. Laughing and comparing rings with each other, the couple is thrilled.

The wedding on the beach, later that day at sunset, is perfect. The bride and groom even pose for wedding pictures in front of Nacho's hulking old backhoe parked nearby.

We all also learned about an interest technicality of Mexican weddings at the end of the ceremony.

When the Delegado and his wife arrived to perform the wedding, they were very nicely dressed and brought with them a plastic table and sheath of paperwork. The table was used as an impromptu altar and, after vows were said and the official municipal wedding script delivered, the newly-weds had to sign the small stack of forms—made difficult because of the wind—before they were allowed to seal the deal with a romantic kiss. This, the Delegado assured me afterwards, is the standard, formal procedure for Mexican weddings. Sign the paperwork and then you get to smooch.

33 - Central Casting, Part 3
(The Vortex Effect)

The longer we're in Mayto, the more I'm inclined to think that we've stumbled into a vortex. The people who show up here, transported through whatever wormhole, just keep getting more interesting.

Take Lina, for instance. The first night I met her, the subject of my book came up and she said, "Oh, Dan, jou have to make me a chapter in your b-o-o-ok. You ha-a-a-a-v-v-v-ve-e to!"

Everything Lina says and does is like that. Muy dramatica. Muy Latina.

But I'm getting ahead of myself.

It started like this:

Returning to the ranch in October 2017, after our annual trip to the States, we immediately started hearing the name Lina mentioned around town, and we could see changes happening at the little shack of a house that she'd rented between us and the beach. This person, Lina, was the latest in a series of transient renters at the property, and hers was a big, noisy presence. Our only reaction, so far, was annoyance at the pack of rescue Whippets fenced in her yard that would come running and snarling —muzzles hard up against the chainlink fence in a torrent of unnerving, violent energy—anytime we happened by.

Instead of stopping by straightaway and getting to know Lina, Holly and I defaulted to listening to the chisme. Without reason we accepted the consensus that she was, at best, a complete 'loca,' and, at worst, a real menace.

"I heard she's asking around for local girls to table dance," was the most popular rumor.

"Someone told me she's hiding out from the Colombian mafia," was another common refrain.

Lina, you see, is Colombian. Her nickname, from the get-go, was "La Colombiana," though others simply called her "La Loca."

May 24, 2017

It's a busy day with tons going on. Holly's away for several weeks visiting her sister, so the load I'm carrying is heavier than normal. On top of the usual work crew being present, a truckload of guys from the Internet company has just showed up, hoping they might relocate the main antenna for Mayto to our property. I'm in the middle of negotiating with them when Lina's car pulls in, her pack of nasty Whippets snarling their challenge out the windows. My dogs are going crazy trying to attack her car.

"Hang on," I say to the Internet guys. Yelling at my two dogs to make them to calm down, I walk over to where she's parked.

Lina is waiting patiently, window down, like she's at a drive-in restaurant and I'm her roller-skating waiter.

"I've been lo-o-o-king for jou," she announces in thick Latina drawl as I approach her car.

I shrug as if to say, Well, here I am. Wad'ya want?

My first impression is of her intense, fiery, Latina eyes. Wearing skin-tight shorts and a wife-beater tee shirt, one leg bent with her foot on the seat, and surrounded by vicious Whippets, she's the epitome of cool.

"I ne-e-e-d jour help," she's says to me, every syllable dripping with drama, dogs snarling in the background for extra affect.

"Uhmmm, OK." I reply. "Para servirle. How can I help you?"

"I was th-i-inking-g-g I could buy jou a beer and jou could help me weeth someting-g-g."

"Uh, well, estoy un poco ocupado ahora (I'm kind of busy right now)," I say, motioning with my head to the truckload of waiting Internet guys plus my regular work crew, all staring back at us. "Is it urgent?"

"No, not urgent."

"Well, how about you come back after four," I suggest. "That's when my guys get off and I stop work."

All the while talking to her I'm wondering and wondering, who the heck is this crazy Latina and what the heck does she want from me? On further, furtive inspection, I notice her face isn't one that's easy to categorize. At first blush, she looks pretty, but in a roughhewn way that suggests a gritty gremlin of character hiding just below the surface.

"OK," she says nonchalantly, "see you later." She drives off.

As I head back to talk to the Internet guys, my worker boys are smirking and joking.

"Hey, Daniel, how come your girlfriend left so quick?" Yamir says in an uncharacteristically brazen taunt.

"She was asking to be with you, but I told her you didn't go with girls." I toss back at him while simultaneously thinking of Holly's and my oft-repeated phrase from years ago: "I'm sorry, my burro doesn't go with burras…"

Yamir grins approvingly at my quick comeback. The rest of the boys laugh.

Three hours later, it's five o'clock. Then six. Around seven, I'm wrapping up the last of the day's chores. I'm still curious about Lina, but, since she hasn't come back, I assume she's found help elsewhere. Without Holly around, my afternoon chores of watering the garden, feeding the goats, putting the ducks and chickens away, and feeding the dogs and Rambo is practically a full-time job, so, although I'm intrigued, I'm also fine with her having not come.

Done with the chores, I'm enjoying the sunset and a glass of wine up on the terrace. It's almost dark now, and Chanchito and Pirata, the best doorbells ever, break into a solid barking, the kind that tells me someone is coming up the drive.

Sure enough, up the road comes Lina, alone and walking barefoot. Lina is now dressed in a flowing, wildly patterned chemise with one, long, yellow-feather earring giving a flash of accent to the ensemble. With the harsh light and shadow of her first visit now mellowed, this new Lina is actually quite attractive.

Up on the terrace, Lina empties a woven bag she's carrying. Out come a designer bottle of raicilla, the local agave-based firewater, and a bag of pot.

Suddenly I'm sitting at an imagined intersection, revving the motor of my '69 Shelby Mach I, the nighttime boulevard ahead a string of green lights, and not a cop in sight.

Oh wait, there is one I realize as the personal policeman of my subconscious steps from the shadows and wraps on the window. Zzzzp. Window down.

"Yes officer?

"Don't even think about it" the policeman says.

"Yeah, yeah, I know you're right" I say to him, knowing my deep love for Holly would never allow me to actually hit the gas.

Snapping me back, Lina is explaining something...

"Dis raicilla is MY raicilla. E-e-s berry special," she says. "I have it make special and I going to sell it all over the w-u-u-r-l-d."

The bottle is special, all right—the upper half solid black and the bottom clear, with a sinewy, half-naked woman and half-flowing tree figure embossed in bright red over the black and clear.

"Oh sure, thanks," I say as she offers me a shot. "But first, tell me, who the hell is this Lina character?"

"Sit," Lina says to me, "and drink my beautiful raicilla, and I wheel te-e-e-e-l-l-ll jou everything-g-g about me."

✶ ✶ ✶ ✶ ✶ ✶ ✶

For the next several hours, Lina talks, and I listen.

Dramatic in that awesome Latina way, Lina paints a picture in bold, colorful brushstrokes of a life straight out of a romance novel. At nineteen, Lina was discovered and soon became a household name in Colombia as a soap opera star.

"I made a lots of money. Soo-o-o-o mu-u-u-uch money," she says. "But I was so young. I deedn't know anything. I spent it all so-o-o fast, just as fast as I could make'd it. I was very famous. Jou can look me up and on the Internet. Naked pictures even!"

After a series of contract issues, and issues with her agent, Lina, I learn, moved on to representing a line of cosmetics.

"They flew me everywhere. I could have whatever I wanted."

On a business trip to Mexico, Lina met a matador, Ignacio, and fell madly in love.

"We meet'ed in January. I deedn't see him again until March. We got married in July. And by the next January, we was'ed dee-vorce-ed."

"Wow, that was a short one. What happened?"

"Oh, we love-ed each other OK. We ste-e-e-l do. But his mother was the ting. She's a very, very bad person. A bruja (witch), actually. She make spell on me, on our house. We couldn't make love, and I begin to have very bad thoughts about hurt myself. One day I even break a big piece of glass and take one of the...how you say...?"

"Shards."

"Yes, dat's it, shar-eds. I take one of those shar-eds and put it to my wrist. Something inside stop-ed me. It tell me, dis isn't you. I was OK den, but I knew for sure that I had to get out."

"Whoa. That's pretty intense. How did you know she was doing all of this to you?"

"I know for sure because I find-ed it. I finded the muñeca."

"A voodoo doll?"

"Yes, yes, that's it," she says, stabbing toward me with her finger. "A voodoo doll. It was made of many strange things—clay, a ball of hair, human bone..."

"How did you find it?"

"I was seeing a physiologist for the depression I was having. I tell'd him I thinks maybe dees ees happening, but he doesn't believe in stuff like that. Finally, one day he tells me, 'Listen, I have a friend who I think can help you.' It is arranged then that this shaman come'd to my house, but he have to bring a helper because he tell me it important I can't never see heem.

If I see heem, the bruja can also see heem through my eyes. If she knows what he look like, she can attack heem too. Dees shaman, he make a big tour of the house and finally comes to a very nice sofa we hav-ed. I'm always having to stay in next room with his helper telling me what thees shaman ees doingg. When he find'ed the sofa, he moved it one way, then another, then showed to his helper the exact spot to find the muñeca. Then he left-ed the room.

His helper tell me bring something to cut with and come in here. I go an' get scissors an' get ready to cut the sofa but he say, no, you can open it from the other side. No ees necessary to ruin your furniture. I turn the cojín over and cut into the back. I reach-ed up around inside and feel something there. I try to pull it out but get weak, like maybe I faint, so I pull my hand out. Calling to the shaman in the other room, the helper tells to me, 'It's OK, I can help you.' He reaches and pulls out that ugly thing then."

"Wow, that's quite a story. What happened then?"

"Then? Then I know for sure I cannot stay with heem. The shaman tells me it best if I cross the ocean. I get on a plane and go to live with my father in Germany. Instantly, when I get on da plane, I feel better. I feel-ed my old self returning, and we get the dee-vorce."

A pause.

"I steel love heem. I re-a-a-l-l-y L-O-V-E heem! We very close friends, you know? It juice we cannot be together. I see him not too long ago in Spain. He doing well, except he get-ed pretty fat. He say he want to get back together but I tell him it cannot work."

"So what's a nice girl like you doing in Mayto?" I ask her.

"I get invited to come'd here with the Spaniards," she says, head motioning toward the beach.

The Spaniards are yet another new addition to Mayto, an odd assortment of three or four Euro business/hippie types and their giant, goofy Great Dane named 'Dr. Hoffman.' Ostensibly, the Spaniards are renting the recently abandoned hotel wedged in between Camille's place and the Mayto Hotel and intend to remodel it into a hip beach bar and resort.

"But they never pay, so I stop the work for them. I fall in love with Mayto, though. Now I'm here for-e-v-e-r!"

At one point in the monologue, the famous Mexican singer Lila Downs comes up on one of my Latin music playlists that's been providing background ambiance to Lina's story. In the song, Downs is singing a sad love song that prompts Lina to get up and start weaving around the terrace, singing along, belting out the song with pretend microphone in her hand—

a wonderful private performance I'm sure Lila Downs herself would have been pleased with.

"Hey, I gotta ask, is it true you're planning on opening a bar with local girls table dancing?" I ask her when she sits back down.

"Ha, Ha, Ha!" Lina laughs hard. "Yes, I wanted to open a bar. I even have it on Google Business. It's gonna be called La Granja (The Farm). But table-dancing girls?" she laughs again, delighted. "I love what everybody talk about me. That's too funny. Ha!"

Next I learn that Lina is only thirty-five years old. I'm surprised and impressed at how much life she's already lived, having figured her to be ten years older.

When there's a pause in the dramatic monologue, I bring up the book I'm working on. Hearing this Lina says, "Oh Dan, jou have to make me a chapter in your b-o-o-ok. Jou ha-a-a-a-v-v-v-ve-e to!"

"Ummm, OK. I'll definitely try to work you in," I tell her. "And oh, hey, I almost forgot. What help were you looking for earlier today?"

"Oh, that," she says laughing. "I have a ceiling that makes leaking. Come by tomorrow so jou can help me know how to fix it, OK? I buy jou that beer I promised!"

It's late. I'm fading, and a steady chill breeze has us both shivering. I walk Lina back to her house and leave her there at the gate, safe with her pack of bloodthirsty wolves.

* * * * * * *

June 7, 2017

Holly is back from her trip, and Lina has invited the two of us to dinner with her and her father Augustin, who's living with her temporarily.

We have a great evening. Holly and I find both Lina and her father to be fun, sophisticated conversationalists, having lived in New York, Florida, and Berlin after leaving their native Cali, Colombia.

The front porch of the house Lina rents is an eclectic, bohemian collection of period furniture; a faux crystal chandelier; cheap, sensual paintings; photographs of her high-society wedding to the matador; and a large, pink rhinoceros coming out of the wall.

Over grilled fish and Colombian rice, the subject of conspiracy theories, and, in particular, Reptilians comes up. Holly tells Lina about a close friend of hers in Vallarta that believes these Reptilians make up the majority of the power elite around the world.

"Of course, of course," Lina jumps in. "I've met one."

"Ummm, OK," Holly says (Holly loves this kind of stuff). "Who was he? What happened?"

"I was at a party in DF, and I meet-ed a very handsome man. Someone was telling me he was a millionairio, so I was curious. He was very nice, and I was thinking we was going to end up sleeping together, but then suddenly he say me, 'I don't feel very good. I jus' go lie down for a few minutes.' After a while, when he deedn't come back, I go look for him and find him in a room. He just standing there, looking very strange. I reached out and touch his arm and it turned all to… how you say…? Like lizard skin?" indicating something small with her fingers.

"Scales," Holly offers.

"Jes, jes, that's eet. Scales!"

We're all busting a gut laughing now, but Lina, I can tell, is perfectly serious.

"How about you, Daniel?" Lina's very pleasant, Harvard-educated father asks. "You haven't said anything yet. Do you believe in this kind of thing?"

Pausing a second to consider, I respond: "I like to keep an open mind, but…well… probably not."

* * * * * * *

Since those first encounters, Lina has grown on Holly and me, and we've become good friends. We've even learned to tolerate her seething Whippets. Always the entrepreneurial innovator, Lina's recently been pushing the shamanistic tourism angle with regular temescal (sweat lodge) ceremonies, curanderos (indigenous healers), and groups of their hallucinatory participants showing up to puke and dance and seek other realms on the golden sands of Playa Mayto. Always entertaining and never dull, Lina is yet another colorful patch in the crazy-quilt of Mayto life.

October 27, 2017

Holly and I met an interesting guy at Rinconcito this evening—Dr. Salvatore.

We've heard much about Dr. Salvatore recently from a friend who's been receiving treatments from Dr. Salvatore in her battle against stage-four lung cancer, so we're curious about him. According to this friend's latest blood work, her cancer is receding at a rapid pace. The treatments Dr. Salvatore provides, mostly in the form of injections that haven't been approved by any government yet and sleeping with a magnetic vest on, are being administered at an undisclosed location in Puerto Vallarta. This all seems plausible because Mexico is so loose on such things as ozone therapy and stem-cell research, and we've heard numerous stories of healers of various ilks based in Puerto Vallarta who provide experimental medical procedures.

Dr. Salvatore, we've been told by our friend, is also part of an elite group of scientists working with the UN on advanced nanotechnology projects ranging from soil-contamination remediation to saving the world's coral reefs.

We've heard, among other things, that Dr. Salvatore and his associates are looking for land in this area to set up a test site for growing nano-enhanced seed stocks (our ears perk up at this), and they're also working on a reef test site in the Marietta Islands near Puerto Vallarta, both part of programs sponsored by the UN in cooperation with numerous other large NGOs.

Dr. Salvatore is a good-looking guy in his mid-fifties to early sixties. The first thing I notice about him—other than his generally fit carriage—is his perfect, gleaming white, glad-ta-meet'cha grin. His hair too, looks perfect, although on closer examination, one sees the telltale, slightly off, rust-colored tint of drugstore hair dye.

Dr. Salvatore goes up to the bar for a round of drinks that he insists on treating us to. After some perfunctory pleasantries, the conversation is off and running—mostly Dr. Salvatore riffing about his work:

"It's all based on the use of nanotechnology," Dr. Salvadore begins. "I've developed a methodology for infusing materials, often precious metals, the platinum group mostly—osmium, ruthenium, palladium, and others—with nanos that vibrate more than a billion times per second and set up oscillating fields of healing energy. The whole process is based on the reality that none of this is what it seems (knocks hard on the table we're sitting at for emphasis, then gestures out to the great beyond). It's all energy vibrating at frequencies that our human filtering systems are adapted to perceive as structure. Without this filtering, we would just be amorphous blobs, perceiving the world as goo!" He laughs deeply at this, exposing for a brief nanosecond, those brilliant teeth.

"All of our existing reality is simply waves of energy and patterns of those waves, creating form and substance, or at least the perception of form and substance. Just like the ancient mystics and philosophers from the Orient, modern physicists are increasingly agreeing that all of our perceived realities are nothing more than waveform occurrences of energy, and that our interaction with them—simply observing—is a dynamic part of the form perceived. My team and I are manipulating rare earth elements such as Yttrium on a molecular and even supra-molecular scale to make them function as a substrate to hold the sub-atomic vibrations we're inducing into them.

"What I do, then, is create molecular data packets of energy, infuse a substrate with the energy vibrations, and turn it into a specialized nano-delivery system. The resulting nanos act as both receiver and antennae, a bridge, if you will, between our own, semi-flat, three-dimensional plane, and higher, more expansive, fourth-dimensional realities by both drawing on and sending out vibratory patterns. Of course, there are many more dimensions in the quantum realm than just four, but, for now, the third and fourth planes give me plenty to work with."

This is followed by another burst of gleaming-teeth laughter.

Clearly, this is a happy guy! And me, I'm thoroughly transfixed at this point. Like nanos themselves, his words draw links between many of the concepts and belief systems I've dabbled with trying to understand, including the recent Sapo experience. Although, truthfully, at the same time that I'm intrigued, I'm also barely hanging on and not quite sure if what he's saying is bullshit or not.

"So, just as each form or structure we experience has its own organized, unique, and well-functioning vibratory signatures," Dr. Salvadore continues, "there are also an equal number of opposing signatures and vibratory patterning that create entropy and dissolution of what we consider the healthy, organized states of matter—be it animal, vegetable, mineral, or even the human psyche. What my nanos do is react with and counteract the unhealthy, decompositional patterns—essentially subduing them, if you will. They recalibrate and rebalance entire systems. Often this requires reseting the cellular time clock and taking systems back to a time before degenerative processes took hold."

"OK, OK, hold on second," I insist. "I think I understand. What you're talking about is basically like making noise-canceling headphones to counteract and nullify vibratory frequencies."

"Exactly!" Dr. Salvatore pronounces, clearly pleased that his work has found an appreciative audience.

"But am I also hearing you correctly that you're manipulating time?"

"Precisely. That too!" he says, even more enthusiastically. "Time is nothing. Time is easy. The perception that time is moving is probably the biggest fallacy that mankind has ever indulged in. I remember once, driving in the Great Smokey Mountains with my son, him saying, 'Look, Dad. Look how fast the trees are going by!' It hit me then, one of my biggest epiphanies ever, that my son's perception of the trees going by was exactly like our perception of time. Like children, we perceive time racing by us, when, in reality, time, like the trees, is actually standing still and we're the ones racing through it.

Our continual string of thought perceptions creates the movement we experience as time. Put us in a prison cell where new perceptions are more limited, and time seems to slow down. It drags by, if you will. But send us on an adventure where new occurrences are generating a massive string of new perceptions, and, voila, time appears to speed up.

The grand irony, yet another trick of the brain, is that, in retrospect, the time that drags by, the jail-cell experience, gets compressed because of the lack of variation and, ultimately, it seems like a relatively short blip, whereas the adventure we went on seems rich and deep as if it had gone on for much, much longer! A really intense experience loaded with sensory perception—a traumatic accident for instance—can take on a slow-motion quality at the time it's happening, but then, after the fact, it becomes an instantaneous blip.

"But I digress. I'm getting off my work with nanos that you asked about. Ha!" (another short laugh).

Who does that laugh and poop-eating grin remind me of, anyway? Jack Nicholson? Dennis Quaid? Paul Newman? All three?

By the time we finish our dinner, my head is spinning and I'm exhausted. Part of the fatigue comes from the mental backflips my mind's been performing trying to get a handle on this guy and figure out if he's a genius, charlatan, or certifiably looney tunes. If half the things he's been saying are true—like he's able to take an Olympic-size swimming pool full of raw sewage and, by applying a small, fingertip-size dot of his nano product on either end, the water will be potable within twenty-four hours —I'm certain that he's a total kook.

Then, at other times, what he says makes perfect sense—like we're all made of electrical impulses and, like anything else electrical, we need proper grounding, without which—i.e. without consistent contact with Mother Earth—we build up an excess of positive charge that creates a detrimental oxidation-like effect on our cells. Some of these ideas seem totally plausible, and I have to once again recalibrate my impression of him.

As we say our goodbyes under the laughing, moonlit palms of El Rinconcito, I wonder once more at the amazing variety of characters who land here. If there's actually such a thing as a cosmic vortex, Mayto must surely be one. I wish I'd thought to ask his opinion on that!

34 - Home Again

Our return to Mayto after visiting the States is always a mixed bag of emotions. The homesick missing of animals and place is tempered by background anxiety—unease about the overwhelming nature of what we've taken on and knowing that, on our return, inevitably things will be in some level of disarray from our having been away. This year's transition has been a relatively smooth one, with two sets of caretakers living at the ranch—one extremely conscientious couple from the UK in charge of our house and animals and a second young couple watching over the lower guest house and common areas.

A changeover we made to having all of our electric systems grid-tied and less dependent on batteries has proved far less problematic than in past years, and I've been working to build a general redundancy into all the other critical systems, which has also meant fewer panicked communiques from the ranch during our time away this year.

Still, inevitably, the longer we're gone, the more things fall apart, and these past couple of weeks have been no exception. In one of the recent news blips from the ranch that we received while wending our way back from the States, we were informed that the couple from the UK needed to leave a week before our return, and the second couple, Luis and Selma, were expecting a baby—a twist that will trash the whole winter plan of having them stay on to run our Education Program. We've also been told that there seems to be a snake having its way with the chickens and they've been disappearing at a steady clip.

Then, just this past week, we received word that Luis severely cut his foot jumping off the pier in Tehua and is now using the moto quad bike—off-limits for all but essential ranch chores—to get around town and the beach.

On top of the unapproved moto use, Luis announces that he's brought his friend Jesús and his two sons to live at the ranch. They're helping him and Selma with their chores, since he's unable to walk. "He's a really great guy," Luis informs us in an email, "and he'd like to talk to you about staying on after you get back.

Selma and I are moving to be nearer my family as we wait for the baby, so having Jesús will be really great for you. He's super experienced in permaculture. Oh, and I also forgot to mention," adds Luis in his correspondence, "the neighbors' pigs got into the garden yesterday and completely destroyed it."

October 17, 2017

"Stay tuned for Season Twelve," Holly laughs as I read her the email from the passenger seat, the truck pointed south toward Mexico.

Talking it over, we decide to let the moto use and friend-staying-for-free slide. We're on the home stretch with this couple and have learned from past experience the value of having things end on good terms. As for this other guy, Jesús, staying on, we decide to punt that ball down the field, particularly since we'll be needing another week of coverage for a Day of the Dead road trip we have planned shortly after getting back. We let Luis know we'll see how it goes with his friend once we've returned to the ranch and have had a chance to meet him.

October 22, 2017

Finally we're bouncing down the last lumpy stretch and turn in through the gate, back at the ranch. At first blush, everything looks stellar. The grounds, which in other years had turned to jungle during the rainy season, are looking as kempt and proper as we ever remember seeing them. Pulling up to the community-building/outdoor-kitchen area, we get out of the car. Luis hobbles out on improvised crutches followed by an abundantly pregnant Selma and their friend Jesús, a classic Mexican Rainbow Fest hippie type complete with long scraggly hair; face tattoos; goofy, 'I Dream of Jeanie' pants; a flowing wrap of Indian fabric around his scrawny torso; and his two clone-like boys, one of whom I find difficult to ascertain whether he's a boy at all.

After a quick hello we break free and head up the hill to survey the situation at the house. "Not terrible," we say to each other, looking around. Like below, the grounds are in good order, but the inside of our new cob house, which has been shut up for three months, resembles Miss Havisham's house in *Great Expectations.*

After unloading the truck and doing a preliminary cleanup, I head back for more of a debriefing with the group down below. I'm with them for just a few minutes when Holly comes flying down the drive in the truck. "It's Oprah," she stammers, jumping from the vehicle. "she's cut. Badly!"

"OK, we'll have to go for Victor," I respond, bolting into action.

"I have some good honey I can put on it," offers Jesús.

Oh, for Christ's sake (literally—Jesús/Christ), I think to myself, *Honey? Is this guy for real?*

Jumping into the truck, Holly and I head to Villa in hopes of finding Victor at the school. Asking some of the students milling round, we find Victor, but he's still teaching a class despite the late hour. He'll be done in half an hour, he tells us. We wait in the car.

Finally, back at the ranch, we find Jesús watching over Oprah, who's in a pretty bad way. One of her huge udders has been sliced wide open. Drained of milk and blood it's now nothing more than a shoe-sized flap of shredded flesh.

Fortunately, our medical supplies are mostly intact, and Victor's able to find the penicillin and analgesic needed. After he gives the sedative, the three of us—Jesús, Victor, and me—lay Oprah out on the wooden milking bench, tongue hanging out of her grimaced mouth. Lacking the proper suture materials, Victor shows me how to easily make do with a broken-off syringe needle and fishing line. "Muy Mexicanada," I say, getting a laugh from the other two.

I've never attended an actual live surgery, and this one's nothing like the doctor shows I've seen on TV. Watching Victor work, it's hard to imagine how the crude, fishing-line sutures will ever make Oprah's grand vessel of milk production whole again. As Victor pierces the mangled flesh over and over with the makeshift needle, the three of us make small talk.

In the past, I've found Victor's impossibly thick accent akin to following an advanced physics lecture—I get fuzzy glimpses of the topic but am clueless about the details. Somehow, tonight, however, I'm able to catch most of what he's saying. I find it's often like this when learning Spanish. Gradually, one at a time, the voice patterns of certain individuals come clear. In this way, I ask about Victor's recent, aborted move to the mountains near Tepic while letting him know how thankful we are that he didn't stay gone.

"It was horrible," he tells me in his intensely thick accent. "Really dangerous. Everyone was growing poppies and lives in fear. The narcos, they were everywhere."

Less than an hour later Victor is tying off the last of the crude sutures by the light of our headlamps in the gathering dark and is giving us instructions for the coming days. This sort of thing, especially having just returned to the ranch, is upsetting for Holly, so she keeps her distance, tending to the chickens and doing other chores. Jesús has been a steady hand throughout the process and, despite my initial skepticism, I find myself beginning to warm up to him. He offers to stay with Oprah while I drive Victor back, massaging and rotating the unconscious Oprah from side to side to prevent her from developing life-threatening, gassy bloat.

"Just keep her moving," Victor instructs us. "She'll be awake in a few hours. She's doing fine."

When I get back, I find Jesús massaging away. Oprah's abdomen, swollen like a timpani drum, has us both concerned. Together, we flip her to her other side until an invisible cloud of powerful, gag-inducing methane gas envelopes us. With that, her belly softens some.

For the next hour or so, the process continues, while, by the light of our headlamps, Jesús and I chat about him and his kids, the ranch, and all things permaculture. His boys are seven and ten and he has them on 'sabbatical' from school for the winter. He's allowing them to learn more of the world and practice surfing. Despite his celestial position on the outer edge of my free-wheeling-hippie comfort zone, I find Jesús to be remarkably knowledgeable and engaging. Forcing myself, yet again, to suspend judgment, I see that I have a good man here beside me, tirelessly massaging the stinky, blood-and-urine soaked Oprah, and seeming appreciative to be having the experience. Like so many other visitors we've had here over the years, Jesús's presence challenges me to rethink my prejudiced biases about freedom and responsibility.

Somewhere into hour three, our conversation is interrupted by a commotion over in the chicken coop.

"I'll be back in a sec," I say to Jesús, getting up to check on the fracas.

Shining my light into the coop, I see there's a good-sized boa constrictor, maybe six feet long, slithering its way up the wall toward the roosting chickens, several of them squawking and flailing about, above on their perch.

Calling to Jesús for help, I look around for the snake catcher I'd made years ago only to find that the main draw cord made of weed-whacker line is completely missing.

"I'll get my gun," I say to Jesús in something of a panic mode, but he assures me we don't need to kill it and asks if I have a box to put it in. Finding a large Tupperware box and a stick with a forked end to suffice as a snake catcher, Jesús and I rush back to the chicken yard.

Inside the coop, the chickens are still squawking but are doing nothing to actually get away from the threat. Chickens are like that once it's dark. Sitting ducks, if you will.

Going into the pen ahead of Jesús, I play the part of the fearless leader. The snake is still moving into position, trying to find purchase from which to snatch a bird. At this point, it has anchored itself in the wire mesh of the window, high on the wall near the roosting perch. The hapless chicken nearest the snake is squawking and flapping but is unwilling to jump to safety.

Lining up the fork of the stick by the light of our headlamps, I make a useless jab, trying to pin the head to the wall. The coiled serpent is now hissing and lunging at the stick.

Jesús steps forward. "I think maybe you're scaring her," he says.

Me scaring her? Are you kidding? I think, while at the same time realizing he's exactly right.

Stepping back, I watch as Jesús takes charge and begins talking to the serpent.

"Shhh-h-h-h, mi amor. Calmate. I'm sorry, but these chickens are not for you. I won't hurt you, I promise. I'm just going to take you to another place…"

Moving gradually closer, Jesús reaches up and gently takes hold of the serpent right in the middle of its two meters' long body and, shockingly, there's little reaction from the creature.

"I will need some help getting her out from around the mesh," Jesús says.

Following his lead, I, too, take hold of the wrist-thick, writhing, bundle of muscle and begin gently pulling and prying the snake away from the window where both its head and tail are securely wrapped in the mesh. After a few more minutes of prying and prodding, the boa lets go its purchase and we have her secured inside the box.

Back in the goat pen, Oprah is starting to stir. It's getting late, and I thank Jesús for all his help this evening and let him know I'll be fine taking it from here.

"Is there anything else I can help you with?" he asks sincerely.

I think I'm really starting to like this guy.

✶ ✶ ✶ ✶ ✶ ✶ ✶

An hour later, after washing up, I'm seated under the palapa, smoking a joint and reflecting on this first day back. Recently I've been aspiring to shedding the über-responsible persona I've been living as for the past thirty years, and am finding that smoking a joint now and then, helps with that.

Taking another hit, I muse about what a day it's been. I especially think about this guy, Jesús, his absolute comfort with nature and himself, and what a terrific teacher he's been for me in only a couple of hours' time. Not only has he given me instruction in moving past one of my deepest fears—snakes—and the blockage to living more in harmony with Nature that fear represents, but he's also given me a wonderful lesson in looking past my useless filters of cultural prejudice. Six hours ago, seeing him through the lens of know-it-all, white-guy bias, I dismissed him as something useless, shabby, and undisciplined. Yet it was I who was useless in the pinch, hiding behind my mask of control.

Inside, in the bedroom, Holly finishes reading and switches off the light, calling out, "Goodnight, mi amor. Don't stay up too late."

A partial moon rising casts a beautiful, pale-blue light over the fields below. Beyond that, a heavy surf pounds the shore, sending up an ethereal, moonlit mist.

Going deeper into the waking dream, I continue picking back through the pieces of the day—blood and injections; startled chickens; the calm, knowing wisdom of Jesús with his scraggly hair and hippie garb; and the tough, slick feel of the muscular snake.

I think about the calm and comfort of the past three months of being in the States. It was a nice trip, to be sure, but relatively boring compared to this. I think about how little inspired I was to write. The fine dinners out, parties with friends, excellent bike rides with my buddies, and warm, fun reconnection with family members was all terrific, but none of it inspired me to write a single word until we'd crossed the border and started having adventures and reconnecting with all the eccentric people that are so ubiquitous here. I know that truly great writers, those relentless miners of truth, can extract nuggets of gold from the most barren landscape, but I'm at a loss to find anything in the last three months in the States that I recognize as treasure.

Now, here at the ranch, in just a few hours, the words of the story have already come rushing to greet me, welcoming me home.

"I've missed you, friends," I say to the night.

35 - Adelante y Atrás
(Forward and Back)

December 28, 2017

Today I turned sixty. It's been a wonderful day. Holly and Hillary helped organize a party for me at our community building. Now the mariachi band is playing and seems to be a big hit, and many of my favorite people are here—gringo friends from Vallarta and the States, and locals including guys from the horse trip, Yamir and Esther, Nacho, Choriz and his wife, and many others on board to help celebrate. Don Juan (Chido) and Lupe are here and are dancing away like they're back in the Talpa churchyard, though I barely recognize Lupe's fancy footwork without his spurs on. To-nio and José Juan have done a masterful job grilling the fish. Hopefully, our local friends understood why we aren't serving the standard party favorite—birria (goat stew).

In between mariachi sets, I've been DJ'ing my favorite playlist of vintage Mexicana music mixed with classic banda (some of which I've grown to almost like over the years) and alternative Latino cuts. Earlier in the evening, we had a lively guest performance by Lina belting out classic ranchero numbers and, just now, the mariachis, who are terrific, had everyone—gringos and locals alike—singing the quintessential Mexican favorite, Cielito Lindo (Beautiful Sky), together.

Song over, I drift away from the group. From out in the darkness at the edge of the party, I feel, for the first time in long memory, entirely at peace. Standing alone under the shimmering cielito lindo, I think back to that other night, one of our first nights at El Rinconcito so many years ago, with Fernando belting out the Cielito Lindo's stirring refrain, 'canta y no llores (sing and don't cry)'.

Looking toward the party glow, I feel as though I'm looking back at every party I've been to since coming here. I see raucous nights of tequila-infused laughter and bonfires on the beach at Rinconcito; campfires on the trail high in the Sierra Madres with true, stoic, Mexican cowboys; talent show nights at our own Rancho campfire ring; and, most recently, glowing coals of temescal sweat-lodge fires heating rocks for the sacred ceremonies.

I also think of the deaths we've experienced since first coming here—Amy, Luna, Lupita, Mrs. Toggenberg, Colorín, Greenfoot, and countless others—those fires of light and soul that were too soon extinguished and that caused us such anguish. I think about what teachers those fires in the crucibles of love have been for us, connecting us over and over with our own mortality and the preciousness of each spark-like instant that we're alive.

Looking fondly into the light, I realize it's been precisely thirteen years to the day that Holly and I first touched down in Vallarta looking for 'a little bungalow near the beach to escape to winters.' Whoa, what a fire that spark of inspiration ignited!

At the time of our arrival, Holly and I were swimming in a heady pool of exorbitant photo shoots, non-profit fundraisers, gallery openings, and jetting about the globe on a whim. Despite the buzz of all that, our lives were always stressed, and I don't recall being particularly happy.

But today, with our house nearly done, our various infrastructure systems getting dialed in, and the food forest and gardens well under way, an increasing sense of calm and contentedness seems to be taking hold. And, as the project becomes less overwhelming, I increasingly find myself excited about the little things—heads of lettuce coming up, dehydrating mangoes, monitoring the nitrogen levels in the aquaponics system, or the anticipation of Holly and I trying to capture our first swarm of native honey bees.

The other thing I'm excited about is that beginning four days from now, after all the build-up, I'll finally be hunkering down and starting my carbon-free year. Even though I feel that reducing my carbon usage to a bare minimum is essential—arguably one of the important things a person can do in this world—it's not my only reason for taking this challenge. I'm also looking forward to exploring the centeredness of staying put in a similar way that I might anticipate a travel adventure.

'OK, enough of that,' the stars all agree, winking at each other while shining down their brilliant wisdom to me. 'Enough with the navel-gazing when you should be stargazing and thinking about nothing but us. Besides, it's time for you to get back to your birthday party!'

* * * * * * *

As I write this final passage, change is afoot in Mayto. The road from El Tuito is finally paved all the way (though the potholes and washouts are already significant due to the crap paving job. I tell people that they didn't actually use asphalt but rather they just spray painted the dirt black. Oh well, 'bad roads, good people' Holly and I remind ourselves as we swerve to avoid yet another bad spot).

The number of tourists finding their way here has grown from a seasonal dribble to a steady, year-round stream. There's also free wireless Internet in town now, and the ragamuffin village youth are rapidly transi-

tioning from kicking soccer balls to passing emojis back and forth on their new, virtual playing field.

Yamir's house is nearly finished, and he's expecting his second baby. Unlike other *chavos* (local boys) who've made bank selling family property and then promptly blown it, Yamir has bootstrapped his way up, constantly constantly working here and selling a cow or two there, always with discipline and vision unusual for a country boy. He's flirted now and again with the idea of going to the States to work, but in the end, the reality is that he loves his life here too much to leave for more than a day or two. Over the years, we've increasingly fallen into a comfortable rhythm, often throwing friendly verbal jabs at each other—old familiar sparring partners in the way of tough guys the world over.

Though we've seen many would-be development projects grind to a halt for various reasons, the group of Spaniards that Lina first arrived with are still hovering around. Supposedly, with the backing of some huge Euro investor money, they're intent on making a play for some of the most prime beachfront real estate up and down this stretch of the coast. Since arriving nearly a year ago, they've brought with them a steady stream of Euro and South American travelers and investors looking to get in on the ground floor the next big Ibitha or Goa-esque travel destination. If successful, their efforts could change life here dramatically.

Another change in the air that I've noticed recently is an internal one. Despite all the drama, trauma, and even fear Mexico has visited into our lives, I feel surprisingly calm, clear, and relaxed these days. I believe this is due to a combination of factors such as growing older (reduction in testosterone?), my Buddhist practice, the steady connection with Nature, plenty of exercise, the reduced time spent in front of screens, reduced exposure to EMFs and other environmental pollution, and our increasingly stable infrastructure here at the ranch.

But I also attribute it to being in the constant congress of Mexicans, with their big-picture perspective on the narco situation and their lack of social pressure to be hyper-productive or keep up with the Rodriguezes in any way. If anything, here in el campo, there's an effort to appear less affluent that your neighbor in order to avoid jealously or theft.

Whatever the reasons, it's great to realize that I rarely get angry or am in conflict with anyone anymore (even with myself!), and I believe I'm greeting each day, and any potential adversity it may hold, with a more open heart. All of this, in turn, creates a positive spiral. The goat I'm milking is calmer when I'm calmer; the clay, wood, wiring, etc., I'm working with is more cooperative; and, though we still hit occasional topes, Holly and I are on a nice roll.

You see, to my way of thinking, everyone benefits by being more Mexican! There's still all of that crazy lack of-planning dysfunction that being so in the moment creates, but, with the right perspective, getting things done, or at least done on time, isn't nearly as important as we gringos usually make it out to be. Hyper-productivity has created terrific opportunity in my life but at an extremely high personal cost that's finally starting to get paid down.

The same goes for thinking I know or need to try to control what comes next. Slowly but steadily, I'm learning to be a human being rather than a human doing. Living in this way is like a taco rather than a complex, well-planned and shopped-for meal. Throw whatever ingredients you have into a tortilla and take a bite. Simple. Easy. Perfecto!

And, finally, I consider the last piece of the puzzle—the endless to-do list I always have. 'How will I get to the end of it if I keep drifting toward being more Mexican and not busting my hump to get everything done?' I ask myself. 'Well,' I answer myself back, 'you know what they say about that—the bright flash of light you see when you die is your to-do list going up in flames!' Ha! Guess I'll worry about that dumb old list mañana...

Epilogue

"Life can only be understood backwards; but it must be lived forwards."
~ Soren Kierkegaard

As this chapter closes, another opens. Despite all of our ups and downs with hosting volunteers and other participants, we're finding our way toward the middle ground and are cautiously optimistically, re-exploring the idea of community forming at the ranch. With Michael Singer's The Surrender Experiment *as an intriguing reminder of what's possible, we're learning to approach the notion of intentional community with more open hearts and lighter hands on the tiller.*

On the homesteading/permaculture front, we're also finding increasing success—the greening of our semi-arid ranch and a sense of abundance we've learned about in our study of permaculture is starting to manifest. When we want milk, cheese or yogurt, we milk a goat. When we want eggs, we borrow some from the chickens. When we want fruit, veggies, or nuts, we are increasingly able to reach into the trees or harvest straight from the garden. Our 'hippie-lux' house, so long in coming, is more comfortable and functional than we ever imagined. Often our days roll out with perfect symmetry—hot in the sun, but cool and comfortable in the lazy afternoon shadows under the main palapa that functions as our living room.

The parade of interesting characters enriching our lives hasn't slowed any either. Our newest friend is a sideshow performance artist who walks on fire and eats light bulbs. "I can get free drinks at any bar in the world," he tells us proudly. He can eat any kind of light bulb, but he prefers the old incandescents. Vintage X-mas tree lightbulbs are his favorite.

Of course, the nice run we're having doesn't come with a guarantee. Just like good sex or a fine meal, one wants life—or at least the current good roll—to go on forever, but no matter how one tries to slow it down and savor every lick or bite, time won't be denied. Meditation helps. For those periods, at least, there is no time—a good compromise and good practice for the eventual dying when our ego-existence will finally slip to nothing. While Holly and I are fully aware that accident, illness, narco-violence, or any number of changes could bring our dream crashing down, we're doing our best to keep a big-picture perspective, while appreciating and living each day fully as if it were our last. And certainly, reading the headlines, what we're doing here seems at least as stable as any other place or way of living we know.

In closing, I hope you've enjoyed the journey thus far and that you'll join me as I write more about the experience of living in Mexico and of stripping life down to its barest essentials. Or perhaps you'll come down for a visit sometime! In the meantime, I'll report back on whatever calm and contentedness that radical simplification may bring, although I realize that being in Mexico, just about anything may happen...

Acknowledgments & Final Message

My sincere appreciation goes out to the dedicated Beta Readers who generously gave their time and love to this project. Holly Hunter, Aja and Cynthia Gair, Camille E. Torres, Catherine Quinn, Vidda Chan, Valery Wait, and Mary Houghton-Barr. You've each provided The Mexico Diaries with much-needed clarity, and a good scrubbing behind the ears. Thank you as well to my excellent navigator throughout the process, Editor Lynn Gray, and to you Tony Cohan for your thoughtful mentoring and endorsement.

As this book goes live on Amazon & Kindle, September 1, 2018, the biosphere, which harbors all life, is under direct attack by climate deniers and is at its most critical moment ever. For the sake of our children and grandchildren, please consider buying less, flying less, and donating to the EDF (Environmental Defense Fund - https://www.edf.org/). This is the organization that I feel is best vetted to put dollars to work where they are needed most.

About The Author

Originally a commercial fisherman, including a stint king crabbing in Alaska and two years as a boat captain in the North Atlantic, Dan traded fish for cameras and left the industry in his 20's. For the next twenty years, Dan was a commercial advertising photographer and photojournalist with a client list that included The New York Times, Unicef, The United Nations, and numerous fortune 500 companies. Dan's photography is represented by Lonely Planet Images and Getty Images.

In the early 2000's Dan became involved in social and environmental issues serving on the Board of Directors of a one hundred bed homeless shelter and chairman of a municipal energy commission.

In 2009 Dan's associates purchased his photography business, and together with his wife Holly Hunter, Dan relocated to the Pacific coast of Mexico to launch Rancho Sol y Mar, the working goat ranch and Sustainability Education Center described in his memoir, The Mexico Diaries, A Sustainable Adventure. Although retired, Dan continues wrangling goats, blogging, and writing articles for Permaculture Magazine.

Dan is currently working on his second book, a novel about a Mexican family struggling to stay united despite borders, secrets, and the narco divide.

Website: https://tinyurl.com/DanGair